RELIGIOUS LIBERALISM
IN
EIGHTEENTH-CENTURY
ENGLAND

RELIGIOUS LIBERALISM

IN
EIGHTEENTH-CENTURY
ENGLAND

BY

ROLAND N. STROMBERG

OXFORD UNIVERSITY PRESS

1954

Oxford University Press, Amen House, London E.C. 4

GLASGOW NEW YORK TORONTO MELBOURNE WELLINGTON

BOMBAY CALCUTTA MADRAS KARACHI CAPE TOWN IBADAN

Geoffrey Cumberlege, Publisher to the University

———

PRINTED IN GREAT BRITAIN

PREFACE

SCHOLARS (and that far greater number who are condemned to be, as Mr. E. M. Forster once rightly
insisted, pseudo-scholars) accumulate numerous obliga-
tions which they vainly seek to discharge in prefaces. They
owe something to men and women they have never met and
never can meet, some long since dead. They can only
acknowledge a handful of the more personal intellectual
influences and express gratitude for some of the more direct
services. Professor Alfred Owen Aldridge of the University
of Maryland certainly did more than anyone else among
personal acquaintances to introduce the author to eighteenth-
century intellectual studies. Other teachers and colleagues
at the same University who contributed helpful suggestions,
valuable guidance, and warm encouragement include Pro-
fessors Donald C. Gordon, Leonora C. Rosenfield, Richard H.
Bauer and Wesley M. Gewehr. The staff at the Library of
Congress, where most of the research was done, were always most co-operative. Thanks are also due to the British
Museum in London and the University Library at Cambridge. The staff of the Clarendon Press aided greatly with
suggestions and in preparation for publication. For the rest,
the friends were chiefly books—save for an indispensable
comrade and assistant, Mary R. Stromberg, who helped in
many ways at every stage of the research, writing, and
preparation.

R. N. S.

COLLEGE PARK, MARYLAND

CONTENTS

INTRODUCTION

> If our first precept should be to study our own history . . . our
> second precept . . . should be to relegate economic and political history
> to a subordinate place and give religious history the primacy. For
> religion, after all, is the serious business of the human race.
>
> ARNOLD J. TOYNBEE, *Civilization on Trial*

THOUGH not all historians might be willing to go as far
as the distinguished one quoted above, his testimony
may be introduced on behalf of the modest survey here
attempted. If not to primacy, religious history ought to be
entitled at least to equality.

Religion was most notably 'the serious business of the
human race', or our portion of the race, during the Middle
Ages and the Reformation; it has become far less so, most
would agree, in modern times. In this study we deal with it
at an important moment of transition. Perhaps, as a ripe
scholar with a sense of humour assures me, all ages may be
called ages 'of transition'. Yet it is hard to resist the conclusion that the eighteenth century was peculiarly so, especially
as concerns religion. Between 1670 and 1830, Paul Tillich
believes,

First among the educated classes, then increasingly in the mass of
industrial workers, religion lost its 'immediacy'; it ceased to offer an
unquestioned sense of direction and relevance to human living.[1]

Doubtless this was less true of England, with which we
are concerned here, than with the Continent—even though
England led the way in 'free-thinking'. Towards the end of
the period we are to examine, the Wesleyan movement provided a Christian revival; and if at the end of the century
Carlyle found 'an age fallen languid, destitute of faith and
terrified at scepticism', this did not mean that Christianity
was finished as a vital force in English life. It is undoubtedly
true, however, that the early eighteenth century produced

---

[1] *Journal of the History of Ideas*, v (Jan. 1944), 66. Paul Hazard, *La Pensée
européenne au XVIIIème siècle*, tome i, préface, admirably states the thesis that 'it is
of the eighteenth century that we are the direct descendants'. M. Hazard goes so far
as to name 1715 the 'critical year' of modern Western civilization.

the first great challenge to the supremacy of that 'Christian epic' which had heretofore dominated Western civilization for more than a millennium. It is a period in which thought and activity are increasingly secularized and rationalized.

England blazed the path. Seen in proper perspective, the religious disputes of the earlier English eighteenth century become of considerable significance. It is well known that these disputes gave rise to an enormous literature. 'England', a foreign visitor noted in 1727, 'furnished sufficient books to supply two daily newspapers, of which one might be entitled Library of English Orthodoxy, and the other Library of English Heterodoxy.'[1] Time was when few historians thought it worth while to take more than perfunctory note of this dull and unprofitable (and interminable) strife of theological controversialists. Most general histories still pass it by. Much of it was subsequently rendered obsolete, so far as concerned the approach to scriptural questions. Deism was perhaps dead long before Burke pronounced its epitaph in 1790, but orthodoxy in the old sense also was to perish not very many years later. However, the rise of interest in intellectual history[2] has rescued the deistic period from oblivion and indeed placed it fairly high in the scale of interest. The task that seems important today is to synthesize an abundance of material rather than to mine a virgin field.

The farther chronological boundaries of our period of 'religious liberalism' are rather clearly marked off by the 1688 revolution, though quite certainly the roots lie much deeper in the seventeenth century. The nearer limits are less clear. It has been frequently argued that we are in another intellectual era in the age of Hume and Wesley—that about the middle of the century scepticism in one direction, and evangelicalism in another, have supplanted the deistic

---

[1] Quoted in Ernest C. Mossner, *Bishop Butler and the Age of Reason*, p. 69.

[2] Intellectual history obviously differs from the history of theology, of philosophy, &c., as well as from the 'history of ideas' as such. Its aim is to establish the 'climate of opinion', in Carl Becker's phrase—to explore the interrelationship between history and thought, to place ideas in the context of history, and to show how history was influenced by the framework of thought. Some good remarks on the nature and purpose of intellectual history may be found in Franklin Le Van Baumer, *Main Currents of Western Thought* (New York, 1952), pp. 3-14.

controversy, as Reason gives ground. It may well be doubted whether there was as much suddenness and finality in this transition as some have implied. Yet there are many landmarks too obvious to miss: Conyers Middleton brought the whole deistic controversy to a new path, and Joseph Butler revolutionized the methods of the orthodox. We must at least seek to close the epoch somewhere short of the period of the revolutions (1774–90), but we ought not to omit some indication of the debate's permanent significance.

'The charge that England cared little about ideas begins to be possible only in the latter half of the century. In the first, she showed at least as much interest in ideas as any other nation.'[1] The period is a stimulating one to the student of intellectual history. England was, in fact, pioneering in modes of thought which would spread later to France and to America, where they would exert a greater practical influence. Paine, Franklin, and Jefferson, Voltaire, Rousseau, and Robespierre—the ideas of these men may be traced to the English deists. Unitarianism flowered as an important intellectual movement in the United States nearly a century after its irruption in England. To trace the ramifications of ideas let loose in early eighteenth-century England lies beyond the scope of this work. It is enough to find that here they were born.

Our subject-matter falls into several categories. Chapters I–III deal with preparations and background for the emergence of a rational approach to religion and a period of bold speculation. Chapters IV–VI take up the radical challenge to orthodoxy—unitarianism and deism. In the next two chapters we discuss the crises within the camp of Christian orthodoxy, a matter of considerable importance, for we shall find that orthodoxy's troubles were primarily of its own making. Chapters IX, X, and XI then make an effort to indicate the social and political implications of this religious controversy, a matter of some complexity which, however, we surely cannot afford to neglect. In the concluding chapter there are some remarks on the final significance of the eighteenth century's religious controversies.

[1] J. M. Robertson, *The Dynamics of Religion*, p. 116.

I

THE NATURE OF THE CRISIS

What we have to realize is that in those years God was on trial.

CARL L. BECKER

I

IT is common to meet the opinion that religion fell into sad decay in England's Augustan age, the victim of complacence and materialism. There is indeed evidence to support this view. Much of it, however, requires criticism and careful weighing; and when we are done, our judgement must be that this age was, in its own way, deeply concerned with religion. How, otherwise, are we to account for the vast body of religious literature produced, and for the great interest religious questions aroused? It will be our thesis that this spate of theological disputation, far from being wholly inconsequential, was actually interesting and important; that the years between 1690 and 1740 were in fact years of crisis in the religious foundations of Western civilization. They were years not so much of languid doubt as of critical tension.

To some who came later, this Augustan theological literature itself became a testimony to the absence of true religion; it was so dry and formalistic. But we must beware of accepting the Methodist indictment, which has helped to shape our picture of this period as irreligious. To George Whitefield, the great evangelist, Archbishop Tillotson appeared to have been no more a Christian than Mahomet. The bias here is all too evident. From Tillotson[1] on, the

---

[1] John Tillotson, Archbishop of Canterbury 1691–4, most famous of those Anglicans who were called Low Churchmen or Latitudinarians. Reacting equally against Puritan fanaticism and Prelatist intolerance, they preached 'moderation in all things', tolerance, and a rational spirit in Christianity; but their search for sanity in religion must not be confused with indifference or heresy. Portraits of other outstanding Latitudinarians, including Edward Stillingfleet, Jeremy Taylor, and William Chillingworth, may be found in John Tulloch, *Rational Theology and Christian Philosophy in the Seventeenth Century*; for a contemporary account

B

eighteenth-century era rejected 'enthusiasm' as the plague; on this alone deist and Christian, orthodox and heretic alike, could agree. The era was not for that reason indifferent or sceptical. From Tillotson, Cudworth, Locke, and Newton to Watts, Doddridge, Law, and Butler, there was always fervent piety, though not ecstatic emotionalism.[1] And if some of the controversialists—the Sacheverells and the Leslies, for example, those furious High Church Tories—impress us less with their piety than with their bitter contentiousness, at least we cannot deny their earnestness.

Heretics there were in this age. But most of them were more than mere scoffers. William Whiston the Arian, even Thomas Chubb the deist, thought of themselves as purifying true religion, not destroying it. So staunch a foe of deism as Timothy Dwight, the American, conceded that the English 'infidels' were less nihilistic than the later French assailants of Christianity.[2] The volume of answers produced, as compared with the mere handful of anti-Christians, tells us how strenuous was the defence of Christianity. 'The strongest intellectual forces of the Enlightenment', writes the foremost student of this period's philosophy, 'do not lie in its rejection of belief but rather in the new form of faith which it proclaims, and in the new form of religion which it embodies.'[3]

True, we must deal with more critics than the Methodists. Hardly a single devout man, indeed, neglected to charge the times with abandonment of religion, and relatively disinterested observers added the weight of their testimony. Daniel Defoe believed in 1722 that 'no age, since the founding and forming the Christian Church, was ever like, in open avowed atheism, blasphemies, and heresies, to the age we now live in'. William Whiston declared that anyone with 'a right sense of religion' must be aware of its 'decay and disesteem in the world'. Swift was fond of noting sardonically how

---

see Edward Fowler, *The Principles and Practices of Certain Moderate Divines Called Latitudinarians* . . . .

   [1] A good discussion of the very real if restrained piety of some Christians in this rationalist tradition may be found in Herbert McLachlan, *The Religious Opinions of Milton, Locke, and Newton*, pp. 209 ff.

   [2] *Travels in New England and New York* (New Haven, 1822; London, 1823), iv. 355. See also Norman L. Torrey, *Voltaire and the English Deists, passim.*

   [3] Ernst Cassirer, *The Philosophy of the Enlightenment*, pp. 135–6.

little the principles of religion were pursued in the world.[1] Bishop Butler concluded that religion had fought a losing battle with unbelief. David Hume, who was perhaps an unwilling sceptic, agreed: England, he wrote, showed the most indifference to religious matters of all nations. This was a period of Robert Walpole and the South Sea Bubble, of many changes both political and social, leading to the conviction in some minds, especially Tory, that the world had 'gone to the dogs'. But much of this was petulance or hysteria.

The testimony of idealists, impassioned or disillusioned, is properly subject to some discounting. In what epoch was it not true that worthy men lamented failures to attain the Christian ideal? At least one contemporary divine (Dr. Gastrell, the Boyle Lecturer for 1697) was able to smile at the tendency of writers to think their own age the most vicious. The charge of atheism and scepticism, obviously, 'included a great deal of what would now be reckoned healthy inquiry'.[2] Indeed, the very bitterness of the self-reproaches about both immorality and scepticism indicates high standards: this age was very careful of both its morals and its beliefs. There were fewer complaints in Restoration times, and yet we know that in most respects the Augustan age was a far purer one than that. If one historian calls it a period when 'religion was at low tide', another quite properly reminds us that it was also a very moral one, symbolized by Steele's *Christian Hero*, by the Societies for the Reformation of Manners and the Society for the Propagation of the Gospel, by Jeremy Collier's assault on the immorality of the stage.[3] Matthew Tindal, the deist, was near the mark when

[1] 'I suppose it will be granted that hardly one in a hundred among our people of quality or gentry appears to act by any principle of religion; that great numbers of them do entirely discard it, and are ready to own their disbelief of all revelation in ordinary discourse. Nor is the case much better among the vulgar, especially in great towns. . . .' 'Project for the Advancement of Religion', *Works*, ii. 175. For a number of other comments on religious indifference, see W. E. H. Lecky, *History of England in the Eighteenth Century*, iii. 11 ff.

[2] John Hunt, *Religious Thought in England from the Reformation*, iii. 74.

[3] H. N. Fairchild, *Religious Trends in English Poetry*, i. 3; F. G. Marcham, *A History of England* (New York, 1937), p. 617. For some defences of the period against various calumnies see the following: Basil Williams, *The Whig Supremacy, 1714-60*, pp. 9-10; Norman Sykes, *Church and State in England in the Eighteenth Century*, pp. 273-4; Rosamond Bayne-Powell, *English Country Life in the Eighteenth*

he denied that England was more dissolute: morality, he held, was vastly improved, and the only complaints came from 'priests' stricken by wholesome examination of their pet dogmas.[1] Morality, to be sure, is not religion; and we are not at all concerned to deny that a vigorous, far-reaching search into the very foundations of religious belief went on. The point is that the debate was a serious one, conducted by people mainly devout and not dissolute, a people anxious about its religion.

It was not so long before, we need to bear in mind, that 'discourse about Divinity' was 'the frequentest table-talk in England'.[2] If this was no longer quite so true—if politics and trade tended to supplant theology as the serious business of life—it still was somewhat true. England's daily newspaper to an extent remained the religious and religio-political pamphlets; and politics was still partly bound up with religion.

We need also to bear in mind that despite lamentations to the contrary there was not, after all, much real disbelief. 'An atheist or a deist is a monstrous kind of creature, which in the country we only know by report', Philip Doddridge wrote in 1726, when deism was at its peak.[3] Perhaps, as Doddridge implied, they existed in the cities; but we need only read the fashionable literature of the day—Spectator, Tatler, or a Fielding novel—to sense the odium in which 'free-thinking' was held. For every heretical tract there were dozens of orthodox replies. Hysterical exaggerations of the amount of 'atheism' sometimes reached the point of the ridiculous, as in the furore over the alleged 'Hell-Fire Clubs' in the early 1720's. (Tales about scandalous 'impious clubs' turned out to be largely fictional.)[4] This was a low-key faith,

Century (London, 1935), pp. 75–111; G. M. Trevelyan, English Social History (London, 1947), p. 353; A. W. Hopkinson, About William Law, pp. 28–29.

[1] The Nation Vindicated from the Aspersions Cast on It . . . , espec. pp. 18–19.

[2] Percy H. Osmond, Isaac Barrow, p. 147. 1673 was the date of this remark.

[3] The Correspondence and Diary of Philip Doddridge, ii. 213. There are abundant indications that the countryside remained far less touched by currents of free-thought, and that indeed 'discourse about Divinity' continued to be its table-talk throughout the century.

[4] See the conclusions of Louis C. Jones, The Clubs of the Georgian Rakes (New York, 1942), pp. 37–55. Jones points out pertinently that it did after all scandalize the nation to suspect that such clubs existed. Defoe began by swallowing the tales and

to be sure, this Augustan religion keyed to neo-classicism and rationalism, abjuring all 'freakishness and enthusiasm'. But it was very real and firm, nevertheless. Blasphemy or radical free-thought were the last things the Augustans wanted to hear.

2

Why, then, *did* they hear them? There are several reasons why, despite an obvious desire for peace and concord, the age was one of controversy. As Carl Becker once put it, God was placed on trial in those years. But it was not because most Englishmen wanted such a scandalous affair.

A document issued by the Church of England Convocation of Canterbury (before it was found convenient to suppress this too zealous body) attributed the 'late excessive growth of infidelity, heresy, and profaneness' to two 'evils': the freeing of the press and the end of the danger of popery.[1] As to the latter, a great many were inclined to look back wistfully on the latter days of James II, when for a time all Protestant factions made peace in a common cause and religious spirit was temporarily much improved.[2] It is instructive to recall that the great Latitudinarians of the seventeenth century, men such as Chillingworth, Tillotson, and the Cambridge Platonists, had based their hopes for Protestant unity not only on a broader spirit of toleration within Protestantism but also on a united front against Rome. But the fear of Catholicism, if not the distaste for it, faded rapidly after 1689. It would revive only for a brief moment in 1714–15. Daniel Defoe pointed out in 1724 that this particular dog was dead, and there was little point in beating it. That they no longer need band together against Papists meant, of course, that Protestants were free to explore their own differences. In point of fact, the first disturbances to agitate English opinion, as we shall see, were within the bodies of the old Christian Churches—

ended, amusingly enough, by suspecting a Whig hoax—see William Lee (ed.), *Life and . . . Writings of Defoe*, ii. 371–8.

[1] *A Representation of the Present State of Religion, Unanimously Agreed upon by a Joint Committee of Both Houses of Convocation of the Province of Canterbury*, 1711.

[2] See Edmund Calamy, *An Historical Account of My Own Life*, i. 194; William Whiston, *Memoirs*, i. 22; Charles D'Avenant, *Essays on Peace at Home and War Abroad*, pt. i, pp. 219–20.

chiefly, the debate about the Trinity. Deists only poured in through a breach already opened by good Christians.

Freedom of the press was doubtless more important. It may be dated from the last days of James II, for opposition to him centred in a 'host of controversialists who scattered pamphlets and tracts from every printing press', with which that harried monarch was quite unable to cope.[1] The licensing system was allowed to expire between 1693 and 1695, never to be renewed despite some efforts in that direction; 'henceforth the English press is free from censorship before publication and enjoys a liberty unique in Europe'.[2] That did not mean freedom in the modern sense; there remained the danger of prosecution for seditious or blasphemous libel after publication. But there was enough freedom, and it steadily expanded. By and large the deists were able to write undisturbed, so long as they exercised a degree of caution. They often disguised their real views somewhat, but this was as much a strategy as a necessity. *The Oracles of Reason*, an early deistic tract written chiefly by Charles Blount, was condemned to be destroyed, which did not appear to prevent the circulation of numerous copies. Thomas Woolston in 1729, and, much later (1763), Peter Annet, passed beyond the limits and suffered penalties for blasphemy. Arthur Bury's *The Naked Gospel*, an important early antitrinitarian tract, was publicly burnt at Oxford in 1690, and the author deprived; Whiston later lost his high university post for his outspoken Arian views; but this did not stop the flow of unitarian pamphlets, or prevent public debates on Socinianism in London. Defoe was pilloried for his famous *Short Way with Dissenters*, and John Tutchin of the *Observator*, prosecuted for libel in 1704, was subsequently assassinated by a Tory mob during the Sacheverell excitement six years later. There were certainly limits to free speech (as there still evidently are in all countries), but deists, Socinians, and other religious dissidents were safe enough as long as they refrained from open blasphemy or extremely immoderate expressions.

---

[1] J. R. Green, *A Short History of the English People* (1895 ed.), iv. 1456.

[2] Laurence Hanson, *Government and the Press, 1695–1763*—a thorough discussion of this aspect of the question.

It was the persecutors who were more often disappointed. In vain did the more rabid orthodox protest to the House of Commons (1701) that 'impudent deniers of our Saviour's divinity' were suffered 'unreproved and unpunished, to the infinite regret of all good Christians'. They secured, in 1698, passage of an act reaffirming the principle that denial of Christianity is an offence punishable by imprisonment. 'Christianity', Sir Matthew Hale had held in a significant decision of 1673, 'is a parcel of the law of England, and therefore to speak in reproach of the Christian religion is to speak in subversion of the law.' The principle stood; but the law of 1698 was laxly enforced. It is generally agreed that free-thought and heterodoxy met little real persecution.[1]

The law of libel, said the Tory *Rehearsal*, is 'a wise and good law'.[2] The Tories, and some Whigs as well, often clamoured for repression of 'dangerous' religious writings. The Whigs for their part undertook to chastise Dr. Sacheverell, and after 1715 conducted a mild terror against the Jacobites. But this was politics, and those persecuted were in this case conservative Christians, not radical free-thinkers. In their brief period of power between 1711 and 1714 the Tories attempted to prosecute Whiston, but proceedings were dropped after 1714.[3] In 1721, a bill to suppress anti-trinitarian writing and preaching was rejected. Matthew Tindal, the deist, was able to keep his fellowship at All Souls until his death. Poor Woolston alone had cause for complaint, and he, it must be confessed, lacked all discretion. As a martyr (he died in prison), Woolston helped advance

---

[1] Act for Suppression of Blasphemy and Profaneness, 9 and 10 William III, chap. 32; Memorial to the House of Commons, 1701. Cf. J. M. Robertson, *Dynamics of Religion*, pp. 111–13. Robertson exaggerates the perils of free thought, and completely misunderstands the position of Locke and Newton, who were certainly not terrorized into orthodoxy. See H. McLachlan, *The Story of a Nonconformist Library*, for instances of repression against the Socinians.

[2] Vol. i, no. 191, Mar. 15, 1707. See also Bishop Berkeley's *Essay towards Preventing the Ruin of Great Britain*, which inquires 'why blasphemy against God should not be inquired into and punished with the same rigour as treason against the king'.

[3] See *State Trials* (Cobbett), xv. 703–16. Accounts of the persecution of the Jacobites may be found in James Sutherland, *Background for Queen Anne*, pp. 182 ff.; David H. Stevens, *Party Politics and English Journalism, 1702–42*; Calamy, *Own Life*, ii. 357–8; Charles Petrie, *The Jacobite Movement, the Last Phase, 1716–1807*.

the cause of free speech: all England seemed secretly ashamed of what had happened.

So Henry Dodwell was reasonably close to the mark in vaunting 'the freedom and liberty, so peculiar to the country wherein we live, of examining the grounds and reasons of prevailing opinions'.[1] The time would come when an Englishman would look back to this era as a golden age of freedom.[2] David Hume was aware of 'a land of toleration and of liberty' as his intellectual environment.

The Act of Toleration, inconclusive and imperfect as it was, had its influence also. The sects that had multiplied under persecution now declined under toleration. It was notorious that the Dissenters began to lose their zeal immediately after the long fight for toleration was won. England gradually learnt the lesson of toleration, and it is instructive to hear Dr. Calamy reflect on a case of religious 'enthusiasm' treated by the new method of ignoring it: 'Being let alone, they by degrees dwindled away, and came to nothing.'[3] 'Toleration is the most successful stratagem', a popular journal announced, to prevent foolish heresies, adding the somewhat more enlightened statement that 'truth does not stand in need of being supported by violence'.[4] Even Tory champions of religious uniformity began to disclaim any intention of persecution for conscience' sake, as may be seen in the language of the first bill against Occasional Conformity.

3

Freedom, then, explains much. Charles D'Avenant complained that while there may have been 'atheism' in the seventeenth century, it then 'did not walk bare-faced, it had

[1] Samuel Clarke, *Works*, iii. 764.
[2] See William Hazlitt, *Political Essays* (1819), preface.
[3] Calamy, op. cit. ii. 108–10. He referred to the 'new prophets', who came to England from France in 1706. See a note on them in Thomas Chubb, *Posthumous Works*, i. 360–5; and James Sutherland, op. cit., 'John Lacy and the Modern Prophets'. It is not true that they entirely escaped persecution, but as compared with the treatment of Quakers a few decades before the contrast is great. Worth noting is the fact that 'enthusiasm' was more apt to be persecuted than rationalistic scepticism in these years.
[4] *Freethinker*, no. 79, 22 Dec. 1718—a conservative journal, despite the title.

no open advocates . . . '.[1] It was open now because of a freer
climate of opinion. Men could write boldly on what had
long been forbidden save in secrecy. For denying the Trinity,
people had been executed but a century before. They were
now free to follow where speculation might lead them.

Nevertheless, this was not all. We have still to account for
the Age of Reason—to explain, that is, the emergence of the
remarkable faith that the world is a rational one and man
a rational creature, from which among other things it follows
that man has a rational religion. Let us defer the effort to
outline such an explanation until the chapter following.

To find the source of religious truth in some blindly
accepted principle of authority was repugnant to almost
everyone in those years, from deist to Anglican. 'It is certainly the duty of every rational creature', Philip Doddridge,
the distinguished Dissenter, remarked, 'to bring his religion to the strictest test, and to retain or reject the faith
in which he has been educated, as he finds it capable or
incapable of rational defence.'[2] This from a clergyman of
irreproachable orthodoxy. It was the keynote of the age.
There might emerge grievous disagreements and confusions
as to the nature of 'rational defence', but all accepted the idea
that rational defence of some sort there must be. On the
extreme right, one finds the non-juring Anglican, Charles
Leslie, conceding that 'God never required any man to
believe anything that did contradict any of his outward
senses'.[3] Francis Atterbury, foremost of the High Church–
Jacobite element, affirmed that the Church of England 'desires nothing more than to be tried at the bar of unbiased
reason, and to be concluded by its sentence'.[4] 'There can be
nothing in Christian Religion which contradicts the clear
and evident principles of natural reason', a popular religious
handbook summed it up.[5]

Socinian or deist would press the claims of 'reason' farther
than most Christians wished to go; and yet the latter met the
former on the grounds of 'rational defence'. 'Fideism', that

---

[1] *Essays on Peace at Home and War Abroad*, pt. i, p. 219.
[2] *Correspondence and Diary*, ii. 423.
[3] Leslie, *Theological Works*, ii, 'The Socinian Controversy Dismissed'.
[4] Atterbury, *Sermons*, iii. 29.
[5] Edward Synge, *A Gentleman's Religion*, p. 74.

'desperate form of faith' which holds that one must believe blindly or not at all, was most uncongenial to Englishmen of this age. They were at length, no doubt, driven to something like it, but only with great reluctance. Our era of intellectual history has perhaps ended when Hume announces that Christianity cannot rest upon reason, when John Wesley and William Law imply that reason is irrelevant to religion or its less important part, and when Butler, seconded by Berkeley, indicates that religious truths cannot really be 'proved'. However, people continued to believe in the rational demonstrability of Christianity long after this. At any rate, nothing shows the faith in reason better than the outraged reception which, in 1743, greeted the scepticism of Henry Dodwell, Jr., who wrote a book called *Christianity Not Founded on Argument*. Christianity to the vast majority emphatically *was* founded on argument—on the rational and positive demonstration of its historical truth and logical consistency.

Men were willing to submit to 'reason' because there was on all hands a sublime confidence that reason and religion were in harmony. It is not possible for a sincere man to be other than a Christian, argued Isaac Watts, the eminent Nonconformist minister; the truth of the gospel is perfectly evident to all whose minds are not closed.[1] Charles Leslie's *Short and Easy Method with the Deists*, a well-known work, was short and easy indeed: 'so sifted and attested' are the facts on which Christianity rests, he thought, that we cannot reasonably doubt them, unless we are prepared to doubt everything.[2] Such was the temper of the age, shared by deist and orthodox alike. Belief in the rationality of the Christian religion was in part traditional, in part newly inspired by the Newtonian world outlook.

A rare flash of humour in the long debate came when the deist Anthony Collins remarked that nobody doubted the existence of God until Dr. Clarke strove to prove it. He

---

[1] See his *Caveat against Infidelity*, 1729.

[2] Cf. Samuel Clarke, 1705 Boyle Lecture: 'A constant and sincere observance of all the laws of reason . . . will unavoidably lead a man to Christianity.' (*Works*, ii. 600.) Thus rational Christianity had the support of the period's foremost metaphysician. For other quotations illustrating the contemporary faith in reason see Mark Pattison, *Essays*, ii. 55–57.

might have added in the same vein that nobody doubted the
doctrine of the Trinity until William Sherlock tried to demonstrate it mathematically. The point is that the Clarkes and the
Sherlocks, men of the gravest respectability, started out se-
renely certain that their religion would be strengthened, not
weakened, by rational examination. We must understand
what a series of jolts orthodoxy had received before it could
rest with Joseph Butler on the uneasy grounds that Christianity may as well be as true as anything else, since all things
are in doubt.

Postponing for the moment any examination of this
optimistic rationalism, we can here merely mention what is
no secret—that the most obvious influence was the new
science, and the support it seemed to give to religion, as
expressed in the views of such impressive figures as Newton,
Boyle, and Locke. Doddridge would give it away when, in
his vindication of Christian evidences, he crowned the whole
argument by pointing out that the above-named men had
been convinced by these proofs.[1] The spectacle of Newton's
science controverting the unbelievers, testifying, as Addison's
famous hymn put it, that

> The Hand that made us is divine,

quite overmastered this generation. Isaac Watts was similarly
moved to sing, inspired by Newton's piety:

> Reason at length submits to wear
> The wings of faith . . . .

It occurred to few that there might be no necessary connexion between the great scientist's piety and his physics.
The connexion seemed established. When Richard Bentley
presented the scientific argument against atheism in the first
Boyle Lecture (1692), atheism became indefensible. Some
years later a youth named Franklin on the far side of the
Atlantic would read these lectures and become converted
not to Christianity but to deism; and at the time a voice
(Whiston's) might have been heard wondering, 'What is
this to the fable of Jesus Christ?' To prove the existence of
God from the laws of Nature, to insist that such an amazing

---

[1] Philip Doddridge, *Three Sermons on the Evidences of Christianity* (1736).

universe must have had a Maker, was a glorious thing, sufficient to silence the followers of Hobbes and Epicurus; only, as it happened, it was as useful to deists as to Christians, and it really did not have much to do with the Bible. But we need only note that at first it produced a supreme confidence that from science, philosophy, and reason Christianity had nothing to fear. Newton, 'the glory of his country and his race', and 'the great Mr. Locke' as well, had made it plain that they considered the new science and the new philosophy buttresses of religion. It was not known to their contemporaries that these worthy men were themselves not exactly orthodox, though pious enough.[1]

Orthodox Christianity, then, gambled on reason. The task of our period was the exploration of the limits of rationalism, in full confidence, at first, that reason and religion were compatible. The sense in which God was on trial may be a little clearer: Christianity was to be subjected to the critique of reason, under relative freedom of discussion, in a more disinterested climate of opinion. As it happened, the Christian God was to be forced into serious straits, though at the start everyone looked for a triumphant vindication. The accuracy of Carl Becker's imagery is attested by the number of tracts which actually did present the controversy as some sort of a trial. There was, for instance, Thomas Sherlock's, whose trial was made to issue in a glorious acquittal of Christianity and the Bible. But in Thomas Gordon's 'trial' the priestly defenders of the Trinity are convicted of deceit and hypocrisy.[2] Deists, Arians, and Erastians will try the priesthood on charges of monumental fraud and trickery; the Bible will be judged as authentic or fraudulent by a horde of scholars and pseudo-scholars; and God himself will be asked to show credentials satisfactory to reason. As a matter of fact, no one will deny the existence of a God; there is no atheism in this age. But Christianity's traditional God is to be subjected to an impudent cross-examination.

[1] H. McLachlan, *The Religious Opinions of Milton, Locke, and Newton*, pp. 117–72.
[2] Thomas Sherlock, *The Trial of the Witnesses of the Resurrection of Christ* (1729); Thomas Gordon, *The Trial of William Whiston* (1739).

II

PREPARATIONS FOR RELIGIOUS LIBERALISM

The Bible, I say, the Bible only, is the religion of Protestants.

WILLIAM CHILLINGWORTH

The denial of reason in religion hath been the principal engine, that heretics and enthusiasts have used against the Faith.

JOSEPH GLANVILL

Knowledge of the works of God proportions our admiration of them ... and our utmost science can but give us a juster veneration of His omniscience. . . . ROBERT BOYLE

I

IT has seemed to some students that we enter another world between 1680 and 1700.[1] It is probably necessary, however, to make this transition less abrupt. The trend towards rationalism goes back farther. It had sources other than Newton and Locke, whose influence, great as it was, is sometimes exaggerated. Reason in religion was primarily a reaction against the social consequences of 'enthusiasm' in the age of the sectaries, that period culminating in the 1650's when the allegedly prosaic Englishmen 'had their great mystical period'.[2] The 'witness of the spirit' so stressed by Reformation theology was highly suspect in Restoration England. The spirit that dwells within being discredited, men turned towards the external evidences of Christianity's truth. They took refuge on what Gladstone was to call (just before it finally crumbled) the 'impregnable rock' of Holy Scripture, as an alternative to both the slavish authoritarianism of Popery and the weird anarchy of private enthusiasm.

As for the former, it is doubtless unnecessary to demonstrate that Roman Catholicism remained, all through this period, as repugnant to the overwhelming majority of

---

[1] Edward Dowden, *Puritan and Anglican: Studies in Literature*, chap. x.

[2] Ernst Troeltsch, *The Social Teaching of the Christian Churches*, ii. 771. A striking interpretation of the origins of rational Anglicanism may be found in Robert M. Krapp, *Liberal Anglicanism, 1636–1647*, where it is clearly demonstrated that it was an aristocratic reaction against popular Calvinistic (Antinomian) enthusiasm.

Englishmen as it had been ever since the sixteenth century; if anything, more so. 'Popery' remained 'a monstrous and most audacious corruption' of Christianity; 'an impious and impudent combination against the sense and rights of mankind'.[1] As for individualistic 'enthusiasm', the proliferation of the 'petulant capricious sects' in the seventeenth century had ended by making them all ridiculous, and *Hudibras* in assailing them with bitter satire became the most popular book of its day. There were to be no more Ranters and Muggletonians, and the Quakers, still under suspicion, quickly grew quiet and respectable.[2] The Antinomian strain in dissent flickered and all but died, as the Puritans passed out of their militant period to become the respectable and decorous Dissenters of the next age. Nonconformism in religion was at low ebb after 1660. It was not so much that there wandered the sons of Belial 'flown with insolence and wine' as that an era of theology had left people weary of such squabbling; and, more important still, dissent was equated with rebellion and civil strife. 'Enthusiasm' was a menace to society.

For a time after the Restoration the spirit of revenge and counter-persecution prevailed. But it was not long before most responsible men could earnestly approve the wish which the martyred Russell might have seen fulfilled had he lived a few years longer: 'That Churchmen might be less severe, and Dissenters less scrupulous.' To the rule of reason both Dissenter and moderate Churchman were eager to return; and the events of 1688–9 registered their victory over the 'high-flying' clergy. It is true that at its inception the Toleration Act was more like a weary *pis aller* than a positive good to most. A truce had been called, but William Penn's radical claim that 'a man may be a very good Englishman, but a very indifferent Churchman', was not yet generally accepted.[3] But as a matter of fact toleration rested on

---

[1] John Taylor, in *A Collection of Theological Tracts*, ed. Richard Watson, iii. 312; William Warburton, in *Chatham Correspondence* (London, 1858), ii. 189. Edward Carpenter, *Thomas Tenison*, chap. ii, deals with the extensive anti-Romanist feeling prevalent during the years around 1688.

[2] Charles E. Whiting, *Studies in English Puritanism, 1660–1688*, chap. vi.

[3] Penn, *England's Present Interest Discovered*, 1675; see the conclusions of W. K. Jordan, *The Development of Religious Toleration in England*, pp. 466–88.

unshakable ground. This ground was partly the deep spiritual belief in toleration of the Cambridge Platonists, partly a more utilitarian outlook. There was Halifax, the genial 'trimmer', whose moderation was eminently practical. 'Circumstances must come in, and are to be made a part of the matter of which we are to judge; positive decisions are always dangerous, more especially in politics.'[1]

William III was also a 'trimmer' so far as concerned religious disputes in England. Fatal to all brands of dogmatism, the approach may be seen in the erstwhile Tory Charles D'Avenant's essays (1704). He returns consciously to the spirit of Elizabeth: wise princes 'make the established religion their principle concern, and yet are indulgent to the weakness of those who cannot comply with it'. He cites Machiavelli: the prince will take care to preserve religion, for 'in the whole world there is not a greater sign of imminent ruin than when God and his worship are despised'. Religion is a very important thing, but more for practical reasons than otherwise. Religious unity is desirable, and the Established Church needs to be sustained; but narrowness and persecution ought to be avoided. The enemy may be found on either Right or Left; it is fanaticism or enthusiasm, whether of Papist or left-wing Puritan.[2] Moderation, as D'Avenant entitled another of his books, is a virtue—a political virtue.

So Machiavelli and Plato each had something to do with the new spirit; so did weariness with old quarrels as well as a new *Zeitgeist* induced by the new science. One should not overlook the extent to which contentiousness was channelled into politics after 1689, rather than into religion. Whig and Tory, *Observator* and *Rehearsal*, exhibited the most violent animosities, and to a degree these were still tinged with religious colours, but the quarrel had really been transposed to a more purely political field. A combination of causes had paved the way for a period in which religion, still regarded as of vital importance, was to rest on reason, not enthusiasm, to be safeguarded by the pen and not by the sword.

---

[1] H. C. Foxcroft, ed., *Life and Works of the First Marquis of Halifax*, ii. 138, 178.
[2] *Essays on Peace at Home and War Abroad*, pp. 179–81, 199, 217–31. Cf. the trimming views of Sir William Temple, in his *Observations upon the United Provinces of the Netherlands*.

2

If both papal authority and inner light were firmly rejected as foundations of religion, so also was tradition. Because that idea subsequently became associated with Anglicanism, there has been a mistaken tendency to assume that Anglicanism always embraced it.[1] But it was not merely a few 'latitudinarians' who rejected tradition as an authority, in the seventeenth and eighteenth centuries. Almost all the clergy shared the view, expressed in a popular religious handbook written by an Anglican bishop, that reason must not be impeded by tradition, for an error may be perpetuated as well as a truth, and 'though the general tradition or testimony of the Church may be a good help, yet it may not always be a certain rule, to lead men to the entire and unadultered doctrine of Jesus'.[2] William Sherlock indicated clearly what a conservative Anglican thought of the authority of 'church guides': 'the Church of Rome will have men believe their guides without reason or understanding; we have guides, not merely to dictate to us, but to teach us to understand . . . to inform our judgment, that we may be able to understand for ourselves'. Thus tradition was interpreted to mean only a source of education, an aid to greater aptitude in understanding the Bible, which is alone the source of truth and salvation.[3] The 'entire and unadultered doctrine of Jesus' could be found in only one place, the Bible.

That what was found there was indeed the Divine Revelation was proved by a variety of external evidences too certain

[1] See the introduction to *Anglicanism: The Thought and Practice of the Church of England Illustrated from the Religious Literature of the Seventeenth Century,* ed. Paul Elmer More and Frank L. Cross, p. lxxii. Numerous selections from this very anthology contradict the claim of traditionalism. Archbishop Ussher, in 1625, categorically denies that 'traditions of men' should be accepted as religious truths (pp. 135 ff.); he quotes Athanasius, 'The Holy Scriptures given by inspiration of God are of themselves sufficient to the discovery of truth.' P. 117, Whitby: the tradition of the Church 'gives no unquestionable assurance of the truth or derivation of these customs from our Lord and his Apostles . . .', &c.

[2] Synge, *A Gentleman's Religion,* pp. 36–40. Cf. Dryden's lament ('The Hind and the Panther', lines 470–1):

> No help from fathers or traditions train,
> These ancient guides she taught us to disdain.

[3] William Sherlock, *A Short Summary of the Principal Controversies between the Church of England and the Church of Rome,* pp. 10–11.

to admit of doubt—mainly by the miracles and the fulfilment of prophecies. It was already realized that there were certain difficulties in discovering precisely what Scripture said, yet there was a firm faith that 'a sober and honest enquirer cannot easily be mistaken in the interpretation of those places of the New Testament, which do contain any necessary part of Religion'. It was a part of the Latitudinarian outlook to hold that these 'necessary parts' of religion were 'few and plain', and that all else might well be left to the theologians. 'There are no real contradictions' in the Bible; and while some things in the revelation are certainly beyond our reason, yet nothing is contrary to reason.[1] This last distinction, held by all the orthodox, was to prove troublesome when explored by the deists.

The right of unlimited private judgement implied in this was recognized and warned against: men had a duty to make up their minds only after consulting all the best opinions. Yet private judgement must in the end prevail, for no one should submit blindly to authority. God will not punish for an honest mistake in judgement. Here was another dangerous doctrine, for the deists could all plead sincerity. But it was simply denied that any honest man could possibly doubt the proofs of Christianity. 'All the arguments against Christianity', it was asserted, 'are so weak and insignificant, that they rather make for it.'[2]

If we ask why such great confidence, and also what was meant by 'reason', we come upon the influence of Locke and Newton. Reason meant lucidity and common sense, not Scholastic obscurities. The latter were somehow associated with that tangled wilderness of sects which had been rejected in disgust. Reason was Locke's 'clear and distinct ideas'. In this tendency, Bishop Stillingfleet perceived, there might lie danger, for Lockean philosophy was impelled to discard all 'mysteries'. Yet when Locke debated with Bishop Stillingfleet on this point, public opinion awarded Locke the verdict.[3] Locke's philosophy led logically to scepticism,

[1] Synge, op. cit., pp. 4, 47, 56.
[2] Robert Jenkin, *A Brief Confutation of the Pretences against Natural and Revealed Religion*, p. xliii.
[3] Hunt, *Religious Thought in England*, ii. 248–50. It seems to have been a common belief that Stillingfleet died of his mortification in failing to meet Locke's argument.

to the acceptance of large areas where certainty was impossible—not least, as Shaftesbury realized, the area of moral truth. But the firstfruit of Locke for most people was not the scepticism latent in his epistemology; it was his own faith in a rational religion, his commonsense revolt against 'mysteries' accompanied, however, by his belief that Christianity could be both simple and clear.

Locke's initial impulse to write his memorable *Essay concerning Human Understanding* came from the desire to know how far men are able to grasp religious truths.[1] His caution, his unwillingness to believe except on the basis of solid proof, his contempt for metaphysical 'fiddling', his disparagement of idle and bootless speculation, of the abstract without tangible content—all this was the new spirit, the ore of Bacon and Descartes tempered in the crucible of wars inspired by rival fanaticisms.[2] But it did not exclude religion. Locke clung to the belief that we can *know* ethical and religious truths (to know meant, for Locke, to be certain). It was his basic trait to scorn the 'vanity' and 'pride' of men who could not be content with a little real knowledge such as was suitable to their limited capacities, but must needs invent fantastic explanations of the whole universe. Yet with all the fervency at his command he felt that this modest stint of solid knowledge did not exclude knowledge about God and His revelation to man. He was willing to simplify this knowledge, but to his 'commonsense' outlook a basic minimum of it was possible and necessary.

Doubtless Locke was glib and inconsistent. 'Had Locke's mind been more profound, it might have been less influential.'[3] The philosopher spoke for his age. It wanted

---

[1] A. C. Fraser, introduction to the 1894 edition of *An Essay concerning Human Understanding*, i. xvii.

[2] See Norman Kemp Smith, *John Locke, 1632–1704*; Bertrand Russell, *A History of Western Philosophy* (New York, 1945), pp. 604–17. What Locke meant to men is discernible more than a century later in a belated defence by an American disciple: 'In the "Essay on the Human Understanding" intellectual science appeared for the first time in a clear and intelligible shape, unmingled with the vain and visionary fancies which had previously disfigured it, and accessible to the plain good sense of every cultivated mind.' Alexander H. Everett, 1829, quoted in Perry Miller, ed., *The Transcendentalists* (Cambridge, Mass., 1950).

[3] George Santayana, *Some Turns of Thought in Modern Philosophy* (Cambridge, 1933), p. 3.

both solid truth and rational religion, and told itself that the two were identical.

For 'grounding all he taught on the phenomena of nature', Locke received the praise of the deists. 'He appealed to the experience and conscious knowledge of every one, and rendered all he advanced intelligible.'[1] Very soon the deists would take Locke's principles to mean that much of traditional Christianity, being 'mysterious', should be abandoned. But the great man himself clung closely to revealed religion, and not from either fear or blindness. It was the most pleasant intellectual experience of his day to contemplate the perfect harmony of Reason and Faith.

Years later it seemed to many in retrospect that John Locke had been the seed-sower for all the 'harvest of rationalist theology'.[2] It is true that Locke's *Reasonableness of Christianity* was a signal for the deists. (John Toland's *Christianity Not Mysterious*, which it had directly inspired, followed it immediately—a work which, as Leslie Stephen wrote, was the signal-gun for the whole deistic controversy.) Anyone concerned to judge of Locke's responsibility for deism must consult this book as well as Book IV, chapters x and xix, of the 1700 edition of the *Essay*. There was the same *ex post facto* criticism of the Cambridge Platonists. In neither case is the criticism justified. Both the Platonists and Locke sought to save religion. To the former, the innate rationality implanted within the human mind, the 'candle of the Lord' as they liked to call it, the structure of universal reason, was a weapon against infidelity, a proof of divinity— the stamp of our Creator on us, as Descartes said, and a bulwark too against the fanaticisms which threatened to bring religion to chaos. As for Locke's sensationalism, it could as readily be used to defend Christianity as to attack it, and indeed it was so used.

The Cambridge group more than Locke were pioneers in rationalism, abjuring both 'enthusiasm' and 'superstition', opposed to dogmatism, their basic mood well expressed in

---

[1] Bolingbroke, *Works*, iii. 52, 405–6.
[2] John J. Tayler, *Retrospect of Religious Life in England*, p. 372. Also Joseph Milner, *Gibbon's Account of Christianity Considered*, p. 154. Milner also (pp. 250–1) reproached the Platonists for the same sin of introducing a fatal amount of reasoning.

Whichcote's aphorism, 'Be rational in your religion.' They contributed the most to a spirit which, in Restoration times, produced a strong tendency to think of religion as 'exalted reason'. The Platonist belief in a structure of abstract, ideal reason, governing or even limiting God, was in fact opposed to Locke's empiricism in some ways, and was a factor independently influencing eighteenth-century deism. Samuel Clarke and Lord Shaftesbury owed more to this tradition than to Locke.[1] The innate moral sense, the structure of eternal reason, the rationalism implanted within man—these were philosophically somewhat opposed to Locke's empiricism.[2] But Locke and the Platonists held in common towards religion a spirit of cool rationality, an anti-dogmatism, an opposition to enthusiasm and to blind traditionalism as well; and also the desire to preserve Christianity while adjusting it to the rational, scientific temper. Thus it is that systems which philosophers find different were in harmony where religion was concerned. Historically, both reflected a religious rationalism induced by the social and political environment, beginning as early as 1650.

In the case of Newton as well as Locke we find that the respect in which science was held, and its assumed harmony with religion, antedated his great discoveries. The biographer of Robert Boyle, 'devout naturalist', has written that 'in his devotion to the laboratory and his loyalty to the altar' Boyle was 'the child of his age'.[3] The soil had been well prepared for Newton's apparent demonstration that when

[1] *Complete Works of George Savile*, ed. Walter Raleigh, pp. 2–7; see also Martin Clifford, *A Treatise of Human Reason*, 1674. Among many writings on the Cambridge group see good brief discussions in Norman Sykes, *Church and State in Eighteenth-century England*, L. I. Bredvold, *The Intellectual Milieu of John Dryden*, E. C. Mossner, *Bishop Butler and the Age of Reason*, and Douglas Bush, *English Literature in the Earlier Seventeenth Century*, chap. x. Longer studies include Tulloch, op. cit., and works by F. J. Powicke (1926) and W. C. Pauley (1937). Alfred O. Aldridge, *Shaftesbury and the Deist Manifesto*, discusses Shaftesbury's hostility to Locke owing to the latter's failure to provide a foundation for moral truth sturdier than mere 'opinion'.

[2] But Locke certainly held that an 'internal sense' exists which provides the source from which moral law is deduced. His belief that there is nothing at all in the mind to begin with did not keep him from believing that men quite generally act rationally, which means morally. Considerations of prudence and the desire for pleasure ensure moral behaviour; men know certainly that God exists.

[3] Mitchell S. Fisher, *Robert Boyle, Devout Naturalist*, p. 23.

we penetrate nature's secrets we find clear evidence of a deity.

It was not merely that the orderliness of Newton's universe implied a Designer; Newton's laws seemed to show not only the omnipotent but the omnipresent God. It was not a naturalism that left God nothing to do once the machine was created. John Toland, deist and (later) pantheist, sought to intrude such a naturalism when he urged that gravitation must be something inherently in matter; but almost no one agreed with him. The 'force' of gravitation, left unexplained, was evidently something sustained by God; thus the very imperfection of Newtonian physics left a convenient function for the Deity. Bentley (directly authorized by Newton himself) argued that 'the principle of gravity is inadequate by itself to explain the systematic motion of the stellar universe'.[1]

To the vast majority, at any rate, Newtonianism indicated, exultantly, the proof of a Grand Designer and Regulator of the orderly universe disclosed by Sir Isaac's experiments. There were a few, indeed, who accused Newtonianism of pantheistic tendencies. But 'physico-theology' carried the day.[2]

Those earnest searchers after the *via media*, the Cambridge Platonists, had been deeply suspicious of Descartes, because his system appeared to exclude God from a mechanistic world-order. On the other hand there was the wholly shocking Spinoza, whose system provided no place for a deity outside the natural order. Newtonianism seemed ideally to avoid both errors. Therefore when Newton urged the complete harmony of his science with religion, all were

---

[1] Aldridge, op. cit., p. 300. In the same place Professor Aldridge discusses Samuel Clarke's argument that motion must be caused by God.

[2] See the discussion in Arthur O. Lovejoy, *The Great Chain of Being*, pp. 133–8; also Meyrick H. Carré, *Phases of Thought in England* (Oxford, 1949), pp. 322–7. Herbert Drennon, 'Newtonianism: Its Method, Theology, and Metaphysics', in *Englische Studien*, lxviii (1933–4), 397–409, is an excellent summary. The great Leibniz accused Newton of leading to pantheism, a charge which Samuel Clarke sought to refute, Englishmen assuming that he had done so. Samuel Miller, *A Brief Retrospect of the Eighteenth Century*, i. 14–17 and 438, refers to the followers of John Hutchinson, who thought Newtonianism subversive in ascribing inherent activity to matter. Plainly this group was an oddity to the Augustans, who were quite convinced that Newton meant no such thing.

convinced. Perhaps had Newton been a Pascal the course of intellectual history might have been changed. But the qualms the latter felt about 'proving divinity by the works of nature' were not much felt in England for half a century. By 1721 Cotton Mather of Massachusetts had accepted the new science as Christianity's handmaiden on behalf of what was surely the western world's most conservative religious body.[1]

3

The inference was that 'reason' is the ally, not the enemy, of religion. What was Reason's role in religious matters? Reason is necessary, in the first place, it was commonly said, to learn whether or not Scripture is truly the word of God: 'My reason must prove to me that it is revealed.'[2] This was evident to all. Reason, wrote Dr. South, 'proves the revelation of it by God; but then, having done this, here it stops, and pretends not to understand and fathom the nature of the thing revealed'. Nevertheless, reason has to test the Bible and is a guide in interpreting it. Another representative churchman agreed that reason must know whether Scripture is revelation and also exactly what truths are revealed there; but it cannot reject what is told there merely because this may be beyond our comprehension.[3]

Socinians and deists will argue that there should be no 'mysteries', for once a thing is revealed it ought to be clear. Orthodox opinion insisted that our reason is too weak for this; God is, after all, wiser than men, and some things remain incomprehensible to the latter. Nothing should be contrary to reason, but some things may be beyond it. The distinction here left some room for argument. The bolder free-thinkers would claim a right to analyse and reject on the basis of internal inconsistency of ideas, refusing all 'mysteries', which the pious could never allow.

---

[1] See Mather's *Christian Philosopher*; discussed by Perry Miller, *Jonathan Edwards*, p. 83.

[2] Robert South, *Sermons*, i. 368. Locke in his *Essay concerning Human Understanding* agrees that reason must judge of the origin and evidences of revelation, though not of its content; see also Joseph Butler, *Works*, i. 198.

[3] Joseph Pyke, *An Impartial View of the Principal Difficulties* . . ., pp. xii ff. See also Luke Milbourne, *Mysteries in Religion Vindicated*, pp. 51 ff.

Having passed judgement on the historical authenticity of the divine revelation, on 'the objective evidence, or rational proof, in which truth is proposed to and assented to by the understanding'[1]—a judgement which orthodox opinion had a sublime confidence must be favourable[2]—reason had one more religious task, and this was to search out and determine the exact meaning of that revelation, a task in which what was wanted was not Platonic or Scholastic mystifications, but the plain sense of the matter. We have spoken of the naïve faith, so widely held, that there could be no contradiction between reason and religion. By this was meant: (a) that the evidence in favour of the divine authorship of the Christian Holy Scripture could scarcely be doubted by a reasonable man, the Bible in its entirety being meant ordinarily; (b) that within this body of revealed truth there are no internal contradictions and nothing contrary to reason, though there are some things above human reason;[3] (c) that the meanings in this body of revealed truth are sufficiently clear and unambiguous, at least on all the essentials of religion, to enable all reasonable men to arrive at substantially the same interpretation. The last proposition involved the assumption that there *are* essentials, the 'few and plain' things absolutely necessary to salvation, not often very carefully defined—the assumption being also that there are a number of more difficult points, again not too clearly indicated, which are not really vital.

With the advantages of hindsight it is not difficult to see pitfalls lurking in these assumptions. Still, what answer was there, then if ever, to the proposition that, unless these things be true, there can be no real Christianity? Was the

---

[1] Thomas Morgan, *A Collection of Tracts* . . ., p. 157.

[2] 'There is no book in the world', remarked Josiah King (*Mr. Blount's Oracles of Reason Examined and Answered*, p. 31), 'whose author can be more plainly demonstrated than that of the Pentateuch.' Such complacent confidence was ubiquitous.

[3] One orthodox writer attempted to illuminate this vexed question by the analogy of a blind man, who could never gain an understanding of light, colour, and vision by his own unaided reason, but who could, with the aid of others, satisfy himself beyond doubt that these things do exist. The analogy was hardly perfect, for it surely left the implication that the truths revealed to us ought to be absolutely clear, and rationally demonstrable, a position soon to be associated with deists and Socinians.

Englishman of Newton's age to be told to stifle his reason
lest he mar his faith? Was he to be directed back to the
Infallible Chair? Or referred again to an infallible inner light
not responsible to reason?[1] These things were quite impossible. If there was a great gamble in the reliance on reason,
it was an inevitable one: the other games were all closed out.

Some few were dubious.[2] John Dryden retreated to
Catholicism, after suggesting that to rely on reason is 'to
take away the pillars from our faith, and to prop it only with
a twig'. Without a principle of authority, Christianity would
become chaos; for reason is

> Dim as the borrow'd beams of moon and stars
> To lonely, weary, wandering travellers.

But Dryden was called a 'monster' for his apostasy to Rome.
Richard Baxter, the great Nonconformist, expressed some
disquietude in the spirit of that older Puritanism which was
little apt to trust the wisdom of men. But the great majority
went forth with a great trust in the Bible and right reason,
splendidly unaware that these might go wrong. They were
not indifferent to religion; they were enchanted by its
apparent agreement with all that human reason might
discover.

Even if reason was as feeble as Dryden said, the Augustans
saw no other support. Deists would press home the point
that, if we cannot trust reason, there is no escape from Rome:
we must have either a Pope or complete liberty of judgement.[3] This was not exclusively an 'infidel' position, but one
the logic of which deists knew no Protestant could resist.
Anthony Collins could quote the distinguished Anglican
Daniel Whitby to the effect that 'we should call no man
guide or master upon earth, no Fathers, no Church, no

---

[1] The tendency to associate the enthusiasts with the Romanists, which at first
glance may seem curious to us, is to be explained by their common reliance on a
principle beyond reason. Thus, the Quakers and later the Methodists were called
'papists in disguise'. The Inner Light and the Infallible Chair might be very
different in some respects but they agreed in their supra-rationalism, and it was this
ingredient which impressed, because it seemed most dangerous to, the Englishmen
of the eighteenth century.

[2] Louis I. Bredvold, in *The Intellectual Milieu of John Dryden*, ably discusses this
group. See pp. 64–71.

[3] Thomas Chubb, *Posthumous Works*, i. 58–59.

Council'.[1] To this faith in free inquiry many within the Church steadily remained true. Religion, wrote Samuel Clarke, 'will not long subsist in the belief of understanding persons', if ever it be separated from its foundation in 'Reason and uncorrupted Nature'.[2] In the author's opinion, this statement is certainly true. If so, the goal of adjusting Christianity to science and reason was nothing less than the project of saving religion for the modern world. The great Catholic apologist Bossuet had long since predicted that Protestantism must fail because it leads to incessant schism. Rational Christians of this age hoped to demonstrate that the right reason of sober men is a stronger fortress for religion than the surrender of the mind to authority.

[1] Anthony Collins, *A Discourse of Freethinking*, pp. 45–46.
[2] Samuel Clarke, *Works*, i. v.

III

THE LIMITS OF THE DEBATE

We must carefully distinguish betwixt what the Scripture itself says,
and what is only said in the Scripture.   ROBERT BOYLE

PLATONIC rationalism, Lockean empiricism, and the
prestige of scientific investigation tended to make old
theological quarrels obsolete and wearisome. It has been
well observed that the Platonists' 'elevation of reason as the
divinely implanted governor of the life of man, and the
arbiter also in the interpretation of Holy Scripture', under-
cut both Calvinist predestination and Laudian reliance on
ecclesiastical tradition.[1] It is true that Dissenters remained,
and also that within the Church of England, after 1688, the
High Church group differed violently from the 'men of
latitude'. But in reality this quarrel was not so much theological as political.[2] Tory churchmen, as well as Whig, ordinarily claimed to trust reason.

Reason was confidently trusted because as yet there had
been no serious challenge to religion from science, or any
other field of inquiry. No major conflict between science and
religion will occur in the first half of the eighteenth century.
Geology offered almost as little opposition to theology as
physics did. Later in the century, the poet Cowper will be
heard murmuring about the impudence of those who 'drill
and bore the solid earth' in order to prove God a liar. But
this was not until 1760, at about which time modern geology
was born. Not until mid-century was the diluvian theory of
the fossils seriously challenged, a theory which so comfort-
ably adjusted Scripture to paleontology that Voltaire chose
to regard fossils as an argument *for* Christianity. Theories as
to the origin of the earth were numerous and fanciful, but,

---

[1] Sykes, *Church and State in the Eighteenth Century*, p. 21.

[2] The essentially political basis of the High Church quarrel with the Whiggish
churchmen is well developed by Sykes, ibid., pp. 285–90. See also below, Chap. IX.
Rural-urban differences were also involved; for a specimen of rural prejudice, see
'A Letter out of the Country to the Clergy in and about the City of London', in
A Collection of Scarce and Valuable Tracts (London, 1712), pp. 213–22.

until such Frenchmen as Buffon, Le Cat, Maillet began to write later in the century, they struggled to vindicate Genesis, and few suspected that this could not be accomplished. Approved by Locke and Newton was Whiston's *New Theory of the Earth* (1696), 'wherein the creation of the world in six days, the universal deluge, and the general conflagration, as laid down in Holy Scripture, are shown to be perfectly agreeable to reason and philosophy'. However, Thomas Burnet's earlier explanation was used by Charles Blount, the deist, to embarrass the defenders of Genesis.[1] Another 'elegant romance'[2] which had a vogue but involved absurdities and entailed a controversy was (1695) Dr. John Woodward's *Essay toward a Natural History of the Earth*; it argued that all geological strata and fossils were the consequence of the Flood. Woodward's hypothesis did not satisfy John Arbuthnot;[3] and it would seem that the more discriminating minds always entertained a certain uneasiness about the fossils. John Toland, the deist, endeavoured to turn the fossils against Christianity in his *Pantheisticon*. But few accepted any real conflict with the Bible; it was assumed that a correct interpretation of nature and of the books of the Pentateuch would reconcile all differences, and meanwhile there were various ingenious 'hypotheses' available to this end. These scientific theories squared very conveniently with Christian theology.[4]

This trial of Christianity, then, differed from later ordeals with which we are more familiar. Science was no great enemy. It seemed, indeed, a very great friend to religion. There had of course been doubts about the new universe. The disturbing notion was especially the plurality of worlds,

---

[1] Blount, *The Oracles of Reason* (1693); Thomas Burnet, *The Theory of the Earth* (2 vols., 1684–90).

[2] Burnet, Whiston, and Woodward are discussed in Samuel Miller, *Brief Retrospect of the Eighteenth Century*, i. 157 ff., along with other theories that followed.

[3] Lester M. Beattie, *John Arbuthnot*, pp. 190 ff. Erasmus Warren and John Keill also entered the argument about Woodward's book.

[4] A striking example of a minister's use of science to prove original sin is in Isaac Watts's *The Ruin and Recovery of Mankind* (1740). The earth was originally smooth, of uniform and equable climate, &c.; the Flood, a consequence of the Fall, brought such examples of divine displeasure as mountains, deserts, devouring animals, insects. Watts uses and praises Woodward's work.

which an orthodox clergyman in 1698 pronounced 'impious, prophane, and unbecoming a Christian', though he was not prepared to say heretical.[1] The vastness and non-geocentric character of the new universe led sometimes to pessimism, but more often and increasingly to optimism, the latter rising to a triumphant crest in Newtonian times. The vastness of the universe did not trouble such men as Ralph Cudworth and Richard Bentley; they gloried in it.[2] And the question of size was overwhelmed by that of orderly design. True, the confutation of atheists by the appeal to Newton's universe soon became less exhilarating; for there were no atheists, and the argument was no good against the deists, who suggested that it eliminated the need for revealed religion— they accepted God willingly enough, but not Christianity's God. Newtonianism can be said to have established that frame of mind which began to doubt all miracles, all instances of special Providence. But it was not taken to be in conflict with Christianity, and remained in common use in Christian apologetics against whatever atheists there might be. . . . In biology, the fixity of species was, of course, assumed throughout the century, Linnaeus fortifying it in the second half; evolution lay some distance in the future. Newtonianism reacted against a mechanistic tendency in Cartesianism on the vital as well as the material level; a spiritual force was at the bottom of all life.[3]

We ought not perhaps to press this absence of tension between science and religion too far. There was always a certain undercurrent of concern; one cannot say that a firm agreement was ever really made, especially as relating to the plurality of worlds and the Biblical accounts of the origins of the earth. Newtonianism cast an effusion of harmony over the relationship between science and religion, but this wore off a little in a few years, and by 1730 a leading clergyman was complaining that 'the men of science . . . are the greatest sticklers against revealed religion'.[4] Neverthe-

---

[1] Josiah King, op. cit., pp. 191–3.

[2] See Douglas Bush, op. cit., chap. ix, espec. pp. 275 ff.; Grant McCulley, 'The Seventeenth Century Doctrine of a Plurality of Worlds', *Annals of Science*, i (15 Oct. 1936), pp. 385–430. Also discussed in Lovejoy, *Great Chain of Being*.

[3] L. Cohen Rosenfield, 'Un Chapitre de l'histoire de l'animal-machine', *Revue de littérature comparée*, July–Sept. 1937, p. 468.   [4] Sykes, *Bishop Gibson*, p. 243.

less, it was easily possible for scientific men to be devout and religious men to be scientific throughout most of the eighteenth century—not only possible but customary. Certainly the impetus to 'infidelity' did not come from any spectacular doctrine of science, such as happened later in the nineteenth century.

What were the areas within which the great debate took place? The religious radicals did not possess the weapons of 'higher criticism', for the day of historical criticism was not yet. Biblical scholarship was indeed formidable within its limits, and something may well be said about it. The years from 1600 to 1660 had seen an extraordinary growth of scholarship, stimulated by the rivalry of Calvinist and Jesuit; it has been said that this scholarship was pursued 'with an intensity of application unequalled before or since'.[1] From Geneva, from France, from Holland and Belgium there came into England the fruits of an international scholarly competition: the works of Scaliger, Heinsius, Grotius, Casaubon, and many others were familiar to English students. England had already by 1690 produced scholars of the stature of George Bull, Robert South, and John Fell, to name only a sample, and in the next few years was to develop many more, including the world-famed philologist Richard Bentley. John Mill produced in 1707 his notable new edition of the New Testament in Greek. There were extremely learned commentators too numerous to mention: among them Whitby, Hickes, Allix, Clarke, Dodwell, and Whiston. Meanwhile works continued to flow in from abroad. Important new advances were being made in textual criticism. These may be dated from the epochal works of the French Catholic, Richard Simon, 'the father of Biblical criticism'. The brilliant Oratorian, who quarrelled with Bossuet over this strategy of confounding the Protestants by casting doubt on Scriptural certainty, was well known in England for his critical histories of the sacred writings.[2] The field

[1] Foster Watson, in *The Cambridge History of English Literature* (1911), vii. 345–6.
[2] *A Critical History of the Old Testament*, translated London, 1682; *Critical Enquiries into the Various Editions of the Bible*, 1684; *A Critical History of the Text of the New Testament*, 1689. Simon took the position that while the doctrinal parts of the Bible were divine, the historical parts were not—a most destructive doctrine. See

of Bible criticism had also proved tempting to the talents of the great critics Spinoza and Pierre Bayle, who must be numbered among its originators.

Here were the beginnings of modern Biblical criticism, and the deist debate would advance them somewhat farther. English deism directly stimulated the great critical movement in Germany in the next century. But as yet the weapons of scholarship were crude, and one may say that the whole furious controversy between deist and Christian about the 'truth' or 'falsity' of the Bible was based on premises now regarded as unscientific. Robert Boyle, as this chapter's epigraph indicates, knew very well that there was a *textual* problem, and so did other educated men. Textual criticism was making rapid strides. The significance of the famous Boyle–Bentley dispute over the Phalaris letters (1699) was that 'historians thereafter began to raise for all the writings of antiquity the preliminary question of their origin'.[1] But textual criticism must of course be distinguished from historical. For example, Newton's *Observations on the Prophecies of Daniel* . . . (published 1732) are bold in textual criticism, i.e. in suggesting that errors may have crept into the received version of the Bible; but the great scientist, a pious Christian, staunchly defended the literal fulfilment of prophecies, declaring that to reject them 'is to reject the Christian religion'. No historical grounds had been discovered suggesting that Scripture was fallible. It might only have been fallibly transcribed.

Cheyne observes that in the eighteenth century only Warburton, Lowth, and Geddes showed 'any talent or inclination for a criticism of the Old Testament which is not merely concerned with various readings of the text'. And only Geddes, the Scotch Catholic who wrote near the end of the century, 'can properly be called a founder of criticism'.[2] Textual criticism of the New Testament advanced, but the approach remained textual, not historical. Of the old exegesis Coppens justly remarks that it looked upon the Sacred Books

Bolingbroke, *Works*, ii. 203, for a deist's favourable opinion of Simon's thesis. Aldridge, op. cit., p. 363, deals with Shaftesbury's use of such ideas.

[1] Joseph Coppens, *The Old Testament and the Critics* (translated by E. A. Ryan and E. W. Tribbe; Paterson, 1942), p. 6.

[2] T. K. Cheyne, *Founders of Old Testament Criticism*, pp. 1–3.

'much as upon documents fallen from heaven', and that it 'virtually denied [better, failed to have any notion of] any process of development in Judeo-Christian revelation'.[1] Not before Conyers Middleton, towards mid-century, was the idea of relating the Bible to secular literature of the same period explored. The problem of scholarship, then, was almost purely one of ascertaining and expounding the meaning of the text, not of discovering the origin and date of it.

Roughly, then, these were the limits within which the debate took place. The deists were not ignorant men. Though few belonged in the highest ranks of creative scholarship (Bentley, Clarke, and Warburton were not deists, though Conyers Middleton perhaps was), they were abreast of the learning of their time, and used it in order to embarrass orthodoxy. Richard Bentley, famous for his textual criticism, was the very pious author of the first Boyle Lecture (1692) on 'The Folly of Atheism and . . . Deism' and later of a famous reply to the deist Collins. But Bentley was sceptical of many things in the Bible; and was he justified in complaining that 'comparatively ignorant and unlearned writers, I mean such as Collins, Tindal, Toland, Morgan, and Chubb', had gone to 'grosser degrees of infidelity'?[2] These deists were, it is true, the natural radicals and iconoclasts. Committed to a religion of nature, they suspected that the whole Christian revelation was no more than a tissue of lies and fables; but they had to prove it. They were prepared to seize upon any contradiction or inconsistency they could find in the Christian case. This might be in theology, in Scripture, in ethics or (more rarely) in science. The deist as scholar and as reasoner was essentially an opportunistic special pleader, looking for anything he could find to wound what he felt (largely on *a priori* grounds) to be a fraud. He did not have the weapons of modern scholarship, though he might make some shrewd guesses; nor did he have the modern critical outlook which seeks not to expose a conspiracy but to understand a growth. Orthodoxy, in any

---

[1] Coppens, op. cit., pp. 3–4.
[2] Whiston, *Memoirs*, i. 109. On Bentley see the biography by J. H. Monk (two vols., 1883) and M. L. W. Laistner, 'Richard Bentley: 1742–1942', *Studies in Philology*, xxxix. 510 ff.

event, had to defend itself on those grounds, committed as
it was to the plenary inspiration of the Scriptures, their
perfect correspondence to natural truth, and their complete
conformity to 'reason'. 'To see the hand of God as clearly in
a long, providential development as in a sudden miracle'[1]
might have been possible then if they had been able to think
of it in that way. But they were not, and neither were their
adversaries.

No one would make the mistake of thinking that all the
criticisms of Christianity brought forward in the eighteenth
century were new. A few random examples will suffice:
(*a*) Shaftesbury's ethical criticisms of Christianity are to be
found in the Renaissance writer Pietro Pomponazzi. The latter's ideas clearly derived from Stoic and Epicurean sources;
and these ideas, the relics of Christianity's first great debate,
were well known to educated Englishmen.[2] (*b*) In the Middle
Ages Averroism was akin to deism in holding reason capable
of full religious truth, revelation being unnecessary except
as a crutch for weaker minds.[3] (*c*) The *Encomium Moriae*
of Erasmus had been deistic in its rejection of any elaborate
theology in favour of a simple, ethical religion. To seek the
origins of deism is a precarious task; it has been well said
that 'deism of a kind may be said to have been alive since
thought began'. Lord Herbert of Cherbury introduced such
ideas early in the seventeenth century, at which time they
were also known in France, but it is unwise to credit him
with too much originality. One student has made a case for
the influence of Montaigne. Tides of infidelity had started
flowing into France and England, to a degree, from Italy,
during the later sixteenth century.[4]

---

[1] W. Robertson Smith, in the preface to the translation of J. Wellhausen's *Pro-
legomena to the History of Israel* (London, 1885). The words seem to sum up the
faith of modern religious scholars, who have abandoned belief in the literal inspiration of the Old Testament books to discover a deeper miracle, the historical development of Israel from savagery to spiritual grandeur.

[2] Aldridge, op. cit., points to the Stoic origins of Shaftesbury's leading ideas.

[3] See Étienne Gilson, *Reason and Revelation in the Middle Ages* (London, 1948).

[4] Douglas Bush, op. cit., p. 322; Pierre Villey, 'L'Influence de Montaigne sur
Charles Blount et sur les Déistes anglais', *Revue du seizième siècle*, i (1913); George T.
Buckley, *Atheism in the English Renaissance* (Chicago, 1932). It need hardly be
added that Socinianism and Arminianism, which arose in the seventeenth century,

If anything was new in this eighteenth-century controversy, it was provided by what real knowledge of the
Bible had been made available, and, second, by the Newtonian frame of reference. Mainly, the debate owed its origin
to social and political factors: the reaction against fanaticism, the achievement of political stability and freedom, and
England's commercial prosperity. The eighteenth century
in English history is an age of repose, in which men had time
to debate religious questions, but few reasons to fight over
them. It was the 'climate of opinion' and the social environment that became favourable after 1689 to the wide propagation of deism.

Professor Lovejoy long ago pointed out the close similarities between deism and the neo-classical spirit in art and
literature.[1] At the root of both lay the conviction that nature
is harmonious, orderly, rational—and man the same. The
positive side of deism, lending strength and courage to its
critique of Christianity, was a peculiar synthesis of the age.

were hardly more than new names for old heresies, if heresies they were. Arianism
and Pelagianism were the older versions of very similar doctrines.
   [1] 'The Parallel of Deism and Classicism', *Modern Philology*, xxix (Feb. 1932),
281–99.

IV

ARIANS AND SOCINIANS

Of the Trinity to reason
Leads to licence or to treason.
                                    ADAM OF ST. VICTOR
Faith is not built on disquisitions vain;
The things we must believe are few and plain.
                                    DRYDEN

I

'THE Holy Scripture is to me, and always will be, the constant guide of my assent', wrote John Locke. 'I shall presently condemn and quit any opinion of mine, as soon as I am shown that it is contrary to any revelation in the Holy Scripture.'[1] But within these limits there was room for basic disagreement. There were some important points on which Scripture was all too vague. In the new atmosphere of reasonably free debate after 1688, the first challenge to orthodoxy came from those who could not find in the Bible, or reason, sanction for the trinitarian doctrine. In this controversy both sides claimed to stand on the Bible as interpreted by right reason.

In the first phase of the debate, the enemy was not considered formidable. The unitarians of the 1680's and 1690's were chiefly Socinians.[2] The heresy that took the form of unorthodox opinions about the Trinity was almost as old as Christianity; older, neo-Arians like William Whiston would say, than orthodox Athanasian doctrine, which they considered a third-century perversion of 'primitive' Christianity. Revival of interest in it accompanied the Reformation, though the great reformers early repudiated and condemned it (Servetus, burnt by Calvin, became the chief of unitarian martyrs). It had been preached surreptitiously in England

---

[1] Letter to Stillingfleet, *Works*, iv. 96.
[2] H. J. McLachlan, *The Story of a Nonconformist Library*, pp. 53–87, points out minor differences between this group and the Polish Socinians, but concedes that they were 'in the main Socinians'. But Stephen Nye, perhaps the intellectual leader of this group, soon reached a position best described as Sabellian.

since the time of Elizabeth.[1] Although we must trace its open discussion in England from about 1675 it became a matter of prominent interest in the 1690's.[2] So scandalous did the contention become that the Blasphemy Act of 1698 attempted, unsuccessfully, to halt it. The Archbishop of Canterbury was forced to forbid Anglican clerics of high renown to quarrel over the Trinity.[3] The writings of a very small and obscure group of heretics had exposed a serious flaw in orthodoxy's defences. These Socinian tracts did cease about 1703, but the heresy broke out anew shortly, in a slightly different form, reaching a climax by 1721, by which time the 'Arian' movement seemed to have infected Anglican and Dissenter alike.[4]

The outburst of Socinian tracts in the 1690's came from an obscure and not very learned little group, who were nevertheless zealous and fairly shrewd in debate; they were aided by at least one wealthy patron.[5] They were sneered at for their ignorance and generally reviled as 'a pestilent crew of subtile and insinuating heretics'.[6] Yet orthodoxy did not ignore them, but rallied eagerly to confute them. An age whose favourite religious textbooks bore such titles as *The Reasonableness and Certainty of the Christian Religion* (Robert Jenkin) was not likely to retreat from a trial by argument.

[1] Earl M. Wilbur, *A History of Unitarianism*, deals authoritatively with Continental unitarianism from the early Reformation to the later seventeenth century. H. J. McLachlan's *Socinianism in Seventeenth Century England* is by the leading student of early English unitarianism.

[2] John Biddle (1615–62), imprisoned many times and banished once (by Cromwell) for his outspoken antitrinitarian views, can claim to be the courageous founder of modern English unitarianism. In the main it was his disciples who carried on the movement, with contacts abroad. Francis Cheynell's *Rise, Growth and Danger of Socinianism* was printed in 1643, but the author was an alarmist who was prepared to accuse even Laud of Socinianism; see Krapp, op. cit., pp. 89–93.

[3] Carpenter, *Tenison*, pp. 297 ff.

[4] J. H. Colligan, *The Arian Movement in England*. See also Robert Wallace, *Anti-Trinitarian Biography*, a useful compilation with a pro-unitarian bias. John Hunt's *Religious Thought in England* deals with this topic in vol. ii, chap. ix.

[5] This was the notable philanthropist Thomas Firmin, who had been influenced by Biddle. Luke Milbourne, *Mysteries in Religion Vindicated*, speaks of 'men of mighty names and interests' behind the Socinians (p. 781) but probably meant only Firmin. Firmin's death was the chief reason for the stopping of the tracts. See Joseph Cornish, *The Life of Thomas Firmin*, pp. 121–30.

[6] Milbourne, op. cit., p. 1; for typical opinions of their ignorance see James Harrington, *An Account of the Proceedings of the . . . Late Visitation of Exeter College in Oxford* (London, 1690), pp. 22–23; Isaac Watts, *Works*, vi. 202.

It was also a fact that the writing of learned treatises *contra infideles* was a way of gaining attention and perhaps promotion, as the preface to more than one churchman's book makes clear; as Leslie Stephen observed, 'the dissection of a deist was a recognized title to obtaining preferment'. So every heretical tract always called forth many answers, a thing frequently deplored by thoughtful Christians as only giving publicity to what otherwise might have passed unnoticed. These abundant answers, moreover, were apt to discover the defenders of the faith contradicting each other, to the great glee of the sceptics. That was what happened here in the trinitarian controversy. Honest men rejoice when thieves fall out—but also vice versa. Trinitarian writers occasionally rejoiced that their enemies were divided, between Arian and Socinian, and thus might cancel each other out. But far greater was the advantage that accrued to heterodoxy when defenders of orthodoxy stumbled and contradicted each other. The doctrine of the Trinity undoubtedly suffered more from Bishop Sherlock's defence than from Stephen Nye's attack.

Before going any farther it may be well to indicate the difficulty and the importance of the question. The Trinity was to become the most perplexing problem of all that plagued the Church in this era of rationalism. It was never settled, and it led honest Christians to despair. Arians and Socinians, wrote that usually confident assailer of heresies, Charles Leslie, were 'the most subtile and hardest to be detected, of any of the Christian heretics'.[1] It is clear that not a few of the moderate, rational clergy of Restoration times had sailed close to the rocks of heresy on this question. (Thus Edward Fowler wished in 1689 to revise the prayer book, making the Athanasian Creed optional, and was a friend of Thomas Firmin's, though he wrote against the Socinians.) Bishop Sherlock, in trying to silence these despised Socinians, slipped into one of the many pitfalls which beset one trying to 'explain' the Trinity, and was himself rebuked and silenced by his own university.[2] The

---

[1] Leslie, *Theological Works*, iv. 22. 'I wish there had been no occasion of reviving this controversy', he wrote uneasily in 1708.

[2] William Sherlock, *A Vindication of the Doctrine of the Holy and Ever Blessed*

formidable William Whiston, whose sincerity and erudition none could dispute, created some consternation when he became converted to Arianism; but it was Samuel Clarke, in the Latitudinarian tradition, who wrote what was at once the mildest and the most devastating of attacks on the Athanasian formula. As an example of a devout Christian and honest searcher after truth whom this question reduced to utter misery, we may take the eminent Nonconformist minister Isaac Watts. Watts puzzled over the Trinity for twenty years, writing book after book. But in the end he had to admit that he had only 'learned more of my own ignorance'; and his posthumous *Solemn Address to* . . . *God* is a remarkable tract wherein the good clergyman is driven to reproach his Maker bitterly for leaving him in such a quandary: 'Surely I ought to know the God whom I worship, whether he be one pure and simple or whether thou art a threefold deity. . . .'[1] Such was the obscurity in which the Bible and reason had left the matter.

But however difficult the orthodox version of the Trinity might be to establish, it was felt to be indispensable. The dispute might be thought trivial, but much really was at stake, as Sherlock pointed out early in the debate. As he put it,

The fundamental mystery of the Christian religion is the stupendous love of God in giving his own Son . . . for the redemption of mankind. If Socinianism be true, God did not give any son he had before, but made an excellent man, whom he was pleased to call his only begotten son.[2]

Socinianism, which frankly made of Christ a creature, sub-

Trinity (1690). The sharp replies were by Robert South, especially *Tritheism Charged upon Dr. Sherlock's New Notion of the Trinity* (1695). Both men were distinguished elder scholars and theologians of the Established Church. Sherlock was considered to have fallen into tritheism; in his explanation there are evidently three distinct beings, though sharing a common consciousness. The real position insisted upon by orthodoxy may be given in Daniel Waterland's definition: 'Each divine person is an individual, intelligent agent; but as subsisting in one undivided substance, they are all together in that respect but one undivided intelligent agent.' (*A Defense of Some Queries* . . ., p. 350.)

[1] Arthur P. Davis, *Isaac Watts*, pp. 120–1. See Watts's *Works*, vi, for his writings on the Trinity between 1722 and 1746. 'Sometimes I seem to have carried reason with me even to the camp of Socinus', he wrote in 1753. But he did not want to.

[2] William Sherlock, op. cit., p. 238.

verted the whole Christian scheme of salvation.[1] Socinianism tended logically to slough off all dogma and stress only conduct: 'a good life is of absolute necessity to salvation, but a right belief in those points that have always been controverted . . . is in no degree necessary'.[2] Since almost all doctrines have been controverted by someone, Sherlock noted, heresy becomes entirely harmless to the extreme unitarian and only good works matter. There is little doubt that this analysis is correct. Original sin must be rejected, along with predestination; God forgives man freely and rewards him for his own actions. The Atonement is not regarded as a satisfaction or payment to the justice of God but as 'only an oblation to the mercy of God'; God could pardon without satisfaction, if he wished. Socinians were entirely orthodox in accepting the Biblical narratives, e.g. the Resurrection and other miracles. But the making of Christ a creature displaces the vital emphasis from faith to works, from salvation by divine grace to salvation by worthy conduct.[3]

The orthodox were firmly convinced, and no doubt rightly so, that Arianism was only a subtler form of the same heresy, leading to the same results. (The older doctrine of Arius, revived chiefly by Whiston, granted that Christ is divine and existed prior to the Creation, but held that he had been created by God, out of nothing, in the beginning, and therefore the Father alone is God.) Dr. Clarke's solution, which was to leave the question open on the grounds that the Bible did not clearly define the relationship between Father and Son, was just as unacceptable. Arians and Socinians were regarded as the same thing virtually: they

[1] Socinian doctrine held that Christ was created by God in the womb of the Virgin and called his son; then raised and exalted ('Adoptionism'). While Arians accepted the divinity of Christ but not his deity, Socinians did not believe in either. W. G. Scroggie, *A Guide to the Gospels* (London, 1948), pp. 525–31, gives a brief account of all the various heresies and confusions about the person of Christ.

[2] Sherlock, quoting the Socinian author of *Brief Notes on the Creed of St. Athanasius* (1689). This was one of the tracts printed by Firmin, authorship in doubt. There is a thorough textual discussion of the tracts in McLachlan, *Story of a Nonconformist Library*.

[3] Other passages on the significance of the question may be found in Joseph Pyke, op. cit., chap. x; Daniel Waterland, *A Vindication of Christ's Divinity*, pp. 206 ff. Also Samuel Worcester's classic statement later, in America, *A Letter to the Rev. William E. Channing* (Boston, 1805).

agreed 'in that one impious error, in denying the Divinity
of our Saviour, a heresy detestable to every sober and intelligent Christian'.[1] Actually the Arians did not deny Christ's
divinity, strictly speaking, but they did make him sub-
ordinate to and separate from the Father Deity, and orthodoxy always assumed that Arianism no less than Socinianism
made of Christ a creature. Undoubtedly this view was well
founded, in that Arianism could not find any middle ground
between the extremes: to make of Christ anything less than
a person consubstantial with God was to strike at the traditional Christian scheme of things.[2] Nor should Clarke have
been surprised when he was denounced as a heretic, for to
leave this important tenet in any doubt was obviously, for
orthodoxy, as good as giving up the game.

The unitarian case was equally strong. One can easily
understand Dr. Watts's confusion, which became very general
as the controversy wore on. The case rested, first, on that
couplet of Dryden's quoted as an epigraph for this chapter;
on that, and on Chillingworth's famous reduction of
Christianity to the Bible and the Bible only. The impulse to
get rid of abstruse theological riddles was a fundamental
one for this age, which Socinians and deists did not create
but only exploited. It was a profound reaction against too
much theology in Puritan times, and it expressed the neo-
classic urge to lucidity. Get rid of the 'metaphysics', this
spirit demanded, and reduce that which we must believe to
the 'few and plain' basic truths, available to all whether
learned or not. (Repeatedly we meet the argument that God
scarcely intended salvation for the Doctors alone.) These
truths are to be found in Scripture—where else?—*clearly
writ*, and all the rest is irrelevant.

'Shall my faith depend on Plato's ideas, Aristotle's subti-
lities . . . and metaphysical abstractions more unintelligible
to poor men than the tongue of angels?' asks an early
Socinian.[3] He thrust here at the weakness of trinitarians.
They could never satisfactorily prove that their doctrine was
plainly scriptural; it was, on the face of it, contrary to logic,

1 Milbourne, op. cit., p. 780.
2 This argument is well presented by Daniel Waterland, *Vindication*, pp. 203 ff.
3 McLachlan, *Nonconformist Library*, p. 79.

and they laboured in vain to make it seem logical; and they were compelled to defend it by 'metaphysical abstractions', if not by appealing irrationally to the authority of tradition. On the accepted grounds of the Bible and reason, they found themselves weak. Moreover, the unitarians succeeded fairly well in putting the burden of proof on trinitarian shoulders. Waterland might argue that it was the other way: if these innovators could not make out a clear case men had better remain on familiar ground.[1] But this was not as strong as the persistent unitarian argument that anything in serious doubt, anything not plainly scriptural, ought to be left optional. Bury's *Naked Gospel*, the work which really set off the controversy in the 1690's, brought forward this argument at the start: here is a 'mischievous controversy' which we may silence by making it no test of Christian orthodoxy. On these grounds, already stated long before by Chillingworth ('The doctrine of Arius is either a truth, or at least no damnable heresy'), unitarians always stood ready to make peace. Their opponents understandably insisted that this would not be a reasonable compromise but actually a unitarian victory. Whiston pronounced the orthodox doctrine to be 'no better than the heretical notions' of 'those ignorant and pernicious heretics, Marcellus and Athanasius, contrary to the sense of the body of the Christian Church in their times'.[2] But even Whiston did not set up a church, though he did organize a Society for the Restoration of Primitive Christianity. It was reasonable, it seemed, to ask that so difficult

[1] *Vindication*, pp. 481 ff. Daniel Waterland (1683–1740) was recognized by 1720 as the successor to George Bull and Robert South as the leading Anglican expert on the Trinity. For a list of his writings see John Nichols, *Literary Anecdotes of the Eighteenth Century* (London, 1812), i. 214–15. His *Critical History of the Athanasian Creed* was the standard work for more than a century. No mystic, he always stuck to the objective evidences, despite his quarrels with what he regarded as the excessive rationalizing of Dr. Clarke, his great adversary not only on the Trinity but also on the ontological argument for God's existence.

[2] Whiston, *Memoirs*, i. 178. The eccentric William Whiston (1667–1752) sacrificed a brilliant scientific career as Newton's successor at Cambridge to pursue his theological heresies, which were numerous but centred in the effort to restore 'primitive Christianity' (he soon became unorthodox on baptism also, joining the general Baptists). He was a kind of Augustan Diogenes, known for his outspoken honesty and his fearless rebuking of all who strayed from the path of righteousness. Along with Clarke, he became a prime favourite of the philosophical Queen Caroline. He was prepared to accuse Clarke (unfairly) of cowardice for going no farther than he did on the unitarian question.

and clouded a question be not included in those items of necessary belief 'few and plain'.

2

The unitarians must be judged to have had the best of the argument, on the grounds as chosen. The Socinians of the 1690's and then the furious Arianism of Whiston did not do much more than arouse a sense of uneasiness; however, they prepared the ground for the formidable Dr. Clarke. His contribution was wholly a matter of Bible scholarship. He asked only one question: what does the Bible say? And he gave the definitive answer. The antitrinitarian position became that of Clarke. Years later Bishop Watson will repeat the position:

> We do not object to the doctrine of the Trinity because it is above our reason, and we cannot apprehend it; but we object to it because we cannot find that it is either literally contained in any passage of Holy Writ, or can by sound criticism be deduced from it.[1]

Socinianism convinced few on scriptural grounds. Such writers as Sherlock, Bull, and Whitby answered it effectively, and in fact Clarke's famous work showed the weakness of the Socinian case.[2] Socinianism did raise the question of reason and religion. The word Socinian came to be loosely used to mean an excessive rationalizer, generally. In Charles Leslie's dialogue the conclusion is that the Socinian will have no 'mysteries', while Christianity, as Luke Milbourne had said, recognizes that some things are above human understanding.[3] Socinians argued that after a thing had been revealed it should be clear; if not, what was the purpose of the revelation? Defenders of the Trinity answered that some things remain 'mysteries'. Socinians agreed that some

---

[1] Quoted by Sykes, *Church and State in England*, p. 353.

[2] A number of passages in Clarke's *Scripture Doctrine of the Trinity* reject the Socinian view of Christ. Daniel Whitby, the noted Arminian and a famed commentator (*Paraphrase and Commentary on the New Testament*, 1703), who assailed the Socinians, eventually accepted Clarke's view of the question (see his posthumous *Last Thoughts*, 1728). A fairly able Socinian rejoinder is *Observations on Dr. Sherlock's Answer to the Brief History of the Unitarians*.

[3] Leslie, *The Socinian Controversy Dismissed*; Milbourne, *Mysteries in Religion Vindicated*, pp. 51 ff.; cf. *Observations on Dr. Sherlock's Answer . . .*, p. 4.

things are unintelligible—the Resurrection, for example—but nothing should be *contrary* to reason, as they claimed the Trinity was, since it involved the preposterous proposition that three is one and one is three. Orthodoxy, agreeing that there is nothing in religion really contrary to reason, laboured to explain the Trinity as a logical possibility. In this inconclusive debate a few things, at least, were clear: that this generation was hardly content to leave the question as the great Aquinas had done, for one thing;[1] and that Socinians, while failing to prove their own case, had set up some thorny problems for the orthodox.

Samuel Clarke's work had the merit of concentrating on a specific and vital point: is the orthodox doctrine of the Trinity clearly given in the New Testament? Prior to this, orthodox efforts to rationalize the Trinity had proved unfortunate. The damage done by Sherlock's mistake is well known. The contemporary ballad, *The Battle Royal*, has been often quoted. While the 'fools' prated about the Trinity, religion 'took her flight' and 'ne'er was heard of since'. The *Letter to a Convocation Man* (1697) says: 'You cannot imagine the mischievous effects, which these opinions and heresies of late published and vindicated have produced among the laiety. . . .'

If even learned divines stumbled, this must indeed be a question too cloudy to make a requirement of faith, and so the unitarians had scored a point. But the vast majority of Christians, whether Anglican or Dissenting, rejected Socinianism. It was too radical and too dubiously supported to win support except among the fringe of 'free-thinkers' who were shortly to take up the more exciting idea of deism. Arianism was slightly different: somewhat more conservative and also better supported, as by the undoubtedly erudite Whiston. The earlier Socinian group apparently did not care for Arianism, and few Arians became deists. Still, while Whiston's studies in Primitive Christianity commanded respect, his inferences were generally regarded as too extreme. 'The pious, learned, but unfortunate Mr. Whiston'

---

[1] *Summa contra Gentiles*, Bk. I, chap. iii: 'For certain things that are true about God wholly surpass the capability of human reason, for instance that God is three and one. . . .'

he was called by one whom Clarke later persuaded, and this about summed up the consensus of balanced opinion.[1]

It remained for Clarke to show the question in a truer light —which was that the Bible unfortunately failed to support any of the theories about the Trinity. Clearly the Church wanted no more discussion of this embarrassing question, and Clarke was to be silenced as Sherlock had been. But he clearly and eloquently showed the need for a thorough discussion of it. Samuel Clarke was generally regarded, after his Boyle Lectures of 1704–5, as the foremost English metaphysician, succeeding to Locke's mantle. He was disliked by both High Churchmen and deists, as he carried on the mild spirit of the *via media* which had originated with his masters the Cambridge Platonists. His rationalism was thoroughgoing; he attempted to prove the existence of God and to derive morality from reason, and he made a sensation at Cambridge when for his D.D. he defended the thesis that 'no article of the Christian faith is opposed to right reason'.

There had been, Clarke now pointed out, a great uneasiness about the Athanasian Creed for some time, on the part of great and learned divines who could hardly be styled heretics: he could cite Tillotson, Cudworth, Taylor, Hammond, and other illustrious names among the seventeenth-century clergy. In the introduction to his famous work he pointed out that Protestantism demands that each individual Christian must 'of necessity at last understand with his own understanding, and believe with his own, not another's, faith'; and that the only grounds of such faith must be the patient, intelligent scrutiny of Scripture.

> The peace and unity of the Church [he repeated later] can be assured but two ways: either by that of charity, and allowing learned men a liberty of examining things, which is the Protestant and Christian method; or by introducing with force an universal ignorance, which is the method of Popery.

So, in the spirit of Chillingworth, he proposed to search

---

[1] Clarke, *Works*, iv. 568. On the engaging Whiston see Hunt, op. cit. iii. 13–20; Nichols, *Anecdotes*, i. 494–506. His volumes on *Primitive Christianity Revived* and such books as *Athanasius Convicted of Forgery* indicate his stress on the beliefs of the early Christians. They drew numerous answers.

and examine the Bible, 'eschewing abstract and metaphysical reasonings'.[1]

This scholarly and non-dogmatic approach had a history before Clarke, whose main contribution was thoroughness. In this same spirit Locke and Newton had secretly dabbled in the question, aiming 'to purge the truth of things spurious'. Other scholars than Clarke made contributions; particularly, the Irish Presbyterian preacher Thomas Emlyn had by 1715 thoroughly examined the important question of the authenticity of I John v. 7, which Newton had secretly challenged.[2] How heavily orthodoxy leaned on that one support may be seen from a reading of Dr. South's sermon on the subject, and from later attempts to defend this text.[3]

But Clarke undertook an examination of every New Testament text (1,251 in all) bearing in any way on the question. Although his opponents were able to turn up some minor errors Clarke was undoubtedly right in claiming that none of these affected his major conclusions. *The Scripture Doctrine of the Trinity* was easily 'the most memorable work in the history of the Arian movement'[4]—except that Clarke was really no Arian, any more than he was a Socinian. He indicted the Athanasian Creed as unscriptural, but he could find in Scripture no support for the Arian version either, much less the Socinian. He properly denied the accusation of Arianism, but he did wish to abandon those portions of the Anglican articles and liturgy that embraced

---

[1] *The Scripture Doctrine of the Trinity*, first published 1712, is in vol. iv of Clarke's *Works* (a revised version) along with other writings and documents relating to the controversy. See also Benjamin Hoadly's preface to this edition of Clarke's works, i. vii.

[2] *A Full Inquiry into the Original Authority of the Text I John v, 7*. Accepted as decisive by Clarke (*Works*, iv. 121, 369). Emlyn, persecuted in Ireland for his unorthodox views, was a notable figure in the antitrinitarian movement.

[3] Robert South, *Sermons*, i. 366–7; cf. Joseph Pyke, *An Impartial View . . .*, pp. 107 ff. David Martin of Utrecht entered the lists against Emlyn in 1719, and Edmund Calamy defended the text in *Thirteen Sermons concerning the Doctrine of the Trinity*. Its spuriousness has long since been generally conceded.

[4] Called so by Colligan, op. cit. It has even been called 'the theological work of the century', but this is a bold claim. Decisive and thorough as it was, the book lacked the scope and originality of Warburton's *Divine Legation of Moses*, or Middleton's *Free Inquiry into the Miraculous Powers*, to say nothing of Jonathan Edwards's *Freedom of the Will*.

the Athanasian Creed, and he wanted to return to the simpler creed of primitive Christianity. As against the Arians he held Scripture to teach that Son and Spirit have existed since the beginning; on the other hand, he found nothing to substantiate the Nicene dogma that Son and Spirit are substantially one with God the Father:

> They are both therefore worthy of censure; both they who on the one hand presume to affirm that the Son was made out of nothing, and they who, on the other hand, affirm that he is the self-existent substance.

God the Father alone is underived, unoriginated; the Son and Holy Ghost derive their being and attributes from the Father and by an act of his will, somehow—but we are nowhere told exactly how.[1]

In effect Clarke had charged all orthodox (Athanasian) Christians with the error of Sabellianism, or allowing no separate identity to the three persons of the Trinity ('which is the same', he declared, turning the tables on orthodoxy, 'with Socinianism'.) He had clearly supported the unitarian position that there is no Scriptural proof for making Christ consubstantial with the Father. He could not understand the orthodox position as Biblical; it was, he said, derived from Scholastic metaphysics, which he deplored. In the ensuing controversy he continued to protest that his adversaries got their meaning not from simple Scripture but from 'hypotheses' of the fourth and fifth centuries or from 'Scholastic notions' of later times.[2] Clarke used the testimony of the early fathers much, but only as witnesses whose evidence had a good deal of value on Scriptural interpretations because they were close to the subject; Waterland, the Clarkites complained, used 'metaphysical hypotheses or opinions of the Fathers' as sacrosanct authority. Clarke, finding no definite Biblical statement to confirm the Athanasian theory, would leave the question open, a non-essential of faith on which each man might reach his own private conclusion. We may amplify our previous statement that the unitarians won this debate by saying that Clarke was

[1] *Works*, iv. 205–6; 328; 475; pt. ii, Propositions XIII and XIV.
[2] Ibid., p. 393. The writer here, as in the next quotation, is John Jackson, who was used by Clarke as his spokesman after 1714.

unanswerable on the basis of the Bible as strictly interpreted. His foes, wishing to save the Nicene Creed, did not by any means concede this, yet they were forced in the end to appeal to the authority of tradition.[1]

To which the Clarkites made the obvious retort, this is Romanism.[2] The indictment against Clarke by the Lower House of Canterbury Convocation simply declared that Clarke's books tended 'to substitute the author's private conceits, and arbitrary interpretations of Scripture, in the room of those Catholic doctrines, which the Church professes and maintains, as warranted both by Scripture and Antiquity'. The appeal to antiquity left Clarke unimpressed, and in replies to Dr. Wells and Robert Nelson he repeated his defence of reason and free inquiry, while arguing forcefully that any other road leads to Hobbism, since authority will be determined by force or convenience. But the more timid were now genuinely alarmed at the havoc Clarke's way might work.

The debate, indeed, 'soon grew very warm', as Clarke's friend Benjamin Hoadly remarked, after Clarke's book. It was attacked vehemently. But Clarke found respectable followers as neither the outcast Socinians nor the 'unfortunate Mr. Whiston' had. (Whiston's disciples, for example Thomas Chubb and Thomas Woolston, were prone to stray off towards deism, earning Whiston's denunciation but discrediting the movement.) Clarke himself, subjected to ecclesiastical discipline in the famous proceedings of 1714, submitted to the extent of stating that he intended to write no more on the subject. But this was really not a surrender, and did not satisfy the conservative clergy.[3] The debate went on, and Clarke kept in close touch with such defenders of his views as John Jackson.

---

[1] Waterland, *Vindication*, Queries XXVIII and XXIX.

[2] John Jackson, *A Reply to Dr. Waterland's Defense of His Queries*, pp. 503, 520; Clarke, *Works*, iv. 525.

[3] See ibid., pp. 540–57, for material on the proceedings. Clarke did not recant, but explained that he was content to rest on what he had written—which was enough. His disciple, John Jackson, who carried on the debate and refused to subscribe to the Articles, lost his chance of promotion thereby. Jackson, as well as Clarke, always argued against the deists, while conceding their right to free speech and a fair answer. The Clarke school was notable at all times for fairness and moderation in debate. For a memoir of Jackson see Nichols, *Anecdotes*, ii. 519–31.

3

After the Established Church passed a crisis somewhat
uneasily in 1714 with the equivocal disciplining of Clarke,
there followed an outburst among the less disciplined
Dissenters of what Dr. Calamy was forced to record as
'bitter animosity and contention', culminating in the famous
struggle at Salter's Hall; writings 'swarmed from the press'.[1]
With one side shouting against persecution and the other
against heresy, the Dissenters voted by the narrowest of
margins against requiring subscription to a trinitarian article. The key figure in this celebrated affair, James Peirce of
Exeter, had been converted to antitrinitarianism by Clarke,
and the latter's book was undoubtedly the cause of setting
off this outbreak of 'Arianism', with 'frightful consequences
of it among our religious people'.[2] The noise at the 1719
synod, and the innumerable pamphlets, added little to the
clarification of the question. But the issue was a vital one for
all Dissenters, completely committed to a rational (i.e. non-
authoritarian) religion.

One result was to shatter the precarious 'happy union' of
Presbyterian and Independent. The Presbyterians were
mostly on the anti-subscription side of the vote at Salter's
Hall, along with some general (Arminian) Baptists, the
latter having been the first to embrace formally a liberal
position on the Trinity. The Presbyterians were influenced
mainly by their traditional interest in 'comprehension',
which meant reducing dogmatic requirements to a minimum; at any rate they took the liberal path. 'By the middle of
the eighteenth century most of the principal Presbyterian
ministers and congregations had silently discarded the old
doctrine of the Trinity.'[3] The Independents, along with the

[1] Calamy, Own Life, i. 407–19.
[2] Defoe (ed. Lee), Life and Writings, ii. 129–30. Peirce of Exeter was so eloquent
and saintly a minister that he contributed no little to removing the obloquy from
antitrinitarianism within Dissenting circles. On the other side a leader was the
intrepid Whig Calvinist Thomas Bradbury; see his Sermons.
[3] Lecky, History of England in the Eighteenth Century, i. 360. More precisely,
Duncan Coomer, in English Dissent under the Early Hanoverians, pp. 78–79,
calculates that by 1770 only one-half of the Presbyterian congregations remained
orthodox on the Trinity. Joseph Priestley in his Memoirs mentions friends who had
to give up their places because of their Arianism; he also indicates that most of his
fellow students at Warrington, the Dissenting academy, were Arians c. 1750–60.

particular Baptists, were more loyal to orthodoxy; but Arianism certainly had a strong foothold within Dissent, where each individual Congregation could determine its beliefs.

After 1720 the debate lost its heat. The coming of deism may be suggested as a reason. But opposition to the trinitarian articles did not die. Within the Established Church the movement to revise the Articles after Clarke's suggestions carried momentum down nearly to the end of the century. It was strenuously debated in 1750–1 and again in 1772 at the time of the Feathers Tavern petition, rejected in Parliament by no very great majority. At that time the grounds for defeating the move related solely to expedience, Burke arguing simply that it is not convenient to disturb what has long existed.[1] A foreign visitor in 1754 observed that many Anglicans did not believe in the Trinity.[2]

Joseph Priestley and his circle, who called themselves unitarians, breathed new fire into an old heresy after 1770.[3] It is the immediate consequences that concern us here. Orthodoxy had been left in some confusion. Waterland, for all his ingenuity, had not been able to answer Clarke, and the Bible alone was seen to have its defects as the sole support of Christianity. Orthodox defenders of the Trinity ended, as they had begun, in confusion and contradiction. For example, we find Calamy, in his sermons on the subject, asserting that any subordination of Son to Father is dangerous and improper. The orthodox position had always insisted upon such a subordination—not one of nature, but of order.

In 1730 a clergyman attributed the decay of religion primarily to 'the contempt which has for many years been cast on the Holy Spirit'.[4] The Trinity was indeed openly

[1] See Sykes, *Church and State*, pp. 333–4, 380 ff. Also A. E. Peaston, *The Prayer Book Reform Movement*. John White, *Free and Impartial Considerations upon the Free and Candid Disquisitions Relating to the Church of England* (1751), an answer to a revisionist tract by John Jones, admits that a majority was satisfied with the existing liturgy for no very strong reason except custom—p. 6.

[2] Duc de la Rochefoucauld, *La Vie en Angleterre au XVIIIme siècle*, ed. Jean Marchand (Paris, 1945), p. 118.

[3] Coleridge regarded Priestley as the founder of Unitarianism; the term was not unknown previously but 'Socinian' and 'Arian' are far commoner in the eighteenth century. Priestley began a new and distinctive phase, which culminated in the distinguished American, William Ellery Channing.

[4] Abraham Taylor, *Lime Street Lectures*; American edition as *The Insufficience*

ridiculed; the left-wing journalist Thomas Gordon published a satire in which fun is poked at churchmen who argue that 'This is trinity in unity; three in one, and one in three; not three, but one; nor one, but three', &c.[1] It was about this time that Newton's views became known; and the confusion of the trinitarians may be said to have been just about complete by the 1730's. By that time, there were more scandalous heresies to combat.

The chief damage to religion lay in the spectacle of clergymen quarrelling hopelessly about an important item of faith. A recent Anglican bishop has well remarked that 'while priest struggles with priest for the mastery, the world outside looks on with contempt and passes by on the other side'.[2] For this reason a basic tenet of Christianity has always been the avoidance of 'doubtful disputations'. Yet, as we know, a rational religion could not well shun the test of reason. Bolingbroke, the deist, drew the moral in writing about this trinitarian controversy that 'the scene of Christianity has been always a scene of dissension, of hatred, of persecution, and of blood'.[3] This was extravagant enough; no blood was shed in this paper war of decorous divines. But of dissension there was plenty, and signs were not altogether lacking that some of the clergy wished to find a safer harbour than reason. The Blasphemy Bill of 1721 was a vain effort to silence criticism by fiat. The tenor of many trinitarian books was a feeling that the Bible should be taken not alone but in conjunction with Church tradition. At the same time the free-thinkers were emboldened. Some pressed onwards to greater heights of infidelity. In the other camp, men such as Berkeley and Butler first began to doubt the adequacy of reason at this time.

4

'Clearly distinct from the Deistic controversy, the Arian movement cannot be altogether separated from it', an

---

of Natural Religion. These popular lectures by a Dissenting clergyman have a certain significance as a sign of the retreat from reason.

[1] Thomas Gordon, *The Trial of William Whiston* (1739).
[2] The Bishop of Chelmsford, quoted by C. E. M. Joad, *The Present and Future of Religion* (New York, 1930), p. 45.
[3] Bolingbroke, *Works*, iv. 25.

authority writes.[1] As a matter of fact, Whiston and Clarke were far from deism. But Whiston himself thought that Socinianism (not Arianism) was a step towards deism, agreeing with an earlier writer who said he could hardly distinguish a deist from a Socinian.[2] Left-wing unitarianism, then, tended to merge into deism. Matthew Tindal wrote two Socinian tracts before becoming a notable deist; John Toland started from his friend Locke's rational unitarianism to reach deism very quickly; Thomas Woolston passed from Arianism to Socinianism and so to deism. Among the little band of Socinians of the 1690's, William Freke eventually showed himself an enthusiast by joining the 'new prophets'; none of the others was prominently associated with any subsequent heresy. Locke, who was certainly a unitarian, is not accurately classified as a deist, but it can be argued that his methods—of unitarianism generally—led towards deism.

The question of the relationship between deism and unitarianism is perhaps an academic one. But, as a prelude to a discussion of deism, it is interesting to note similarities and differences in their outlook. Deists found the trinitarian idea rather fantastic, and could not take it seriously.[3] They dismissed it not because it was unscriptural, however, but simply because it was too inconceivable to a pure rationalist, and because they thought of God as almost impersonal. For this reason the whole controversy was relatively meaningless to them: Toland could not see that Socinianism or Arianism were any more 'reasonable' than trinitarianism, and he sneered at their compromises.[4] The nature of Christ, wrote Chubb, whether God or only sent of God, does not matter, since we need only know that 'the word of the Lord in his mouth was truth'; here speaks deism's view of Christianity as pure morality, and Jesus as only a wise man repeating moral truths which are ancient and universal.[5] In this, of course, deism pursued a unitarian tendency much farther. It might be added that the two could agree that Christianity had been

1 Colligan, op. cit., p. 92.
2 Milbourne, op. cit., p. 782; Whiston, *Memoirs*, i. 231–5, 276 ff.
3 Thomas Chubb, *Posthumous Works*, i. 169 ff.—a passage of obvious irony.
4 *Christianity Not Mysterious*, p. 27.
5 *The True Gospel of Jesus Christ Asserted*, pp. 46–47.

corrupted since its primitive era.[1] But deists made sweeping charges against all the 'priesthood' of organized Christianity, while unitarians only protested against the Athanasian usurpation. The unitarian of this period accepted the Bible's literal truth, and sought only to purge all subsequent accretions to it, in order to get back to the simplicity and clarity of early Christianity. But the deist took the Bible allegorically if at all, and certainly was not much interested in a return to the third century. Still, unitarianism had introduced the habit of 'impertinently meddling' with time-honoured versions of Christianity.

The deist's plea for absolute freedom of inquiry, and the right of individual judgement, would echo Clarke's. (Anthony Collins's *A Discourse of Freethinking* followed Clarke's *magnum opus* by one year.) Most of all, deism was nourished by that confusion among Christians on important questions, of which the doctrine of the Trinity was the chief. In an early anti-deist tract, remarkable for its fairness, the deist is made to say that he is little read in such matters, 'further than to observe how the gladiators in dispute murder the cause between them, while they so fiercely cut and wound one another'.[2] The characterization was apt. But in assailing Christianity nothing was more effective than to set one priest against another. The greater part of Anthony Collins's *Discourse of Freethinking* is given over to a devastating exposition of the extent to which the divines differed.[3] In one thing, if no other, the deist agreed with the Papist: both delighted in the confusions of liberal Protestantism struggling to build Christianity on reason and private judgement. One of them thought that this demonstrated the futility of Christianity except upon the basis of established authority; and the other thought that it demonstrated just the futility of Christianity.

---

[1] Toland, op. cit., p. 163: 'Mystery prevailed very little in the first hundred or century of years after Christ. . . .' Bolingbroke admired early Christianity because it had not become an official state religion enforcing its beliefs; but he also shows the influence of Conyers Middleton (see further below) in thinking the early Christians to be extremely credulous. *Works*, iii. 476 ff.; iv. 89, 237.

[2] Robert Jenkin, *A Brief Confutation* . . ., p. 51.

[3] Collins lists, pp. 61 ff., all the conflicting versions of the Trinity.

V

THE DEFINITION OF DEISM

[The deist's] religion is the most ancient and the most widespread; for the simple adoration of a God preceded all the systems of the world.
VOLTAIRE, *Dictionnaire philosophique*

I

WE are here concerned with English deism from about 1700 to 1750. Like unitarianism, deism had an earlier history, as well as a later one.[1] It can hardly be called important in seventeenth-century England, however, unless we are to make Hobbes a deist. The author of *Leviathan* was, of course, extremely influential if generally disliked, and in 1694 Bentley, aiming his Boyle Lecture at the grim realist of Malmesbury, thought that 'not one English infidel in a hundred is any other than a Hobbist'. But Hobbes had little in common with later deists; he was known in the eighteenth century as an atheist, along with Spinoza, and atheism was always distinguished from deism. The ancestry of eighteenth-century deism is usually traced to Lord Herbert of Cherbury.[2] (But see the remarks above, p. 32.) Herbert's philosophy was quite obscure in his time. Charles Blount and the group that published *The Oracles of Reason* in 1693 echoed Herbert's ideas, and added some bold if crude jibes at the truth of Scripture.[3]

It can be argued that subsequent deists added nothing of importance to the ideas and methods of these pioneers. True, Herbert based his theory of a universal religion, available to all without need of a special revelation, on the doctrine of

[1] See E. C. Mossner, *Bishop Butler*, pp. 46–51; John Orr, *English Deism*, chaps. i–iii; Lechler, *Geschichte englischen Deismus*, Bk. I.

[2] Harold R. Hutcheson, ed., *Lord Herbert of Cherbury's 'De Religione Laici'*. For an example of French deism in 1622 see F. Lachèvre, *Le Procès du poète Théophile de Viau*, ii. 105.

[3] Some of Blount's other writings are listed in the bibliography at the end of this book. His father, Sir Henry Blount, was a traveller famed for his reports on the Near East; see Boise Penrose, *Urbane Travelers, 1591–1635* (London, Philadelphia, 1942). In at least one of his books Charles was supposed to have had his father's collaboration.

innate ideas, one which went somewhat out of style with Locke. But Locke as well as Descartes, sensationalism as well as rationalism, arrived at the idea that all minds are alike and therefore capable of natural religion.[1]

We begin our study of deism when, in the free and rational climate of Augustan England, it first became widely known —with the English edition of John Toland's *Christianity Not Mysterious*, in 1702, which Leslie Stephen termed the 'signal gun' for the deistic controversy. John Toland, political pamphleteer and amateur philosopher, was so much more the former than the latter that his character is discussed below, in a portion devoted to the political aspects of religious liberalism (Chapter XI). Deistic ideas were then taken up and exploited by a very few men, who succeeded in making a noise out of all proportion to their numbers and even their talents. It seems evident that this was more because of Christianity's weakness than because of deism's strength.

Anthony Collins (1676–1729) was probably the shrewdest of all the deists, a man of genuine philosophic talents (as his contribution to the free-will debate exhibited), but especially talented in preying upon the inconsistencies of the Christians. Born of 'good estate', educated at Cambridge, like Toland a disciple of Locke, Collins was a most amiable and esteemed public servant (justice of the peace in Middlesex and then Essex) and a 'philosopher' by avocation. He suffered, in 1714, a severe assault at the hands of Dr. Bentley, who riddled his pretensions to advanced scholarship—a famous example of literary mayhem, but hardly a philosophic answer to deism.[2] Collins recovered to

---

[1] Shaftesbury's 'moral sense', and Clarke's rational Christianity as well, were certainly derived from the doctrine of innate ideas; Locke was not so ubiquitous and all-conquering as is generally assumed. But both doctrines led deists in the same direction: away from revealed religion and towards a universal religion of nature. There are some useful remarks on Locke's relation to deism in Andrew Brown's article, 'John Locke and the Religious Aufklärung', *Review of Religion*, xiii, Jan. 1949.

[2] *Remarks upon a Late Discourse of Freethinking.* J. M. Robertson disputes the common view, presented among others by Leslie Stephen, that the great philologist thoroughly lacerated Collins. The truth would seem to be that while Bentley discovered his less scholarly opponent in some embarrassing errors of detail he did not exactly meet his major arguments.

write in 1724 the most effective of all deistic critiques of Christianity (*The Grounds and Reasons of the Christian Religion*). It was about this time that deism reached its peak. Thomas Woolston's violent assaults on Christianity and the clergy were widely sold; so were Thomas Gordon's anticlerical pamphlets and *Independent Whig*; a third 'doubting Thomas' was Thomas Chubb, the self-taught journeyman glovemaker. Matthew Tindal sought to define deism as a positive creed, in addition to the usual attacks on Christianity, in his *Christianity As Old As the Creation*, 1730. Thomas Morgan, the self-styled Moral Philosopher, entered the debate, adding little to Collins and Tindal but reaching a wide audience. To the writings of all of these, and others, we shall refer in an effort to define deism.

By about 1733 the cumulative effect of such deistic attacks on Christianity, abundantly aided by the confusions of the faithful, led to a real sense of despair among many of the latter.[1] We have not mentioned all the deistic influences: Lord Shaftesbury, for instance, who wrote no theological polemics but only a few polished essays, was regarded by many as the most subversive of all, thrusting as he did at the adequacy of Christian ethics. Boldest of all was the disciple of Bayle, Bernard Mandeville, who did not deny Christianity's truth so much as its relevance to contemporary society, and is perhaps not properly to be classified as a deist; he inquired, like Bayle, whether formal religious belief does after all have anything to do with the morality by which society functions.

The result of all this was certainly a crisis in Christianity. Destructively, deism was a success, or rather orthodoxy was a failure, and Christianity began to beat a retreat from the field of reason. But deism was not a success on its constructive side, in seeking a firm basis for its alleged natural religion. The mid-century sceptics, David Hume and Conyers Middleton, are left without any real faith in either natural or revealed religion.

---

[1] See, for example, *Weekly Miscellany*, a conservative religious journal, 1733-4, which shows constant grave concern over the spread of deism. The decade of the 1730's produced an alarmed flight from reason, reflected in the notable works of William Law, Joseph Butler, George Berkeley, and John Wesley.

2

In 1722 William Wollaston, a retired clergyman of independent means, wrote *The Religion of Nature Delineated*, a work widely designated since as deistic, which was, however, a fairly orthodox effort to show how far reason and nature alone can discover true religion—an exercise which was neither new nor heretical. This, as Wollaston remarked, 'is so far from undermining true religion, that it rather paves the way for its reception'.[1] The point is worth making as a step in clarifying some difficulties in the definition of deism. Orthodoxy no more rejected 'natural religion' than it rejected reason, and it always used arguments from natural religion to refute atheism.[2] It liked especially well in this age to dwell on the purely rational or natural arguments for the truth of Christianity; but that did not mean it thought revelation either spurious or unnecessary. What distinguished the deist was not an interest in natural religion, but the belief that natural religion *alone* was sufficient, without need for any Christian revelation. Confusion on this score is found in some writers on deism.[3]

Dr. Clarke's effort to define deism stands out from many such, then and later.[4] The 'true deists' he thought to be those who believe rightly in every respect, 'but profess to believe only so far as 'tis discoverable by the light of nature alone, without believing any Divine Revelation'. He did not think this position tenable, and in fact there was certainly none who accepted all of Christianity on the basis of nature alone

---

[1] *The Religion of Nature Delineated*, pp. 382–3. Cf. Alan Richardson, *Christian Apologetics* (London, 1947), p. 112: the classic view was that 'natural and revealed theology were complementary to each other, and together they comprised the sum total of our knowledge of God'.

[2] See, for example, Robert Jenkin, *A Brief Confutation of the Pretences against Natural and Revealed Religion*, espec. p. 44. The atheist is first confuted by arguments for natural religion; then the deist by arguments for revelation. This was standard apologetic method. Daniel Waterland in his *Vindication of Scripture* (against Tindal) was prepared to assert that a deist could be no real friend to natural religion—for revealed and natural religion are so bound up together that an enemy of one is sure to be an enemy of the other.

[3] See, for example, G. A. Koch, *Republican Religion*, p. 16, for an instance of misuse of the term 'deism'. The term is extended to embrace arguments for natural religion, or Newtonianism in any sense. Newton, Locke, Clarke, and Bentley thus become deists, which is impossible to justify.

[4] 'A Discourse of ... Natural Religion', in *Works*, ii. 595 ff.

—though the deists claimed (dubiously) to accept the essentials. Clarke mentioned those who deny immortality and that God concerns himself with the governing of the world. He thought that these were logically atheists. To say that God exists yet cannot interfere with the laws that govern the universe is really impossible, for a God so limited by a higher power would not be God at all in any real sense. So Clarke defined away deism—which, logically, may have been correct, for deism was never really successful, all will agree, in developing a stable and consistent position. But we do by usage classify as deists a group who thought, at least, that they occupied ground between traditional Christianity and atheism. They believed in some august First Cause, and in some sort of natural religion without a special act of revelation.

Clarke also noted that there was 'no such thing as a consistent scheme of deism', a judgement generally approved. With this caveat in mind we may attempt to summarize the philosophy of deism. We might first essay a brief imaginative tour into the mind of a typical deist. He had been impressed by Newton's discoveries—too impressed.[1] This vast universe controlled by immutable laws, this wonderfully constructed machine, undoubtedly had a Maker. The deist was not an atheist. But would such a Being as headed this marvellous world-machine condescend to reveal himself to Moses, an obscure man of a benighted race on a petty planet? The deist could not see the majesty of this, always heretofore regarded as the greatest wonder; it was unworthy of God. We meet here an *aesthetic* quarrel possibly at the root of the whole matter: what had once seemed infinitely pleasing and wonderful and inspiring now (to some) began to seem infinitely ridiculous and degrading. The deist could not reconcile Newton's master physicist with the Jehovah who had wrestled with Jacob—and it must be admitted he had a point. This last, he assumed, was all a tale made up by ignorant barbarians and then imposed upon mankind by priests, known to be a deceitful and

---

[1] Professor Aldridge, op. cit., argues cogently that there should be a distinction between 'scientific deism' and 'humanistic deism', Shaftesbury being the best example of the latter. However, even Shaftesbury felt the Newtonian impact.

mercenary class. This inference of a conspiracy was perhaps not necessary, but it was plausible and indeed very nearly inevitable at a time when the historical sense of a development in human affairs was notably lacking. Perhaps the Judaic sort of religion was necessary for the literal-minded mob, but no 'philosopher' could believe it. God revealed himself to man, no doubt—but was not Nature enough of a revelation? Eagerly the physico-theologians had proved the existence of God by pointing to his masterly works; the deists now inquired why it was then necessary to go any farther.

Jesus, the alleged Messiah and self-styled Son of God, seemed to the deist an excellent moralist, but not a superhuman agent. That he was the Son of God was only another Hebraic myth. The excellent moral code taught by Jesus was not a divine revelation, but could be found in Nature, surely, if one searched. Just how and where, the deist was never able to state clearly, but he believed strongly in the idea nevertheless. The moral rules, everywhere alike, could perhaps be found in universal reason, or perhaps in the heart of man, a divinely implanted instinct. In any event they were discernible independently of any special revelation. The proof of this was that all men had arrived at a similar code of morals, though theologies differed; and Europe was now aware of the existence of other religions apparently similar to but quite independent of Christianity.[1] Christianity, had it not been corrupted by priests and metaphysicians, would have agreed perfectly with this 'natural religion'.[2]

[1] Much has been written on the influence of new knowledge about various non-European peoples during this period: the Far East, the Near East, and the 'noble savages' of North America and the Pacific Isles. R. W. Frantz, *The English Traveller and the Movement of Ideas, 1660–1732* (Lincoln, Nebr., 1934) attempts to appraise the influence of the travellers on deism, in chaps. iv and v. His evidence does not seem very conclusive. Chauncey B. Tinker, *Nature's Simple Plan: A Phase of Radical Thought in the Mid-Eighteenth Century*, discusses the deistic idealization of the Noble Savage; he thinks the visit of Omai, the South Sea Islander, in 1774 marked the end of this illusion. Awareness of the Chinese and of Mohammedanism doubtless helped in the formulation of the notion of a universal religion of nature. But on the whole the existence of a universal natural religion was an *a priori* assumption which the ugly facts finally slew.

[2] Bolingbroke, *Works*, iv. 281.

3

All this was much too radical to say out at once, and so the deists spoke by indirection. They were often wholly unscrupulous and deceitful in their methods. Thinking that the priests and their preachings were fraudulent, they felt justified, it seems, in using fraud to fight fraud. Unable to proclaim all the truth, they would introduce it in small doses. They used mildly disguised sarcasm or satire, a method disconcerting to sober Christians. 'When you expect an argument, they make a jest perhaps', it was noted early.[1] 'Ridicule', Thomas Woolston later stated bluntly enough, 'will cut the pate of an ecclesiastical numbskull, which calm and sedate reasoning will make no impression on.'[2] Above all, deists took a delight in interfering mischievously in any argument between Christians, in order to compound the damage done by such disputes. All this makes it a little difficult to interpret the deists. But it is usually not hard to discover when they are writing with tongue in cheek and when not.

They were sincere in believing in a God. Serious writers always distinguished atheism from deism; Spinoza and Hobbes were considered the only real atheists.[3] 'The deists as a group either assert God's existence as an absolute certainty, or use the teleological argument to demonstrate it.'[4] Atheism seemed untenable to the rationalists; in theism there are perhaps difficulties, but in atheism there are absurdities.[5] In such a statement as the following the deist spoke sincerely:

That there is a Deity, or governing mind, who gave being to all

---

[1] Jenkin, *Brief Confutation*, p. 40. This allusion in 1702 makes it plain that ridicule was a deist weapon before Lord Shaftesbury's writings were widely known; the latter made it more popular.

[2] *Mr. Woolston's Defence of His Discourses*, p. 20. Cf. Anthony Collins, *Discourse concerning Ridicule and Irony in Writing*.

[3] Samuel Clarke, *Works*, ii. 513 ff. John Toland became a Spinozist or pantheist in 1720, and exerted an influence on the materialist-atheist school of D'Holbach in France. But in England it was not usual for deism to develop into atheism.

[4] Walter M. Merrill, *From Statesman to Philosopher: A Study in Bolingbroke's Deism*—a valuable work on the philosophy of deism.

[5] Bolingbroke, *Works*, ii. 465 ff.; see also Hazard, op. cit. i. 153 and iii. 66.

things external to himself, and who exists by, or from, an absolute necessity, is, to me, most evident and plain. . . . I think atheism, in point of argument, is insupportable.[1]

We had best remember that to conceive of a world without a creator, without a plan, and without a purpose, was an incredible thing, until nineteenth-century science made it more plausible. The deist was as a rule an optimist who believed in an orderly, rational universe. Order and reason implied an intelligent, purposeful creation.

It may be worth adding that there is some justification for the charge of atheism against the deists (we recall that Theodore Roosevelt, to the indignation of some, called Tom Paine an atheist). This has already been mentioned: later deists, such as Peter Annet, developed the impossibility of miracle so that God was evidently completely enthralled to natural laws which he was powerless to alter. As John Jackson, following Clarke, wrote, it would seem that 'God did not form them, nor is the author of nature, which is atheism'.[2] However that may be, all deists of course paid tribute to a Supreme Being, remote or purely formal though he or it might tend to become. They thought him 'eternal, immaterial,[3] infinitely perfect . . . wise, powerful, just and good', possessed of 'the most perfect intelligence, goodness, and boundless power'.[4] Yet they rejected any anthropomorphizing of him, and any 'particular Providence', as superstitious. The notion that God 'talks to all mankind from corners' was as absurd as the idea that he showed his back parts to Moses.[5] He was a remote deity, tending towards the impersonality of an abstract First Principle,

---

[1] Thomas Chubb, *Posthumous Works*, i. 157.

[2] John Jackson, *An Address to the Deists*, p. 14.

[3] Deism did not generally deny the immateriality of the soul and of God until the time of David Hartley and Joseph Priestley, after 1750. Collins's intervention in the debate on the soul between Clarke and Henry Dodwell seems to indicate that he was prepared to take up the idea, however, if the occasion was opportune.

[4] Chubb, *Posthumous Works*, i. 158; Anthony Collins, *A Vindication of the Divine Attributes*, a pamphlet in which Collins is concerned to deny, against the alleged views of Archbishop King, that human passions are properly attributed to God.

[5] Collins, *Discourse of Freethinking*, p. 38.

though milder deists did not deny that he might occasionally, 'to answer some great and good ends', interfere in the affairs of the world.[1]

Had this Deity inspired the Holy Scripture? Deists from the beginning denied that this was as evident as the orthodox insisted. Standing as it were on Locke's shoulders, they desired to push the claims of 'reason' farther than orthodoxy found comfortable. Toland in *Christianity Not Mysterious* declared that he would believe only what he could clearly understand. There should be nothing either contrary to reason *or* above it in the Bible, the latter an addition orthodoxy could never allow. Revelation is 'not a motive of assent, but a means of information'—i.e. we have a right to test revelation by reason and need not accept it untested. These were bolder claims for reason than orthodoxy thought reasonable! They were, in fact, somewhat doubtful. One could hardly avoid accepting the revelation if it was attested as truly from God; and it seemed reasonable to most people that man had no right to suppose every truth to be available to his own weak reason, unassisted. Christians moved to meet this attack with great confidence, a confidence exhibited in all the answers to *Christianity Not Mysterious*. The very titles are proof of this, for Charles Leslie had a 'Short and Easy Method' to confute the deists, and Robert Jenkin a 'Brief Confutation of the Pretences' against revealed religion. 'No man that truly and impartially considers things', the latter announced, 'can be either an atheist or a deist.' It was inherently reasonable, first, that God should declare the truth to man; and then it was quite certain, according to abundant evidence, that the sacred writings of the Jews and Christians were indeed that revelation. Finally, the Christian doctrine as thus divinely announced proved to be infinitely pleasing and rational. On these three legs the case for Christianity rested. But the deists began to hack away at each of them.

As for the first, deists found it repugnant to reason and morality to believe that one group of men had been singled out to receive the word of God. To suppose that God has

[1] Chubb, 'A Short Dissertation on Providence', appended to the 1738 edition of *The True Gospel of Jesus Christ Asserted*, p. 202.

'favourite nations' is a form of superstition.¹ God has
doubtless spoken, as Voltaire would say, but to the universe.
Why not simply through the reason he has given men,
together with those miracles of nature with which he sur-
rounds them? If there was a prophet, deists implied, it
was more apt to be Newton than Moses. ... The unfairness
and irrationality of a special revelation vouchsafed only to
the Jews was something quite a few others had worried
about, now and then, before the deists. There was the almost
unavoidable inference that the heathen must be damned
without even an opportunity to know the way of salvation—
an orthodox view, but most embarrassing to orthodoxy; 'of
all objections', admitted Dryden,

> this indeed is chief
> To startle Reason, stagger frail Belief.²

So deists were exploiting here a Christian weakness. The
theory of a universal, indirect revelation succeeded in discrediting the classic *a priori* argument for the Bible, that
God must have revealed himself to man, and substituted for
it an *a priori* argument for doubting the Christian revelation, namely, that God must have revealed himself to all
men through his works. The ramifications of this are
numerous throughout the deistic debate. Deistic writers
laboured to disparage Jewish civilization in order to empha-
size the irrationality of awarding it the honour of being a
favoured nation.

The real question, however, was the second. Was it really
true that the evidence for the revelation could not be
reasonably doubted? If so, all other objections became
irrelevant. If God *did* reveal himself to the Hebraic prophets,
and left unimpeachable proof of it, there is no need to go
farther. However seemingly incomprehensible or unjust, the
word of God must be accepted if it is indeed the word of

¹ Bolingbroke, *Works*, iv. 310; Collins. *Discourse of Freethinking*, p. 38—examples
of a general deist position.
² *Religio Laici*. See Chubb, *Posthumous Works*, i. 177 ff.; Jenkin, *Brief Confutation*, pp. 48–49, where considerable embarrassment is evident in the orthodox defence
of this unpleasant corollary. The pious Cowper could not digest the 'outrageous
wrong' of

> Ten thousand sages lost in endless woe
> For ignorance of what they could not know.

God. However, deists were prepared to subject the credentials of Christianity to as searching an examination as was
then possible. Here we come to the heart of the matter, and
to its greatest length as well. We confront that mountain
of literature (now largely obsolete) in which a few challenged,
and many defended, the authenticity, consistency, and inherent probability of the Bible as the direct word of God.
We shall for the moment postpone any summary of this
long argument. It is enough to say that the deists doubted
the divine inspiration of both the Old Testament and the
New, in the Christian sense;[1] and that they perhaps gave as
good as they took in a debate bound to be inconclusive.

Certainly the deists, profiting heavily from the disputes
within Christianity, gave some sharp shocks to orthodoxy.
The deists asserted that the Bible is a work of many hands,
uneven and contradictory, and by no means all divinely
inspired. But they were not really alone in this. Great
scholars were coming reluctantly to the same opinion. By
1740 the brilliant scholar Conyers Middleton took it upon
himself to tell the pious bluntly that the game was up for
the old view of Scripture. These were the years when, as
Dr. Johnson recalled, the Apostles were tried once a week for
forgery and acquitted. We may add that the litigation at
least gradually damaged their reputation. By 1740 William
Law and Joseph Butler had found ways of shifting the case
for Christianity on to other grounds than those of external
evidences. And David Hume had remarked that Christianity
must rest 'on faith, not on reason'.

The final proof of Christianity was said to be its excellence. That it had, after all, won the civilized world; that it
had survived for many centuries hence, and had equipped
men with a most useful moral and political code, was a prime
orthodox argument.[2] Along with the claim that Christianity

---

[1] It was possible for a deist to claim that he accepted the divine inspiration of
Scripture; see Thomas Woolston, *Mr. Woolston's Defence of his Discourses*, p. 27.
But he could only have meant that he accepted it in the sense that he accepted any
lofty thought or writing as of divine inspiration—not in the Christian sense as
applied to the Bible.

[2] The utilitarian argument is heavily stressed in so conservative an apologetic
piece as Berkeley's *Alciphron*—see Dialogues I and V. See also John Leland, *A View
of the Deistical Writers*, pp. 12–13.

had improved the world went the converse, that deism would worsen it morally. ('Why, if it be as you say,' Swift imagined the common response to deism to be, 'I may safely whore and drink on, and defy the parson.') Christianity, a religion 'so suited to all the necessities of man', had succeeded as the basis of civilization; and the amazing success and utility of the Gospel was commonly listed as proof of its divinity. The 'excellency of its doctrines and precepts', its tendency to provide a perfect morality and to promote 'the well-being of man' above all other religions were said to be as good proofs of Christianity's truth as the miracles were.[1] Here we may note first that the deists were quick to take advantage of this utilitarian, moralistic argument for Christianity by declaring that the *only* true criterion of a religion is the production of virtue—sufficient social virtue.[2] If next they could show that morality was attainable without revealed religion, they might beat orthodoxy on its own ground. The suggestion presented first by Pierre Bayle, the great French sceptic, that even an atheist might be a good citizen, was bound to be pushed by the deists.

The boldest way to challenge Christianity's claim to moral excellence was to deny it altogether. Shaftesbury and Mandeville in their different ways did so: both implied not only that morality is independent of Christianity but that the Christian ethic has serious flaws (to Mandeville, the flaw was evidently only this, that the ethic was too perfectionist for the secular world). Bernard Mandeville, the Anglicized Dutch physician who became the most shocking writer since Hobbes; and Lord Shaftesbury, scion of the noted Whig family and pupil of Locke, whose ethics were as much deplored as his prose was admired, stand in a way outside the deist stream, in that they entered very little into the theological or evidential debate, yet they were very much a part of it in so far as they suggested a natural foundation for morality. As a rule, the deists chose not so much to quarrel with Christianity as a moral system as simply to deny that this morality was peculiarly Christian, that it had need of a special revelation to install it. The moral code of Jesus was

---

[1] Isaac Watts, 'A Caveat against Infidelity', in *Works*, iv. 77–78.
[2] See, for example, Thomas Morgan, *A Collection of Tracts*, preface.

splendid, and was the reason for such success as Christianity had had; but theological 'mysteries' had been smuggled in by scheming priests, and were not merely dispensable but positively pernicious to the ethical truths at the heart of the religion. Priests, for selfish reasons, had corrupted a plain and simple creed. Paul, one of the deists' *bêtes noires*, had been the first.[1] Expel the mysteries, and Christianity, the deist was ordinarily prepared to agree, was quite pleasing, proper, and rational. 'No religion ever appeared in the world', wrote Lord Bolingbroke, 'whose natural tendency was so much directed to promote the peace and happiness of mankind.'[2] But this gospel of Jesus had not been new or unique; it was only an effective statement of the 'religion of nature': 'that good old way which always was, and always will be the true way to life eternal . . .'.[3]

4

Deism found it easier to criticize Christianity than to erect its own positive philosophy. What has been called constructive deism is commonly recognized to have been a failure, and indeed never advanced beyond the stage of a theory both inconsistent and absurd. What did man need that religion provided? That he needed emotional satisfaction, or an inward spiritual experience, was beyond the range of the deist's view; or he was content to get it in contemplating the marvels of Newton's universe, wonderfully run by natural law. But man clearly needed morality. If the Law had not been revealed to him immediately from God, whence came it? Sharing to the full the unhistorical character of this

---

[1] All the deists were anti-clerical, dwelling on the villainies of 'priestcraft'; it would be superfluous to cite the many passages of this sort from Chubb, Woolston, Bolingbroke, and Toland. Peter Annet's *Critical Examination of the Life of St. Paul* expresses the deistic dislike of Paul, which was not, however, shared by Thomas Morgan. Deists' admiration for Mohammedanism, a characteristic often noted, was mainly due to the smaller role assigned by Islam to church and clergy.

[2] Bolingbroke, *Works*, iii. 396, 500. To Bolingbroke, Plato and Platonism were chiefly the 'mystifiers' who had corrupted simple Christianity, the equivalent of 'natural religion'.

[3] Chubb, *The True Gospel*, p. 30. Even in the stronger *Posthumous Works* (i. 136–40) Chubb exhibits the deists' profound respect for Jesus, the Jesus they saw, which was a simple, rational, moral Jesus, not the passionate mystic (which modern scholarship regards as historically the more valid). The latter trait they attributed, ordinarily, to Paul.

age's outlook, deists before Hume could scarcely imagine a gradual historical evolution of morals. Morality must be derived from the 'light of nature'. What was this light of nature? Deism never really knew.

The 'true religion', every deist insisted, is something written clearly in reason and nature, so clearly that no man in the world could possibly mistake it. Only thus could it be independent of Revelation. 'It is as bright as the heavenly light, and free from all ambiguities. . . . The common understanding inherent in man's nature is sufficient, without skill in books and languages, to lead him to the necessary knowledge of his faith and obedience.'[1] Left vague were the key phrases: 'true religion', 'common understanding inherent in man's nature', and 'necessary knowledge'. Deism never succeeded in defining them. The deist was committed as an article of faith to the claim that all mankind may read religious truth clearly: it 'admits of no doubt', 'no man who is able to read the plainest characters can mistake it'.[2] But he never could precisely state what this universal religion was, or how it was so evident.

The confusions in deism came under effective Christian counter-attack. In general this happened later, after 1725. It is somewhat misleading to say, as is rather common, that deism suddenly entered upon its second or constructive phase about 1729, with Tindal's book *Christianity As Old As the Creation*. Lord Herbert had, after all, stated the principles of positive deism at the very beginning, a century before. Yet it is true that between 1700 and 1730 deism succeeded in keeping Christianity on the defensive, and was pretty successful in embarrassing the confident proponents of a rational Christianity. Matthew Tindal's effort to state the deist creed brought that creed into attention. Was the Gospel indeed, as his challenging title affirmed, no more than 'a republication of the religion of nature'? There were effective replies. Tindal received a barrage of answers, and the verdict must be that he was fairly routed. From this time on, the battle approaches a stalemate. The critical or destructive sort of deism did not stop, though it soon ceased

---

[1] Peter Annet, *The Resurrection of Jesus*, 1744, p. 9.
[2] Bolingbroke, quoted by John Leland in *View of the Deistical Writers*, ii. 29.

to arouse much interest. Constructive deism, however, no longer commanded the support of intelligent free-thinkers. Hume and Middleton cannot really believe either side.

Perhaps the basic fallacy in deism was pointed out by John Leland: it was the (unwarranted) assumption that *because nature itself is clear and unalterable, men's moral inferences from nature must be equally so.*[1] Bishop Butler would even declare that nature herself is not so clear, a claim that somewhat puzzled his contemporaries, however. In any event it was obvious that the Light of Nature did not lead deists to think alike, for they differed on many points when they came to construct a faith. In controversies with the pagan philosophers of the Roman world many centuries before, the Christians had employed the strategy of pointing to the variations and inconsistencies of their critics, and they now did the same to the deists, thus turning the tables. If the question is one of consistency, Christians are not apt to be worse off than their less disciplined adversaries, the philosophers. Some deists denied, for instance, that a future life is necessary to morality, but others thought it was. In what way the religion of nature was written clearly in every heart was another matter in dispute among deists: Shaftesbury's innate benevolence was ridiculed by Mandeville and Bolingbroke, who found the guiding principle in self-love; while both of these schools laughed at those who followed Wollaston and Clarke in supposing that morality was deducible by abstract reasoning.[2]

For positive proof that all men can 'naturally' know true religion, deists set forth the argument that Cicero and other pagans had reached the same moral truths as Christianity. It was not hard for Christians to show that this was false, and also beside the point—since Cicero was not, after all, a savage, 'without skill in books and languages'. And he himself had thought a rational religion attainable only by

---

[1] Leland, op. cit. ii. 33. Almost every argument used against the deists may be found forcefully stated in the works of this Nonconformist minister and scholar, the son of a Lancashire business man.

[2] Ibid. ii. 271; cf. Hume's *Treatise of Human Nature*, Bk. III, pt. i. Chubb, in whom the inconsistencies of deism may readily be studied, adopted each of these views at various times. It is notable that none of the really first-rate students of ethics in the eighteenth century was a deist, unless we so classify Hume.

the few.[1] It remained for David Hume to point out in his *Natural History of Religion* that savages are not enlightened deists.

Deism faltered under these attacks, as well it might. The myth of the 'noble savage', the 'uncorrupted man' of earliest times when 'reason and benevolence' were law, was suitable for poets, perhaps (such as the sentimental Thomson), but hardly for philosophers. Thomas Morgan (*The Moral Philosopher*, 1737) shows us deism in partial retreat, for he seems to repudiate the theory that the light of nature is planted in every heart, while still insisting that religious truths depend on eternal reason and must therefore 'be always and everywhere the same'. It remained for David Hume and Conyers Middleton to dispose completely of this 'constructive deism'; and the key to an understanding of their scepticism is their realization that both Christianity and deism had come up against a blank wall in searching for absolutely certain proof. If Christianity had been damaged as an objectively demonstrable proposition, constructive deism had failed to set up a credible alternative. The 'universal religion of nature' which 'has always been the same, and must for ever be alike apprehended by the understandings of all mankind' had become, by mid-century, about as believable for advanced intellects as that God took Moses by the hand.

5

Hume especially struck a blow at deism with his *Natural History of Religion*. Though many then and since have thought Hume an atheist, there does not seem to be any good reason to question his sincerity when he writes that 'the whole frame of Nature bespeaks an Intelligent Author'.[2] This was surely as self-evident for Hume as it had been for Boyle. Hume was certainly not a Christian, though we quite often suspect he would have liked to have been; in him we have reached the stage where the enlightened philosopher does

[1] Isaac Watts, *The Strength and Weakness of Human Reason*, in *Works*, v. 399–401; also Leland, op. cit. ii. 57 ff.

[2] David Hume, *Essays and Treatises on Several Subjects* (Edinburgh, 1817), ii. 383. The ensuing summary and quotations are from this text, pp. 383 ff. *The Natural History of Religion* was first published in 1757, as part of *Four Dissertations*.

not even think it worth while to bother refuting something so patently absurd as a special revelation. He even ridiculed Christian ethics. But to him the claims of constructive deism were equally foolish. So far from there being a single faith available to all men, 'no two nations, and scarce any two men, have ever agreed precisely in the same sentiments'. So far from there existing a natural state of enlightenment in man, the savage is always an idolater, and the majority of men even in contemporary Europe are incapable of arriving at a rational conception of Deity. That the 'mind rises gradually from inferior to superior', Hume had grasped. Deism is false, since man is not a rational creature in the sense deists imagined. Hume was left with the conclusion that there will be one religion for the philosophers and another for the masses. The enlightened few will be deists, if anything; the masses never were, and perhaps never will be capable, of such enlightenment.

By mid-century, then, deism had been deflated as a credo. Destructive criticism of Christianity would, of course, go on. David Hume and Conyers Middleton, representing the most intelligent stratum, were left, for the moment, high and dry: they could believe neither in Christianity nor in the 'light of nature'. Voltaire's 'principes de morale communs au genre humain' were in a parlous state; and if deism be defined as such a belief in the common, universal light of nature making for a clear natural religion, it died almost as soon as it was born.

In a broader sense, deism never died. The critical spirit endured; so did the search for a moral order independent of any special or miraculous revelation. But the idea, broached by Hume, of what Lessing called 'the education of the human race'—the idea of moral evolution, of a *progressive* revelation—moved the frame of reference away from those who had called themselves deists. The true deists were committed to the static concepts of an immutable reason and immutable human nature, always and everywhere the same.

To arrive at a concept of moral evolution meant to leave a place for Christianity. Turgot was more logical than Voltaire: if man is making gradual progress through developing his rational powers, how can you dismiss the whole Christian epoch as a regression? It was more reasonable to conclude with Turgot that Christianity had been 'a powerful agent of civilization', even if now perhaps obsolete. Christianity was not a republication of a hypothetical religion of nature; neither was it a monstrous fallacy. It was a step in the moral evolution of man.[1] And it was still a useful one, though a minority of 'philosophers' could not believe it literally. It is important to note that when the belief that all men possess reason enough to spell out religious truths faded, those who had been militant deists preferred to keep silent. Benjamin Franklin is a good example. He relates in his autobiography how he came to think that his youthful deism, 'tho' it might be true, was not very useful', and thereafter he encouraged a Christianity he clearly felt to be very useful though it might not be true. Middleton and Hume would agree with him that the masses still needed Christianity— perhaps they always would. This view was not a casual cynicism; it was the logical outcome of the deistic debate.

This might well be called the basic dilemma of deism, on which it fell: if all men can see religious truth so easily and naturally without Revelation, why is it that they do not, and never have? The deist could only answer by referring to a monstrously successful conspiracy of the 'priests' to keep all the world wrapped in ignorance. The answer was hardly credible.

[1] John Morley, *Biographical Studies* (London, 1923), pp. 24–25; J. B. Bury, *The Idea of Progress* (London, 1920), pp. 156–7. Ronald S. Crane's articles, 'Anglican Apologetics and the Idea of Progress, 1699–1745', *Modern Philology*, xxxi (1934), 237–306, 349–82, show how the idea of moral evolution appealed to some orthodox Christians (notably Edmund Law) as a weapon against deism.

VI

HIGH LIGHTS OF THE DEISTIC CONTROVERSY

So spins the silk-worm small its slender store,
And labours till it clouds itself all o'er.

POPE

I

IT becomes evident right away that deism was successful on the destructive side mainly because it profited by Christianity's own apparent weaknesses as a rational system. The strategy of exploiting the 'divisions of the Christians' was very skilfully employed by Anthony Collins and his cohorts. Such divisions were many, as Christians submitted their faith to the test of reason and scholarship.

The attack by Daniel Whitby on Mill's New Testament, pounced upon by Collins in his *Discourse of Freethinking*, indicated a certain crisis in the interpretation of Scripture. Men were beginning to wonder exactly what the Bible did say—indeed, exactly what it was. In 1707 William Whiston touched off a long debate when he admitted that the Bible as it stood was not good enough to support Christianity, and claimed the need for a sweeping revision in the canon and text of Scripture. The messianic prophecies of the Old Testament, said Whiston (whose sincerity was beyond question), must be literally fulfilled; a mere allegorical interpretation exposes Christianity to ridicule. Yet literal interpretation would not stand, Whiston believed, and so he saw nothing for it but to conclude that Scripture as it stands is defective, and the true books remain to be restored. He believed with his usual firmness in his own theory as to the proper reconstruction of the Bible, but few others could share his eccentric views. He had, however, inadvertently dealt the prophecies a sharp blow.[1]

---

[1] *The Accomplishment of Scripture Prophecies*, printed in the Boyle Lectures (*A Defense of Natural and Revealed Religion*, ed. J. Nichol and S. Letsome), ii. 259–348. Also *An Essay towards Restoring the Truth of the Old Testament*, 1722.

The prophecies were universally regarded as the strongest support of Christianity's truth. It was beyond dispute that Christianity as revealed truth rested firmly on Judaistic foundations, the New Testament on the Old, Jesus on the prophecies.[1] Christ believed in, and justified himself by, and found his purpose and inspiration in the Old Testament; no one can reject the divine interpretation of the Old Testament without also rejecting the New. That Christ was the Messiah foretold was both central to Christian doctrine and its strongest, indeed indispensable proof. Many other prophecies in the Bible were thought to provide, in their precise fulfilment, the best evidence for the supernatural character of the Bible period. Since Grotius, orthodox Protestant Christians had grown accustomed to interpreting the prophecies in a 'double sense', a view which Whiston now pronounced fatal to Christianity. Was it not true that the 'allegorizing' of deists like Woolston led straight to infidelity?[2]

For Woolston, soon to become the most scandalous of the deists, had started on the primrose path by allegorical interpretations under the influence of Origen. To Whiston the lesson was clear: there must be no smuggling in of allegory in any form, there must be precise and literal fulfilment of every prophecy.

The confusion of some divines may be illustrated by Calamy's suggestion that the prophets were inspired but possibly their transcribers were not, and had erred.[3] Clearly this way led only to confusion, to the discrediting of every line of the Bible. The suggestion that the Bible might be of human origin, not divine, anticipated later criticism, but few were yet prepared to accept such a disconcerting conclusion. Neither was there any serious support for Whiston's theory that the pure revelation had been extensively

[1] A. A. Sykes, *An Essay upon the Truth of the Christian Religion*, p. 2; William Warburton, *The Divine Legation of Moses*, pp. 5–6. Thomas Morgan and Matthew Tindal, the deists, tried to detach ethical Christianity from its Hebraic roots, calling themselves 'Christian deists', but their Christianity was not, of course, supernatural.

[2] See Woolston's *The Old Apology . . . for the Christian Religion . . . Revived.* Many of the early Fathers were fond of allegorizing, and so indeed was so devout a Christian as Pascal. This could never be considered heretical unless carried to great extremes, as Origen and Woolston did carry it. See Carré, op. cit., p. 33, for comments on the development of allegorizing tendencies in Christianity.

[3] See his *Fourteen Sermons* (1710).

corrupted, presumably by the later Jews. (This, too, fore-shadowed subsequent awareness of great chronological and textual confusions in the Old Testament.) In some intelligible sense, the Old Testament prophecies must have been ful-filled. Many Christians were reluctant to give up the 'double sense' interpretation (by which prophecies had a literal application to their own times but applied to the coming of the Messiah in a secondary and allegorical sense only); but not a few agreed with Whiston that prophecies must have a single, literal sense only.[1] Both ways were dangerous: to be satisfied with partial allegory, and also to attempt to defend the literal fulfilment of every prophecy.

Anthony Collins, tongue firmly in cheek, hastened to step into this breach. Ridiculing the idea that the prophecies were literally fulfilled, Collins informed Whiston that to insist upon this is 'most destructive of Christianity'.[2] He mar-shalled all the discrediting evidence against literal fulfilment. Implying that he shared Whiston's opinion that allegorical interpretation would be detrimental, Collins hoped to leave Christianity damned either way, and damned out of the mouths of its own conflicting supporters. Christians were understandably irritated by this mischievous intervention in their problems by a deist, but could hardly deny the embarrassing dilemma he had pointed up. Collins surely was, as Philip Doddridge exclaimed, 'one of those unhappy people who have made it their interest to disbelieve Chris-tianity, and are therefore searching out for any shadow of argument to support their consistency'.[3] Nevertheless, Collins had struck at a sore place, and hit it hard. The *Grounds and Reasons*, first published in 1724, made a sen-sation, and has been called the most effective of all deist tracts. 'The minds of many are intent upon this important subject', Sykes wrote in 1725.[4] This was the most turbulent period of the deistic debate.

---

[1] See A. A. Sykes, op. cit.; and George Benson, in Richard Watson, ed., *A Collection of Theological Tracts*, iv. v–viii, 481–513. But the shrewd William Warburton thought Sykes 'rash and mad' to give up the double senses. (Nichols, *Illustrations of the Literary History of the Eighteenth Century*, ii. 826.)

[2] *A Discourse on the Grounds and Reasons of the Christian Religion*, p. 234.

[3] *Correspondence and Diary*, i. 457.

[4] *Essay upon the Truth of the Christian Religion*, pp. iii–iv.

Collins's shrewd and barely disguised attack on Scripture itself was followed by Thomas Woolston's assault on the miracles, still less disguised. The former, Whiston noted, made 'a very great noise' when it appeared. An even greater noise was made by Woolston, though some dismissed him as mad. Possessed of a lively and vigorous style, the author of *Free Gifts to the Clergy* and *Discourses on the Miracles of Our Saviour* excelled all previous deists in boldness, and paid for it in deprival, ostracism, and finally imprisonment. He was no very weighty arguer. Although it is thought that no fewer than 30,000 copies of his attack on the miracles were sold, that it did the deist cause much good may be doubted. A shocked respectability whispered that Woolston was both insane and ignorant—an enthusiast and a poor scholar, the two worst crimes in this age. Anyone troubling to read his works finds too much shrewdness and wit to believe that a madman wrote them; yet he also finds that Woolston was incapable of careful argument, and, though he had been a scholar, he had reached a stage where, as he said, he did not care whether his learning was correct or not. It is easily demonstrable that he was insincere in his claim that he wished to save Christianity from the literalists.[1] 'I am resolved', he wrote, 'to run down the *letter*, in order to make way for the *spirit* of the Scriptures.' He purported to follow the early Fathers; but it is evident that he had ended in hostility to the whole of Christianity.

Woolston, who had dared to make fun of the Gospels themselves, drew innumerable replies.[2] So did Collins and Tindal, whose book *Christianity As Old As the Creation* now appeared. Deists were growing bolder, and were at the peak of their success between 1725 and 1733. The effect of Woolston's death in jail, where he languished on a charge of criminal blasphemy, scarcely hampered the cause, for the blood of martyrs is notoriously the seed of any church, and England seemed abashed at this persecution. If deism none the less quickly declined, the fault lay in the sterility of its own creed rather than in the failure of its criticism.

[1] N. L. Torrey, *Voltaire and the English Deists*, pp. 48–49.
[2] Some are listed in Nichols, *Literary Anecdotes*, i. 405. Replies to Tindal set a record, evidently numbering more than a hundred.

Strongest of the critics of Christianity was Collins. There were plenty of defenders of the prophecies against his attack, but they were not very effective. Thomas Sherlock believed that each prophecy need not be precisely fulfilled; it is enough to say that 'Jewish religion itself, as containing virtually the hopes of the Gospel, is a Prophecy'.[1] This was sensible enough and surprisingly modern, but not apt to seem adequate at a time when it was generally assumed that supernatural proof was required to attest the supranatural revelation. Sykes agreed with Whiston that literal fulfilment had to be shown. Samuel Chandler, and later John Leland, attempted to deny that the Old Testament prophecies are indispensable to the truth of Christianity. But Christian apologists had been making explicit statements to the contrary too long and too recently.[2]

Weak as Woolston was, his daring had opened up a field very tempting to the talents of deists. Annet, Morgan, and Chubb took up the case against the miracles, including the central miracle itself, the Resurrection. Richard Smalbroke and Gilbert West, among others, felt obliged to defend the miracles of Christ with exhaustive examinations of the evidence; the vivid summation of Thomas Sherlock was a bestseller.[3] It appeared that the deists were not even willing to accept the possibility of such miracles. Annet found 'inconsistencies, improbabilities, absurdities and contradictions' in the testimony for the Resurrection, as did Chubb; but

[1] *The Use and Intent of Prophecy* (1724), a very popular work.

[2] Samuel Chandler, *A Vindication of the Christian Religion*; Leland, *View of the Deistical Writers*, ii. 102–3. On pp. 104–9 ibid. Leland mentions the chief replies to Collins. Samuel Chandler was a well-known Dissenting minister; Edward Chandler, Bishop of Durham, also wrote against Collins. It was in replying to the latter's *Defence of Christianity from the Prophecies of the Old Testament* that Collins made what ultimately proved to be a sound surmise about the date of the Book of Daniel —a good example of deistic shrewdness; see his *Scheme of Literal Prophecy*. For a modern view of the prophecies see N. W. Porteus, in H. W. Robinson, ed., *Record and Revelation* (Oxford, 1938), pp. 248–9.

[3] Smalbroke, *A Vindication of the Miracles of Our Blessed Saviour*; Peter Annet, *The Resurrection of Jesus Considered by a Moral Philosopher*; Chubb, *Posthumous Works*, i. 332 ff.; Thomas Sherlock, *The Trial of the Witnesses of the Resurrection of Christ*. Smalbroke (1672–1749) was a fruitful controversialist who wrote also against Whiston and the Arians, against Dodwell on the soul, &c. Peter Annet, the last English deist of any importance, was also the most radical, and influenced strongly the later American movement associated with Tom Paine and Elihu Palmer.

beyond this they had the argument, derived from Newtonianism, that the course of nature is not to be altered. The earlier deists had not presumed to challenge the very miracles of the Saviour; Chubb had even accepted them as adding 'greater weight or power' to His message.[1] Now it was said that the Resurrection was so *inherently* unlikely that hardly any amount of circumstantial evidence would be convincing.[2]

It was this that John Jackson and Samuel Clarke thought rank atheism. Jackson, replying to Annet, remained confident that the prophecies and miracles could stand the test of any fair criticism.[3] Perhaps the deists had gone too far. Sherlock's famous 'Trial' was recognized as a popular success even by deists.[4] It seemed as if orthodoxy had carried the day after all; but then from an unexpected quarter Conyers Middleton launched a series of bombs. This Cambridge scholar, a disciple of Bentley and the equal of any in learning, returned a devastating rebuttal to a book Daniel Waterland had written against Tindal.

2

Whether Middleton was a deist or a Christian has rather unnecessarily troubled some writers.[5] Clearly, whatever you choose to call him, his significance was in his relative disinterestedness. A scholar and a rationalist through and through, deep piety was remote from him, yet he possessed

---

[1] *The True Gospel*, pp. 52–53. That earlier deism was merely more cautious is indicated by the fact that while Toland's remarks on the miracles had been very ambiguous in *Christianity Not Mysterious* (pp. 144 ff.), he later made his scepticism more explicit—see Walter Merrill, op. cit., p. 63.

[2] Annet, op. cit., pp. 75–77. Hume's famous essay on miracles appeared later, in 1748 (in *Philosophical Essays concerning the Human Understanding*), though he had written it earlier. For Lord Shaftesbury's bold insinuations as to the doubtfulness of miracles, see Aldridge, *Shaftesbury and the Deist Manifesto*, pp. 361–3.

[3] *Address to the Deists*, p. 71 and *passim*.

[4] Annet, op. cit., p. 3. Gilbert West's long and thorough defence of the Resurrection (1747), which may be found in vol. v of Watson's *Collection of Theological Tracts*, was also regarded as very successful.

[5] Leslie Stephen accused him of 'conscious insincerity'; Sykes (*Church and State*, p. 421) is inclined to defend Middleton's 'sincerity'. George Sherburn (in A. C. Baugh, ed., *A Literary History of England*, p. 1083) characterizes Middleton's best-known work as 'unintentionally subversive', which is not strictly accurate. Torrey, *Voltaire and the English Deists*, pp. 155–71, discusses Middleton. That Middleton was somewhat embittered by failure to receive promotion in the Church is clear from some of his letters (*Miscellaneous Works*, vol. ii) as well as from a note in Nichols, *Literary Anecdotes*, iii. 165–6.

none of the malignancy of the carping deist who delighted in smashing Christian idols. He would have been orthodox if he could. He had taken the measure of the debate between deist and Christian. He knew very well that the deists were neither fools nor villains, and could not be defeated by invective—or even by argument, on the grounds chosen. It annoyed him to hear Waterland call Tindal an ignoramus, and he reminded that divine astringently that Tindal was at least his match! He said bluntly that the clergy had nothing to offer against Collins 'in which a man of sense could reasonably acquiesce'.[1] This was not the propaganda of an inveterate anti-Christian, but the cool judgement of a great scholar. Faithful to the 'plain historical method' of Locke, Middleton had been led by this method to abandon the view that the Scriptures are perpetually inspired. To insist on complete inspiration will only bring Christianity into ridicule.[2] It is absurd to try to vindicate every text in its literal sense. Yet he also saw the foolishness of the deist claim that 'the light of reason' is enough to give, as Tindal had said, 'a perfect and complete rule of duty in all cases, both towards God and Man'. Reason, Middleton pointed out, had never in all history been a foundation for popular religion. In short, this sensible if unemotional don perceived that both literal Christianity and constructive deism were unbelievable.

What then remained? Middleton did not go beyond the facts in the case; he was not a Law or a Wesley, or even a Hume. He could only say that while Christianity is not strictly true it is useful, since the masses must have mysteries in their religion. Like Buffon, he was prepared to admit 'il faut une religion au peuple', and draw a line between *peuple* and *philosophe*. This apparently cynical view (of which Karl Marx for one was to make a great deal) should not be interpreted as malicious; it was rather the dilemma in which he and others had been left. The controversy had deposited them on this awkward ledge, and they knew not how to get off.

Middleton's *Letter to Dr. Waterland* led eventually to the *Free Inquiry into the Miraculous Powers* ('which are supposed

---

[1] *Miscellaneous Works*, ii. 138–43, also page iii.
[2] Ibid., ii. 19, 73–74, 163–4.

to have subsisted from the earliest ages through several successive centuries of the Christian church') (1749). On this attack on the reliability of the Fathers of the early Church in their claims of miracles, the admission of Bishop Warburton is a sufficient comment: it 'had given the miracles of the early ages such a blow as they would not easily recover from'.[1] The implications were evidently outrageous. John Wesley, to be sure, was unfair and inaccurate when he wrote:

> It is easy to observe that the whole tenor of your argument tends to prove . . . that no miracles were wrought by Christ or his Apostles; and that these too were fools or knaves. . . .[2]

For Middleton had not attacked the integrity of the Apostolic Fathers, though he did attempt to show that they themselves had claimed no miracles. It was the Christians of the second and third centuries whom he indicted for gullibility. It is significant, however, that good Christians thought as Wesley did, and doubtless it was natural.

In other writings Middleton denied that the apostles (also the prophets) were incapable of error, and detected inconsistencies in the Gospel accounts of Jesus.[3] This was surely carrying the critical spirit to the brink of impiety.

To Middleton, whose *Letter from Rome* was a famous assault on Catholicism, there were 'superstitions' he was attacking, better suited for Romanism than for rational Protestantism, and he certainly did not think of himself as anti-Christian, though he was bitterly attacked as such. But there was absolutely none of the *haereticus esse nolo* spirit in him. He followed where scholarship led, and no one showed so lucidly that it led away from Biblical literalism. It is safe to say that after Middleton educated men could no longer hold to a belief in the plenary inspiration and complete

---

[1] Nichols, *Illustrations*, ii. 179–81. Warburton could only salvage one or two miracles from the carnage Middleton wrought; he sought to vindicate one in his *Julian* (1750), for which, however, he had a naturalistic explanation.

[2] 'Letter to Dr. Middleton', in *Works*, x. 1.

[3] See *Miscellaneous Works, passim*; e.g. 'Reflections on the Dispute between the Apostles Peter and Paul' and 'Reflections on the Variations or Inconsistencies which are found among the Four Evangelists'. In the latter he sees a general harmony which is strong evidence for the truth of the story, but he denies that the evangelists never erred.

accuracy of Scripture. In his keen-sighted historical method the higher criticism had been born, though it would be a long time maturing. The century between Chillingworth's *Religion of Protestants* and Middleton's *Free Inquiry* marked the rise and fall of Biblical Christianity. It is interesting that the *Free Inquiry* had not said a word about the Bible, but its method, the historical one of placing sacred history in the context of secular history, was revolutionary.

If the Bible was still the religion of Protestants, it must be on some other terms than Chillingworth had meant when he penned that famous phrase. Yet Middleton's sane scholarship slew the deists in the same stroke, for no educated man could now think that Tindal was either credible or relevant. Middleton's criticism of deism shrewdly pointed out all the fallacies of this creed.[1] The way was cleared for the long task of reconstructing Christianity on a historical basis. It must not be supposed that Middleton abruptly ended all the preceding controversy. Deists continued to attack the external evidences of Christianity, and Christians to defend them. Middleton was furiously assailed, and lived long enough to dispose of only one or two of his critics. The debate about miracles and prophecies went on.[2] How far orthodoxy was from accepting any historical view of religious development may be judged from Warburton's comment that Hume in positing an original polytheism was guilty of an 'atheistic naturalism'. Orthodox Christianity thus agreed with deism as against the radical new naturalism of Hume's historical method: Christians and deists could agree that monotheism had always existed.

3

To detach Christianity from its Old Testament roots was always a strategic goal of the deists. If Tindal was 'the first English deist to attack the Scripture in detail from the point of view of morality',[3] no deist had ever neglected an opportunity to cast aspersions on the Jews, their Law and their

---

[1] Ibid. ii. 175–6.
[2] For some later tracts on the prophecies and miracles see Watson's *Collection of Theological Tracts*, vol. v.
[3] Torrey, op. cit., p. 128.

prophets, their society and their view of God as exhibited in the Old Testament. The reason for this intellectual anti-Semitism of the deist movement is obvious: to discredit the Jews was to discredit Revelation, for they were its instruments. We need not question the sincerity of the deist when he argued that Christianity is sound, if it is a Christianity that 'does not stand on the legs of Judaism' (Annet). It should stand instead on 'the rock of nature', it ought to be just the 'republication of the religion of nature', not a special revelation vouchsafed to the Jews. On these terms deists were always ready to embrace Christianity; the terms, of course, amounted to a demand that Christianity as a special religion abdicate. Thomas Morgan, the 'Moral Philosopher', tried to define the two parties as the 'Christian Jews' and the 'Christian Deists'.

To Tindal's and Morgan's disparagement of the Jews there were a number of replies in the expected manner.[1] The unexpected one was William Warburton's *Divine Legation of Moses*. Over this famous work a furious controversy broke out among the clergy, to the renewed delight of the deists (1738–40). Morgan thanked Warburton, ironically, on behalf of the deists.[2] Warburton's book reflected the man himself: it was a brilliant yet evidently perverse *tour de force*. The learned friend and theological tutor of Alexander Pope (after, not before, the *Essay on Man*) seems to sum up in his personality all the brilliance and oddity of theology in the age of reason. He had a horror of being thought unorthodox, but, carrying on the Clarke tradition, he nearly reasoned himself out of orthodoxy. *The Divine Legation*, called 'the most learned, most arrogant,

---

[1] For example, Francis Webber, *The Jewish Dispensation Considered and Vindicated* . . . (1738); Moses Lowman, *A Dissertation on the Civil Government of the Hebrews* (1740); John Leland, *The Divine Authority of the Old and New Testament Asserted*, vol. i (1739).

[2] *A Brief Examination of the Rev. Mr. Warburton's 'Divine Legation of Moses'*, p. 1. Morgan was regarded by Warburton as a 'senseless and abandoned scribbler' who only repeated Tindal. The judgement seems sound; yet Morgan had a flair for popularization, and *The Moral Philosopher* was widely read. Thomas Morgan was, like Chubb, a poor boy (Welsh), educated by a Dissenting minister; he became a Presbyterian minister but was dismissed about 1721 for his extremely unorthodox views. He then became, evidently, a physician, and, most certainly, a prolific pamphleteer.

and most absurd work' produced in English theology for
a century, had a main thesis both 'simple and ingenious'—
in the opinion of half his fellow clergy, over-ingenious.
Warburton, they declared, was either a subtle enemy to Revelation or else a very indiscreet friend.[1] Echoes of the controversy were to be heard as late as 1766, when the great scholar
Lowth attacked Warburton's thesis; and the bitterness of it
may be judged from Warburton's own remark that he had been
more reviled than any deist.[2] Among the sharp replies *The
Divine Legation* drew was one by the great William Law, who
had supposedly abjured all such argumentation. Here was
another Sherlock–South affair to scandalize Christianity.

Warburton was scarcely as eccentric as William Whiston,
and was most anxious to be considered an orthodox Christian,
unlike his friend Conyers Middleton. But there is much
evidence that those who admired his abilities feared his
inclination to singularity. In his *magnum opus* he had, as he
thought, invented a new method of proving the truth of
Scripture, at the same time striking a clever blow against the
deists. The new method was what Warburton called using
internal evidence rather than (exclusively) external.[3] In this
method, which involved a certain idea of growth and development in religion, later students might detect the faint gleam
of modern historicism. But Warburton had only one idea
in mind: to show that the absence of belief in immortality
among the Hebrews proved they must have been under
divine guidance directly. He was aware that deists had often
disparaged the moral and religious concepts of the Old
Testament, supposing that this weakened the plausibility of
the Jews' being the chosen people. But Warburton held that
it demonstrated the opposite. The Jews must indeed have
been chosen, else they could not have survived without a
belief in immortality. Thus Warburton hoped, as he said,

---

[1] See A. W. Evans, *Warburton and the Warburtonians, passim*—the most autho-
ritative study of an important figure.

[2] Nichols, *Anecdotes*, ii. 176–7. The quarrel over the Jews flared up again in 1761
when Peter Annet (?) published a strong attack on David, always a favourite target
of the deists among Old Testament characters. A number of divines, including
Samuel Chandler, John Francis, and William Cleaver, felt obliged to defend at
length the moral character of the Israelite king.

[3] *The Divine Legation of Moses* (1738), pp. 1–2.

to show the truth of Christianity on the deists' own principles.[1]

For most of his contemporaries, the argument was too paradoxical. It resembled the old *joke* about the infidel converted to Christianity after a look at the Papacy because he reasoned that nothing so corrupt could endure unless indeed divinely protected! It was at any rate in conflict with strongly held beliefs—that immortality had always been believed in since Adam, that the Old Testament gives proof of such beliefs, that this idea was not hidden from the Jews by God and Moses.[2] It opened up a fresh argument, also bound to be inconclusive in the absence of greater knowledge about ancient history, one which could only delight the deists, puzzle the orthodox, and perhaps disgust the public. In subsequent volumes of *The Divine Legation* Warburton extended his range to write interestingly on many questions; the work is an uncommonly rich one. He was a learned and ingenious man, though alleged to be disputatious, arrogant, and a lover of paradox. He was a stout champion of orthodoxy on many questions, a keen exposer of the inconsistencies in deism. No one, for instance, argued so well (though the argument was scarcely new) that the deists cannot prove their alleged natural religion to be really natural; for they really have the advantage of the Christian revelation in arriving at principles which they falsely take to be attainable by unaided reason. As we should put it, there is no such thing as an abstract content of 'reason' outside the social and historical milieu. Warburton had a gift of shrewd thinking and trenchant expression beyond most others of his day, dull as his theological paradoxes may seem to a modern. But it was the fate of his best-known work to do, in the opinion of many of his contemporaries, more harm than good to the Christian cause.

[1] Warburton recognized an inconsistency of the deists when they also argued that pre-Christians were all quite moral, and capable of adequate religious knowledge (see ibid., pp. 412–14). To deism the Jews were a people apart too, it seemed: they alone were *in*capable of even natural religion. Christians, Warburton says, must hold that pre-Christians were neither too weak nor too strong in reason: not strong enough to discover the true principles of religion unaided, yet not so weak as to be unable to appreciate those truths when they were revealed.

[2] William Law, *A Short but Sufficient Confutation of the Rev. Dr. Warburton's 'Divine Legation of Moses'* (1757).

4

Of these lengthy disputes pursued with so much intellectual labour, most if not all seem to be obsolete; and our modern verdict on them is apt to be the same as that which Gibbon, only a few years later, pronounced on Warburton's book: 'a monument, already crumbling into dust, of the vigour and weakness of the human mind'. The ingenuity lavished by both deist and Christian on the external evidences was mainly wasted, since both wrote largely without that factual historical knowledge of the Bible and its times since uncovered. Their unhistorical approach renders their quarrels meaningless. What point is there in asking whether the Jews were moral or immoral, whether they did or did not believe in a future life, as if there had been no change throughout their history? Warburton was evidently right, roughly speaking: the Jews developed the idea of a future existence quite late, and then not in the Christian sense. But he did not deal with the question as a development at all. Out of all this discussion, however, there did slowly emerge the foundations of modern criticism. Middleton and Warburton bring us to its threshold. The Germans were stimulated in their scholarship by the English debate. Is it not always true that in human history a vast amount of irrelevant intellectual energy is required to distil a little intellectual progress? The deistic debate was not wasted.

There were many other disputes growing out of deism, some of which had only a personal interest, others of which led away from the Bible to general philosophic and moral discussions. As an example of the former, there is the much-discussed question of Alexander Pope's deism. The general significance of this is that the poet, while innocent of any heretical intent, had absorbed deistic currents of thought unknowingly, so pervasive were these. Pope could pillory Toland and Tindal, yet absorb and convey the ideas of Leibniz and Bolingbroke. That the *Essay on Man* is loosely deistic seems evident, thought the fact had to be pointed out before it was recognized. Warburton was able to attack the Essay as 'rank atheism' first, and then change to lead the vindication of Pope. Atheism, Pope thought (so did the deists), is absurd. But so is theology. Why should there not be a universal 'commonsense' religion, so that all this vapid theologizing might be avoided? Why should man strive to grasp the supernatural, anyway? Doubtless it exists; but human reason is too weak to grasp it, being proportioned to positive facts alone, and so 'the proper study of mankind is man'. To 'look through nature up to nature's God' is only common sense, but to go any farther leads to foolishness. Catholicism, scepticism, and genteel deism blended in Pope's admittedly confused but significant philosophy. What it meant above all was that men of taste were profoundly bored with theological disputes. They did not want to be branded heretics or infidels, not at all—this was enthusiasm. The disputatious 'free-thinkers' disgusted them; but so did disputatious divines, and they did not want to have to defend their orthodoxy in this way. Their tendency to belittle reason sprang from such motives.[1] One may say that they wanted the advantages of orthodoxy without the burdens, and that they proposed to solve the problem by dismissing it. But one may not deny that they represented a deep revulsion against the barren and interminable debates about the proofs of Christianity. The more popular journals learned to avoid all theological controversy.[2] A great English historian has written that this period was marked by 'a general indifference to all questions of religious speculation or religious life'.[3] The statement is much too sweeping; but it is true that both

---

[1] In an article on 'Pride in Eighteenth Century Thought', Arthur O. Lovejoy once noted that the most influential authors of the early and middle eighteenth century 'made a great point of reducing man's claims to "reason" to a minimum, and to belittling the importance of that faculty in human existence . . . '. This was in large part the literary reaction to rational divinity. We observe it in Bolingbroke, the deist, who taught it to Pope. However, reason was rejected only so far as it attempted to probe the supernatural and to wrestle vainly with unanswerable questions.

[2] Defoe, *Writings*, ed. Lee, ii. 128–30: in 1719 Defoe apologized for inserting a theological note into his paper. 'Religious things are sometimes tiresome to many of your readers, who generally expect something more diverting. . . .' The *Spectator*, of course, made a point of avoiding theological abstruseness in favour of entertaining moral edification. Benjamin Franklin reflected the boredom with theology as he related in his *Autobiography* how he could take no interest in the 'polemic arguments' of the Pennsylvania Christians, which he found 'dry, uninteresting, and unedifying'.

[3] John Richard Green, *A Short History of the English People* (London, 1921), p. 735.

the general public and the men of letters increasingly ignored the theological combatants, finding the debate most tedious.

The third Earl of Shaftesbury, who died in 1713 but whose ideas exerted an influence throughout the century (being carried on by Francis Hutcheson especially), was above all a man of taste, willing to say genially that 'the most ingenious way of becoming foolish is by a system'. He did not make a system, and he abhorred the rationalistic moralists as well as the theologians, but his essays contributed to the deist cause, both negatively and positively. Shaftesbury was really neither very original nor very acute, but he was a consummate literary artist in the prose style. He revived the Pomponazzian argument that virtue is its own best reward, from which it was inferred that Christianity's reliance on future rewards and punishments is a false or inferior morality. Whether false or inferior makes a difference, to be sure; if the latter, then Shaftesbury must find himself in the familiar position of saying that an enlightened few do not need revealed religion, but the rest do, and it is necessary for society; Christianity may not be the highest teaching but it can surely do no harm. Evidently this was indeed Shaftesbury's view. He was quite willing to accept the Church of England as a useful institution. The deists, however, were soon arguing that a belief in a future life has no value for anyone, and that man as a 'sociable animal' has sufficient natural morality.[1] This idea they had received from Shaftesbury.

Hutcheson, developing Shaftesbury, would teach that 'the ethical ideal is possible of attainment by man without the acceptance by him of a theological basis'. A 'moral sense' exists instinctively, anterior to all religious beliefs. Benevolence is a part of human nature, Shaftesbury supposed, using the analogy of moral approbation with aesthetic pleasure. More definitely naturalistic in Hutcheson, this theory was really directed against the egoism of Hobbes and

---

[1] Thomas Chubb, *Some Observations* . . . [on] *Mr. Warburton's Divine Legation of Moses*, in *Posthumous Works*, i. 69–94. It was a part of Warburton's argument, of course, that belief in a future life is indispensable to society, except under a special and divine dispensation.

Mandeville, who asserted the impossibility of disinterested benevolence. Nor did Shaftesbury claim that the instinct of benevolence operates automatically; he thought it had to be carefully educated and cultivated. But the deists were quick to take over and exaggerate the idea.

Orthodox Christians immediately detected a dangerous heresy in the essays of Shaftesbury. They were considered as 'very artfully' attacking revealed religion under cover of 'fine language and beautiful sentiments'.[1] The 1709 Boyle Lectures were directed against them. Pope told him, said Warburton, that 'the *Characteristics* had done more harm to revealed religion in England than all the works of infidelity put together'.[2] For one thing, the essayist gave an impetus to the use of ridicule, which tendency deists had already shown, but in which they were now much encouraged. They could quote the eminent Lord Shaftesbury that ridicule was nothing less than the 'test of truth'.[3]

Shaftesbury's attack on immortality and his assertion of an innate moral sense were both embarrassing to Christians. They were hard to meet, because set forth in terms of the highest sort of ethical ideal. Possibly Christianity had laid too much stress on the usefulness of its doctrine, as its greatest proof. A belief in immortality had been declared indispensable to morality and social order—the only way to hold in check men's passions. Locke, and later Bolingbroke, observed that immortality cannot be proved, but is most useful.[4] Shaftesbury questioned whether the idea was even useful. Did it really make men better? He thought not. Might society get along very well without any such thing as a Christian Church? Shaftesbury led to the implication that it might, though he himself would not have gone so far. Strictly speaking, no doubt, it is irrelevant for a Christian

---

[1] Doddridge, *Correspondence and Diary*, i. 62. A. O. Aldridge's work, *Shaftesbury and the Deist Manifesto*, not only analyses the question of Shaftesbury's deism but includes (pp. 371 ff.) an extensive list of the references to Shaftesbury in the eighteenth century.

[2] Evans, *Warburton*, p. 200.

[3] Professor Aldridge has pointed out that Shaftesbury did not actually claim that ridicule was *the* test of truth; but he did insist that it was a legitimate device to use on religious subjects.

[4] Locke, *An Essay concerning Human Understanding*, ii. 192; Bolingbroke, *Works*, iv. 327.

to inquire whether Christianity has made the world a happier place.[1] Yet the Christians of this age had said the opposite too many times.

Shaftesbury was answered many times, not often with outstanding success by Christians.[2] The shrewd Bernard de Mandeville stabbed at him and Christianity both. Man, as he saw it, is neither rational nor benevolent, but simply selfish.[3] So he is, indeed, to many Christians; Mandeville himself, like Pierre Bayle, owed much to the Calvinist tradition. The optimistic Christians of this era, however, were not Calvinists. In arguing that good and evil impulses have nothing to do with formal belief or religious doctrine, that a society of atheists might be as virtuous as a society of (presumed) Christians, Mandeville naturally shocked respectable opinion, and it was no wonder he was universally reviled. He did not believe the great majority of men to be rational, or benevolent, or capable of Christian salvation. But human selfishness is socially harmless; viciousness cancels out, 'private vices equal public virtue'. In appearing to sanction wickedness Mandeville so disturbed a righteous generation that even Edward Gibbon applauded the pious William Law for refuting such a 'licentious doctrine'.[4] This harsh realism did not even appeal to the average deist, who generally thought of man as both rational and good. He was not above using it, however, to discomfit Christians.

Perhaps this whole generation owed a debt to Mandeville for exposing the hollowness of its pretensions to virtue. William Law found himself forced to agree with Mandeville that mere morality is about as good on infidel terms as on Christian. 'He brought the great question, whether "right" and "wrong" mean anything, to an issue.'[5] Mandeville did

[1] Jenkin, A Brief Confutation, p. 46.

[2] For example, Isaac Watts, Self-Love and Virtue Reconciled Only by Religion (1739); part ii of Berkeley's Alciphron; John Leland, letter v in A View of the Deistical Writers, where (i. 71–72) numerous other answers to Shaftesbury are listed. See also Aldridge, op. cit., pp. 371 ff.

[3] The Fable of the Bees, or Private Vices Public Benefits was first printed in 1714; its modern edition has been edited with a scholarly introduction by Frederick B. Kaye.

[4] Gibbon, Autobiography, pp. 16–17.

[5] William Law, Remarks on the Fable of the Bees, edited with an introduction by F. D. Maurice, p. ix.

not so much attack Christianity as deny its relevance to eighteenth-century England. And it is certainly true that to the great majority, Christianity meant a rather complacent creed of bourgeois morality. The deepest Christians saw that if it were no more than that it must perish at the hands of deism. The crisis was really one within Christianity. A handful of deists could not slay her, unless she had already mortally wounded herself.

VII

ORTHODOXY AT BAY

We are outrageously attacked from both within and from without, by
open enemies, and false brethren; with pretext of Scripture and in
defiance of it. . . .   FRANCIS SQUIRE, 1723

I

DEISM was never respectable. To an overwhelming majority of Englishmen, rank unbelief was abhorrent.
If Christians had presented a firm and united front
against the scoffers, the outcome would never have been in
doubt for a moment. The 'false brethren' were more dangerous than the open enemies; or, to put it more fairly, it was
confusion within the orthodox camp that rendered its cause
desperate. We have already seen how persistently deists
dwelt on the discords of the faithful.

It is best to define an orthodox Christian as one who
'considers it important to be what he regards as an orthodox
Christian'.[1] This included nearly everyone; it included, for
instance, Whiston the Arian, who thought Socinians and
deists scandalous, and it included so unusual a sect as the
Quakers, who did not like to be associated with deism.[2] But
the objective standards of orthodoxy were increasingly in
doubt. 'Heresy' was becoming harder to define. Dissenters
from the State Church were officially recognized; force as
an instrument of conformity was *passé*; there was no unassailable seat of authority to be appealed to.

Orthodoxy was certainly not Romanism, for all remained
staunchly hostile to the Catholics. Cruder Whig propaganda

---

[1] Fairchild, *Religious Trends in English Poetry*, i. 23.
[2] A Quaker attack on deism is Alexander Arscott's *Some Considerations Relating
to the Present State of the Christian Religion* (London, 1731; reprinted in Philadelphia
by Benjamin Franklin, 1732). The apostate Quaker George Keith brought charges
against his former brethren of affinity with deism, but these were very loose. For
an interesting discussion of the relationship between eighteenth-century Quakerism
and deism see F. B. Tolles, *Meeting House and Counting House*, pp. 171-4, 210-12,
except that Tolles is confused as to the definition of deism and classes Locke, Clarke,
and Wollaston as deists.

continued to accuse the High Church Tories of 'papist' tendencies, but this was as wide of the mark as the Tory hint that all Dissenters were bloody revolutionaries. Far into the eighteenth century, all sides employed the appeal to prejudices against Rome. The conservative apologist Berkeley asked if all this undermining of the true faith would not leave an opening for 'Popish emissaries'.[1] Quakers and Methodists were quite commonly accused of being Papists in disguise. Free-thinkers and moderate churchmen were quick to label any appeal to authority as Romanism. The deists dwelt on 'the absurdity of opposing faith to reason', but here they spoke not for the deists alone. There was never any question of closing the debate by an appeal either to an infallible chair or to blind faith.

It was Protestant Christianity, then. But the Protestants in England were deeply divided. The dominant Church of England was bitterly torn into factions. Those Whiggish Anglicans who had inherited the mantle of Tillotson and Stillingfleet, including such as Benjamin Hoadly and Samuel Clarke, incurred the reproaches of the High Church element, as betrayers of the true way; there are no severer strictures in this period than those passed by one Anglican on another, mainly by the disgruntled Tories on the victorious Whigs. Doubtless this was chiefly a political quarrel —yet it is well to remember that politics and religion were still connected. A 1704 pamphlet stated accurately enough that 'all this noise about High and Low Church . . . signifies no more than Whig and Tory'.[2] But after all, the question of Church and State was religious as well as political. High Church Tories sincerely believed that the Whiggish political

---

[1] Berkeley, *Works*, ii. 117–18. See also James T. Hillhouse, *The Grub Street Journal*, p. 242, for some strong anti-Romanist views of a High Church organ.

[2] See *A Dictionary of English Church History*, ed. S. L. Ollard (London, 1912), p. 115. Aside from his loyalty to the Stuart cause and disgust at the appointment of Whiggish bishops in lieu of those who refused to swear allegiance to the new government, the marks of a 'high-flyer' were his suspicions of toleration, with demands for strict enforcement of laws against Dissent; his inclination to like more ceremony in the Church, though this was vague and scarcely doctrinal; and perhaps his attitude towards Reunion, though this was also no very clear criterion, since projects for alliance with the French (Gallican) Church were advocated not only by High Churchmen like Hickes and Leslie but also by Archbishop Wake (1717–20), who was surely not a Tory.

doctrines dealt a mortal blow to the position of the Church, and hence to all religion. To these embittered reactionaries, the Church of England had been ever since 1689, in Dryden's phrase, 'a meer mock queen of a divided band'. Toleration had begun it; this was, to Charles Leslie, 'a sacrificing of God to Mammon'. All subsequent evils they regarded as stemming from the events of that year, which had devastated their cherished principles of hereditary monarchy, non-resistance, and especially the firm alliance of Church and State. The Revolution, they believed, had substituted in religion the mere fiat of man for the authority of God; utility in place of Scriptural command; and 'Erastianism' in place of the proper equality of Church and State. 'I say it is a necessary and infallible consequence', wrote Francis Squire, 'that if we take not our faith and our manners implicitly from the authority of God, we must do it from the fancy and caprice of man.'[1]

In the mythology of non-jurors and their sympathizers[2] this is what had happened when an anointed monarch had been deposed by Parliament, and, most of all, when bishops who refused to recognize the act were deposed by the State.

> For how can she constrain them to obey
> Who has herself cast off the lawful sway?

The Church was no longer a true one. Dr. Sacheverell, leader of the Tory uprising of 1709, denounced the Whig bishops as 'factious and schismatical imposters'. This intrepid soul, a true 'fanatic' in the view of Whigs and other moderates,[3] only stated in extreme terms what a great many Anglicans were thinking. Such invective was treasonable

---

[1] Squire, *An Answer to the Independent Whig* (1723), p. 10. Thomas Gordon, the crude but popular 'Independent Whig', gave an extreme version of the Whig position, embarrassing to moderate Whigs, which was deistic and cynically Erastian (justifying the Established Church on grounds of political expediency alone).

[2] I.e. those who refused the oath of allegiance to William and Mary in 1688 and were deprived. To the extreme non-jurors, the Church since 1688 was without legitimacy, and their own society the only true Church. Many who sympathized with them and grumbled at Whiggism did not carry defiance so far.

[3] The pamphlet *Faults on Both Sides* (London, 1710), though moderate, blames Sacheverell as a 'fanatic' and as a priest meddling in politics. Ordinarily these were unpopular characteristics; Sacheverell won support mainly because of hostility to the incumbent Whigs on the war issue.

after 1715, and several people paid with their lives for repeating it a few years later. But many Anglican clergymen went on thinking it and saying it privately. In 1717 George Hickes, foremost of the non-juring bishops, said it for the last time, publicly: the clergy cannot be deprived by any secular power, and it is blasphemy to pray for a Hanover, whose alleged Church of England is a schismatical imposture.

Benjamin Hoadly, most 'political' of the Whig bishops, replied that James II was properly excluded, and the Non-Jurors properly deprived for not swearing allegiance to the government. But he went on to define the Church in such terms as few honest Anglicans could accept. Hoadly's sermon of 31 March 1717, on 'The Nature of the Kingdom or Church of Christ', defined the Church as no more than the body of sincere believers, and repudiated all authority over its members' 'consciences or conduct'. It led to a famous quarrel which ended in a dean and a bishop giving each other the lie direct. It was the general view that this unhappy affair did much damage to religion generally.[1] Hoadly was widely suspect as a political bishop. That he earned his appointment by political writings on behalf of the Whigs, and that he shamefully neglected his diocese, are reproaches that ought not to prevent a recognition of his intellectual honesty and ability as a liberal clergyman. But the so-called Bangorian controversy in which he was involved left the Church still hopelessly divided and confused. If the Bangorian controversy presented the alternatives, there was evidently a most unpleasant choice between treasonable fanaticism and semi-deistic Erastianism.

Hoadly's version of the nature of the Church was so broad that even Edmund Calamy, the Dissenter, saw in it more of Dissent than of Anglicanism; it seemed to define away the Church of England as a recognizable body. Hoadly went beyond the limits that his fellow Latitudinarians thought discreet. But his position was shared in the broader outline by others of the moderate clergy. 'Mutual charity, not . . . a pretense of uniformity of opinions' was to be the basis of the Church; the right of private judgement, reduction of neccessary beliefs to a few fundamentals, and a tendency towards moralism (expressed as a concern for 'virtue and holiness' rather than theological opinions)—these were tenets of the liberal wing.[1] The only other road, they argued, led to Rome—or, as Clarke said, turning the Erastian charge against his accusers, to Hobbes.[2] But this mild and complacent spirit was a red rag to High Churchmen. They reserved their choicest epithets for Gilbert Burnet, and then Benjamin Hoadly, and then Edmund Gibson. Whig Anglicans could answer quite as bitterly in ridiculing High Church doctrines of apostolic succession and 'infallibility'.[3] Yet differences of doctrine were almost non-existent. The question was one of Church discipline and government, with a heavy overcast of political animosity. True, High Churchmen were aware of the threat of moralism, and insisted that religious duties were more important than good deeds. They never trusted private judgement quite so far, displaying a readiness to demand conformity and to exercise discipline against any cleric who strayed beyond the Thirty-Nine Articles.[4]

Circumstances were against the 'high-flyers' in the age of Walpole. Even before that, the Act of Union (1707) had dealt a severe blow to the theory of religious uniformity, by conceding that Scotland might retain her own (established) Presbyterian Church.[5] After 1718 the Occasional Conformity and Schism Acts, passed in the late years of Anne, were repealed. (The Test and Corporation Acts remained, but were scarcely enforced.) The intransigent spirit of Sacheverell, Leslie, and Atterbury gradually departed, the failure of the 'Fifteen' being of course the critical

[1] A. A. Sykes, *The External Peace of the Church*, is a good brief statement of the liberal Anglican position, by one of the more notably liberal Anglicans, scarcely less distasteful to the conservative faction than Hoadly.

[2] Samuel Clarke, *Works*, iv. 240 ff.

[3] See Hunt, *Religious Thought*, iii. 1–31.

[4] Seen in the Clarke case, discussed above. Arthur W. Hopkinson, *About William Law*, pp. 35–38, contains a good brief summary of the High Church position, as reflected in Law's critique of Hoadly. Fleetwood, *Works*, iii. 4–40, 143–73, 186–210, sheds light on certain differences concerning baptism and Holy Communion—particularly the performing of baptism by laymen, defended by liberals.

[5] See Leslie's laments over this act, *Rehearsal*, vols. ii–iv (1707–8), *passim*. It is worth noting that in America this precedent was immediately used to challenge the legality of an established church beyond England proper.

event; and Thomas Sherlock, who becomes the leading Tory Churchman in the 1730's, is a far milder figure. When purged of its intolerance and political prejudice, the High Church tradition contained a core of real Christian piety unique in this age. Out of it issued the religious revival; it is hardly accidental that William Law had been a non-juror and that Wesley's family drew on the same tradition. (John Byrom was also the son of a non-juror.) Likewise Butler and Berkeley, greatest of the Christian apologists, must be ranked with the element in the Church that had always mistrusted the glib rationalism of the Whig bishops. These men really cared about religion, whereas the others cared only about morality or scholarship; and after they had at length learned to stop blaming the decay of piety on 'the downfall of Monarchy and Episcopacy', they proceeded to constructive thinking.

In *Alciphron*, Berkeley traced the infidels back to Latitudinarianism. By this time even Bishop Gibson was convinced that the men of latitude were 'semi-infidels, who . . . were destroying the whole work of our redemption by Christ and making Christianity little more than a system of morality'.[1] The progress of deism led to a certain reaction against such weak-kneed Christianity. Defeated on the political field, the high Anglicans were eventually to prove victorious in the religious. Yet the eighteenth century was no time for Anglo-Catholicism. A stricter adherence to the rubrics was about the only message High Church had, and it was not a very vital one (we remember Wesley's obsession with ritual in his student days). John Wesley and William Law emerged from this tradition, but they were beyond the pale of Anglican orthodoxy; for the high as well as the low Anglicans remained victims of that terrific prejudice against 'enthusiasm' which caused Wesley and Whitefield to seem like the worst of monsters. Meanwhile the Church remained strongly rationalist, if not Hoadlean. In 1738 the famous Bishop Warburton, advising an aspiring young theological student what to read as his basic education, recommended Locke, Cudworth, Wollaston, Stillingfleet, Grotius, Pufendorf, and even Bayle.[2]

---

[1] Berkeley, *Works*, ii. 45; Sykes, *Gibson*, p. 264.
[2] Nichols, *Illustrations*, iv. 849–50. The letter is a most interesting one.

Between the (orthodox) Dissenters and Anglicanism there were no particular differences of doctrine.[1] There was a tendency, especially after 1725 (and in the New World as well as the old), for Dissenters to conform, possibly in accordance with Emerson's observation that no Dissenter rides in his coach for three generations. Certainly there were many signs of the decay of Dissent, mainly from an excess of prosperity and respectability; the alarm became great around 1730.[2] Nothing better indicates the temper of the age than the almost complete disappearance of the multitudinous sects of the seventeenth century, and the absence of any new ones. Presbyterian, Independent, and Baptist, along with Quaker, persisted but in all cases showed signs of diminishing vitality. Clearly the decline of persecution and the growth of their wealth softened the Dissenters' zeal. Still, the 'dissenting interest' survived, a vigorous and prosperous 10 per cent. of the nation; in terms of knowledge and ability, Nonconformity proved the equal of Anglicanism.[3]

Dissent, as well as Anglicanism, lacked unity. It had been split in 1695 by 'perfectly scandalous' quarrels between Calvinists and Arminians (the former called Antinomians and the latter Arians by their enemies). In the doubtful days under Anne, they drew together again from fear of persecution, but again were torn apart by the Arian question, 1719–21. The 'happy union' of 1690–1 between Independents and Presbyterians was one casualty of these disputes. The stormy meeting at Salter's Hall where that question of the Trinity was debated was the triumph of disunity and the defeat of any effort to impose a doctrinal unity on Dissent. The local Church determined the creed; and within Presbyterianism, for instance, one found Calvinists, Arminians, and Arians. Independency remained more orthodox, with perhaps more

---

[1] See, in addition to Henry W. Clark, *History of English Nonconformity*, the useful little book by Duncan Coomer, *English Dissent under the Early Hanoverians*.

[2] E.g. Strickland Gough, *Enquiry into the Causes of the Decay of the Dissenting Interest*, 1730; Philip Doddridge, *Free Thoughts on the Most Probable Means of Reviving the Dissenting Interest*, 1731. Dr. Calamy observed (1728) that many Dissenters of all sorts were concerned 'about the decay of the Dissenting interest, and the occasion of it' (*Own Life*, pp. 529–30).

[3] H. McLachlan, *Essays and Addresses* (Manchester, 1951), includes a defence of the learning and qualities of civilization of the eighteenth-century Dissenters, by a veteran historian of that subject.

religious zeal and a warmer spirit of faith, expressed in Watts's hymnody which flourished among these gathered covenanters. Doctrinally the trend in Dissent—as indeed elsewhere—was against any precise theological definiteness; towards a spirit broad-minded and tolerant but passive and negative.

Watts's hymns, and the suggestion of Dr. Doddridge that preaching might be changed in favour of more plainness and warmth, must not be confused with anything like the evangelical spirit. English Dissent was to show nothing to compare with the Great Awakening in America, and evangelicalism had to emerge from within the Church of England. 'The enthusiasm of the Methodists shocked the staid Independents of the 1740's.'[1] A leading authority on the subject, J. H. Colligan, attributes the decay of Dissent to a neglect of 'churchmanship'—the elevation of individual opinion and rationalism above all elements of form and tradition—which seems to be another way of saying that these eighteenth-century Dissenters were true children of the age of reason. Doddridge and Watts were fine neo-classical gentlemen and scholars, pious but restrained, abhorring enthusiasm. They were the leaders of a community not noted for its religious vigour in this period. Dissent had become respectable; and though it is surely not true that all Dissenters had grown very wealthy, their upper strata were among the leaders in the rise of a new wealthy class.

Certainly the movement relaxed before the warm fire of Whig tolerance and prosperity. After 1715 they had little to complain of. Some, in an effort to arouse the group from complacency, tried to stir up a new attack on the Establishment between 1732 and 1736, and made a drive to repeal the Test and Corporation Acts. It is most doubtful if this unsuccessful campaign resurrected much zeal among the Dissenters. 'I desire to be thankful for the liberty we have', one of their ministers wrote in refusing to become a militant fighter for new rights at this time.[2] The reaction was typical. Dissenters

[1] Davis, *Watts*, p. 49. Watts joined the bishops in denouncing Whitefield. He and Doddridge wanted a far more chaste revival than this. See Watts's *Guide to Prayer* with its rejection of all 'enthusiasm' in worship.

[2] *Letters to Dissenting Ministers and to Students for the Ministry from the Rev. Mr. Job Orton*, i. 156. Daniel Neal's partisan *History of the Puritans* was a reflection

of this period wished to stir up no trouble, and were complacent. Not until the days of Price, Priestley, and Cartwright would Nonconformity show vigour, in a new direction somewhat, and then hardly with the approval of the great majority. Aroused by the struggle of their co-religionists in America, these militant battlers for liberty and democracy revealed that the major genius of Nonconformity was still resistance to arbitrary rule—a political rather than a religious genius. In the earlier part of the century that spirit had little chance to exhibit itself.

2

An uneasy feeling that all was not well within Christianity spread in the 1730's and after. Orthodoxy of all sorts could agree on the negative points of opposition to Romanism, to rank infidelity, and to enthusiasm. It had been alleged to be unassailable on the grounds of reason and evidence, but this seemed less certain. Unlimited rational inquiry, as well as the drift to a Pelagian moralism (treated in the chapter following), began to alarm some Christians. Indifference among the nominal Christians as well as the shrewdly aimed barbs of the deists disturbed the pious.

What was Christianity, and what was wrong with it? A new and radical diagnosis, which might not wholly accurately be described as a 'retreat from reason', emerges in the 1730's under the leadership of remarkable men—Law, Butler, Berkeley, Wesley. Before dealing with that significant movement, we ought to make note of the defeats orthodoxy had suffered. Some of these have been mentioned in previous chapters.

The belief that the grounds of Christianity were rational had been shaken by the emergence of several quasi-heresies which had established themselves within the camp of Christianity on these grounds: Hoadleanism, Arianism, extreme Arminianism. The very nature of the Established Church, the very nature of Christ's identity, the terms of salvation—all these were issues at best unresolved, at worst

of this campaign against the Establishment, 1730–6; it stirred up a violent literary war between Anglican and Puritan—see, e.g., the numerous articles on it in *Weekly Miscellany* during Dec. 1733.

hopelessly confused by the parade of rational divinity—and many another lesser perplexity had been raised. This made for theological indefiniteness to the point where some were ready to throw up hands in despair, while the public had been wearied and perplexed. Theologically, Christianity was evidently what any ingenious writer said it was. This encouraged the tendency to define Christianity as simply living a good life.

More vital yet, the Biblical foundations of Protestant Christianity had been undermined. In 1736 an Anglican bishop wrote an essay on *The Difficulties and Discouragements Which Attend the Study of the Scriptures* which seemed to abandon, in despair, the classic Protestant foundation of Christianity. To be sure, Bishop Hare doubtless wrote in irony when he suggested that to study the Bible is the best way to become a heretic.[1] Hare, a liberal, had in mind the calumny to which his friends Clarke and Whiston had been subjected for their honest inquiries. His intention was certainly to satirize the already evident retreat from reason. But there were many who took Hare seriously, and in fact Hare himself clearly felt that the study of Scripture *was* the cause of difficulties. The book is really an argument against any such thing as a fixed standard of 'orthodoxy'. Hare was saying that uniformity of belief on the basis of the Bible is impossible, and subtly pleading for complete freedom of belief. Whichever way the book was taken, it was much discussed, and is most significant. Faith in a firm foundation, Biblical, for a single, basically uniform Christian creed was wavering. The Bible as interpreted by reason seemed no longer a very sure guide to Christian orthodoxy.

This was hardly the achievement of deism alone. Orthodoxy implicitly recognized this by its habit of disparaging the deists. 'Had a hundred such pens as these been employed on the side of religion', wrote Swift, 'they would have immediately sunk into oblivion and silence . . . .' If the deists were so slight, why had they succeeded? It becomes evident that deists had only carefully pointed up the pitfalls that lurked

---

[1] See the preface to Warburton's *Divine Legation of Moses* (1738), pp. iv–vi. Hare's work is printed in the anti-clerical compilation, *The Pillars of Priestcraft and Orthodoxy Shaken*, vol. iv.

in the way of rational Christianity. Doubtless it was true
that the deists were not great men.[1] But they had wit enough
to arrange in their most damning form facts and ideas already disclosed by orthodoxy itself.

Toland's *Christianity Not Mysterious* had capitalized on
Locke's *Reasonableness of Christianity*, subtly exaggerating
its thesis. The question of prophecy, opened up by William
Whiston, had proved a deist windfall. From William Sherlock to William Warburton, well-intentioned Christians had
done the real damage. Toland and Tindal entered into the
question of Church and State only after High and Low Anglicans were already at each other's throats.[2] Anthony Collins
intervened mischievously to good effect in the Dodwell–
Clarke controversy on immortality.[3] Collins was the master
of such tactics, and therefore the most effective of the
deists; his *Discourse of Freethinking* and *Grounds and Reasons*
are simply clever textbooks of orthodoxy's contradictions.
It is not easy to think of any deist, however, who did not
spend most of his time cataloguing the 'divisions of the
Christians'; Tindal and Morgan were other specialists in
this art.

Clearly the confusions of the Christians turned on the
effort to find clarity and certainty, and a clear standard of
orthodoxy, in the Bible aided by 'reason'. During the 1730's,
immediately after the great outburst of deistic controversy,
it is not surprising that we find a few leading Christians so
dissatisfied with this method that they are seeking for a new
way. Complacency gives way to troubled thought. In general
there was very little of this sort of searching for the root of

---

[1] Leslie Stephen, the great nineteenth-century student of English thought in
the eighteenth century, helped to perpetuate the view that the deists had no ability at
all, which is surely false. The sanest remarks on this are those of Conyers Middleton,
in his 'Letter to Dr. Waterland' (*Miscellaneous Works*, ii). Middleton observed that
while Collins and Tindal were neither great scholars nor great thinkers, they were
the equal of most of their orthodox opponents, and were shrewd students of religion
who knew perfectly well how to exploit every weakness in the Christian position.

[2] See Toland's *Memorial of the State of England* and Tindal's *The Rights of the
Christian Church*.

[3] Which may be followed in Clarke's *Works*; it occurred in 1706–7. The distinguished Non-Juror Henry Dodwell argued against Clarke's scornful opposition that
the soul achieves immortality only through the Church, through being baptized
by an episcopally ordained minister. Collins's *Essay upon the Nature and Destiny
of the Human Soul* pretended that Dodwell had denied the immortality of the soul.

the trouble, earlier in the century; no trouble was sensed. There was stubborn persistence in the view that Christianity could defend itself rationally, and defeat every criticism. Perhaps there might be doubt whether Leslie's method was quite so 'short and easy'. But in 1723 the conservative Anglican Francis Squire, while protesting against the deistic demand that 'everything must be made plain and easy', held fast to reason; he proposed to demonstrate that Thomas Gordon's deistic position was really far more irrational than the Church of England doctrine.[1]

High Churchmen used the Revolution as a scapegoat, and seemed to feel that all would be right with religion if only a Stuart sat on the throne. As an example of how a rather typical (in this respect) Augustan Anglican considered the question of reform in religion, take Swift's remarks: he could only suggest that the royal family and social leaders should strive to make infidelity unfashionable, and that more churches might be built. Ministers should be better trained, but they are warned against emotionalism; 'a plain, convincing reason' is all they require.[2]

But in the 1730's the need for 'a new way with the deists' emerged strongly. It appeared in William Law's *Case of Reason* (1731), George Berkeley's *Alciphron* (1732), Joseph Butler's *Analogy* (1736), and in John Wesley's first evangelical work (1738). The sense of crisis was strong. There was great concern over the apparent successes of deism; still more, perhaps, over the indifference of Christians.[3]

There was no way out of the dilemma on the assumptions of the age of reason. Berkeley, Law, and Butler each broke through these assumptions. None of them had such immediate influence, but all were of the utmost significance. In one way or another they show a disappointment with Swift's 'plain convincing reason'—because it is neither plain nor convincing. So deism at length created in Christians a discouragement with the grounds of the debate, with the treatment of Christianity as a problem in legal evidence;

[1] *Answer to the Independent Whig*, p. 29.

[2] 'Letter to a Young Clergyman', and 'Project for the Advancement of Religion', in *Works*, vol. ii.

[3] See *Weekly Miscellany*, 1733–4, for signs of alarm among the pious at the spread of deism and of indifference.

likewise with its dependence on proofs furnished by science and 'nature'.

Later generations were to express amazement tinged with disgust that any Christians could ever have viewed their religion in this light. What, make a spiritual question no more than a problem in historical scholarship? Yoke it submissively to the grim chariot of science? Before venturing on some discussion of the pioneers of a new way, it would be well to repeat the Augustan position. The men of the eighteenth century failed to understand how Christianity, whatever its meaning might be—and they were aware of its 'stupendous wonder'—could exist if it was not *true*. The definition of truth as simply conformity to experience they were not unaware of; Christianity, they believed, was admirably suited to human needs; but they did not seriously think that Christianity could endure unless it was true in some solider sense than this. To rest it on no more than individual experience was to revert to antinomianism and anarchy. Blind faith was ruled out as popery. There could be no coercion of the free mind. Admittedly encouraged by Newton, they firmly grasped what seemed the only alternative, and proudly proclaimed that no test of investigation or logic could prove Christianity other than the literal truth: attested so by all historical evidence and all scientific knowledge. The claim, it soon appeared, was rash, perhaps. It was not so clear what other rock of refuge remained.

Indeed, the men we have named who began to challenge this view were hardly comprehensible to their age, and were probably not at all times quite certain themselves what they meant. Their restlessness and their probing for a wholly new path was symptomatic of a feeling of crisis and a struggle. It did not really bear its fruit until much later. The vigorous Wesley did win disciples, but they were beyond the pale of respectability, and Evangelicalism came into its own only in the nineteenth century. Butler's *Analogy* came to be accepted as the greatest of all apologetic tracts only in the nineteenth century. The immaterialism of Berkeley grew to have meaning as a religious philosophy, as something more than a mere paradox for logicians, only, again, at the much later date.

3

William Law rejected reason the most boldly. He was, without much doubt, the finest religious writer of his age, perhaps the only one who bears comparison with the great seventeenth-century divines. Law did not doubt the Bible, but he had come to doubt the wisdom of testing the authenticity of Christianity by Bible analysis. It was his opinion that to treat religion in this way, as a problem in evidence, was to play the deists' game. He had himself been a redoubtable controversialist, but, as he wrote, 'the more books that were written in this way of defending the Gospel, the more I was furnished with new objections to it . . .'.[1] At length he came to the radical conclusion that to trust in reason is gross idolatry. Thus the great mystic turned and rent not only the deists but most Augustan Christians as well: those whom he named 'nominal Christians', 'historical Christians', and 'literal Christians'—all, that is, who did not know 'the true life of the new birth'. To be formally orthodox, in the merely outward sense, is utterly worthless. Law fled back to the 'witness of the spirit', and with his advice to 'turn inwards', to give up the academic defence of Christianity, and with his bold assertion that 'the Gospel is within you, and you are its evidence', he seemed 'enthusiastic' even to Wesley. 'If you are afraid of reason hurting your religion, it is a sign that your religion is not as it should be. . . . Complain therefore no more of want of evidence; neither books, nor study, nor learning is wanted. . . .'

It was impossible to accept such advice; it was equally impossible to ignore Law's tremendous prose, and his charge that true spiritual Christianity was not to be found anywhere in England. We are not Christians, Law said, unless our life 'is a common course of humility, self-denial, renunciation of the world, poverty of the spirit, and heavenly affection'. To live as a Christian meant 'dying to the world'—much to ask of the eighteenth century. To live as a Christian was, indeed, an accepted ideal; but Tillotson, the great Latitudinarian, had made it easy, while Law made it quite another

[1] *Mystical Writings of William Law*, ed. W. S. Palmer, p. 122. Other quotations herein are from this excellent selection of Law's writings.

thing. 'The whole duty of man' had been a prudent, sober life—easier, said Tillotson, than the way of vice and wickedness.[1] Law did not think it was easy.

The magic of Law's prose, as is well known, exercised a spell over even such unlikely mystics as Edward Gibbon and Samuel Johnson. Deploring the fact that Law's mind was 'clouded by enthusiasm', Gibbon remarked that 'a philosopher must allow that he exposes with equal severity and truth, the strange contradiction between the faith and practice of the Christian world'.[2] This new version of piety was, however, much too strenuous for most. And Law's rejection of reason was much too extreme. He became one of those writers, it seems, whom everyone praised, many read, but few followed.

John Wesley was much swayed by Law's writing in his restless search for a programme for the revival of Christianity; and we see the influence above all in the Wesleyan conviction that 'Though you bear the name, you are not Christians. You have neither Christian faith nor love.'[3] Nevertheless, Wesley could not accept the radical personal mysticism of Law either as sound Christian doctrine or as the basis for that great revival which Wesley, above all an activist, wished to bring about. A practical Christianity suited to the masses must have a creed, though a simple one; and Wesley of course never doubted the literal truth of that creed. Wesley's spiritual odyssey began in the High Church home where spiritual earnestness was joined to a severe rationality, the family evidently acceding eagerly to the request of Emilia Wesley 'that things may be clearly and plainly proved before you demand my assent to the truth of them'. There is no evidence that Wesley ever felt Christianity beaten on those grounds. There is every evidence that his mind constantly and naturally turned away from all those questions which did not have the power to move the human heart; he was by instinct (in the highest sense) a great propagandist. The urge to action led him at Oxford to the

[1] See chap. vi of Sykes, *Church and State in England in the Eighteenth Century*, for an excellent presentation of the dominant Tillotsonian concept of a Christian life.

[2] Gibbon, *Autobiography*, pp. 16–17.

[3] *Christian Examiner*, July 1847, p. 14.

'Holy Club' to promote Christian living, at first conceived as fasting, prayer, attendance at Communion, and charity. Later on it led him to seek the hearts of simple people with passionate preaching. He never thought, but always denied, that this was 'enthusiasm'. It was only clothing the demonstrable truth with the warmth of emotion, which alone could bring it to life in the souls of simple men. He never shunned the test by reason.

The same was in fact true of Berkeley and Butler. To the important observation that all of these men sounded a cry against their age and its view of religion, against worldliness and rationalism and mechanistic science, must be attached the equally significant warning that they remained in part children of their age, and used its very methods. The wilder forms of passion or irrationalism were not for them. They did not predict Romanticism in their style or form. 'I, for my share, declare the world to be no machine!' Carlyle will exclaim a century later, excoriating the whole eighteenth century. He is repeating Berkeley and Butler, but in very different accents. Berkeley was content to follow 'the dry light of reason' (G. Dawes Hicks). He had begun by protesting against what seemed to him Locke's outrages not against mysticism but against common sense. Both he and Butler seem most of the time to be arguing that deism and mechanism are *less* rational than faith; they would show us that mystery is logical. They appeal to the reason altogether —from reason drunk to reason sober, they would have said.

Law was doubtless the most enthusiastic; for that reason he received the least credence. Wesley rejected Law; and Bishop Butler rejected Wesley, on the grounds that his enthusiasm was 'a most horrid thing'. On the great evangelist's strong admixture of common sense we cannot do better than to quote this appropriate comment:

His head was as clear and utilitarian as Franklin's, without the least particle of mysticism or extravagance; whilst his heart flowed with a zeal like Loyola's, and glowed with a charity like Fénelon's.[1]

If Wesley was assailed with bitter invective for arousing the poor, it is clear that Berkeley and Butler, arguing with

[1] *Christian Examiner*, July 1847, p. 14.

great intellectual subtlety for a new way in religion, were, as Franklin observed of Berkeley in America, 'not very well understood'. Lord Hervey's was a typical comment on Berkeley: too metaphysical and abstruse, and assailing a straw man in attacking 'atheism'—which last showed that Hervey completely misunderstood Berkeley. On familiar rationalist grounds, atheism was indeed a straw man: no one doubted the existence of the Great Watchmaker. But Berkeley felt that all who thought of the universe and God in this way were really atheists: insist as they might on God, their conception of Him really excluded real religion.

Berkeley's *Alciphron* is an uneven work, and at times reads like conventional apologetic, while at others it is most ineffectual (as in the attack on Shaftesbury).[1] But breaking through, especially in section vi, is the perception that God cannot be 'proved' by rational means, that 'faith alone is required'. Berkeley keenly felt a major crisis, and so did Law, Wesley, and Butler. 'Our prospect is very terrible, and the symptoms grow stronger every day.' What all these men sensed, Law and Berkeley perhaps the most acutely, was that something was drastically wrong with the whole outlook of the age of reason—that 'his enemy was nothing less than the age itself'.[2] It had eliminated all the 'mysteries', in a deeper sense than that in which the word was ordinarily used even by those who pretended to believe in them (they meant merely rational enigmas). It tried to prove God mathematically, and it divorced morality from religion. Scepticism about the rational proofs, in a way that often anticipated Butler's work of a few years later, was combined in *Alciphron* with Berkeley's idealistic view that the human mind can directly apprehend the Divine.

Berkeley in *Alciphron* ridiculed the free-thinker, the 'minute philosopher', as a narrow and shallow creature. But clearly the philosopher was indicting not only deists. All who followed Locke and Newton, the way of sensationalism and science, were guilty. Berkeley was able to foresee the day when Laplace would calmly announce, for science, that

---

[1] Berkeley also misunderstood Mandeville, who replied most effectively in *A Letter to Dion* (1732). See Dialogues II and III of *Alciphron*.

[2] John Wild, *George Berkeley; a Study of His Life and Philosophy*, p. 497.

it had no need of the hypothesis God. He saw no answer save to strike at the root by denying matter's reality. In certain remarks Berkeley anticipated the line of argument that Joseph Butler was shortly to follow; while his relationship to Law and Wesley may be observed in the comment that faith is not mere logical acceptance, it is 'an operative persuasion of mind, which ever worketh some suitable action, disposition, or emotion on those who have it'.[1] He also recognized that faith cannot be blind; he noted that pure subjectivism leads to deism, for then all beliefs stand on the same level, measurable only by their intensity. His great remedy, which was to him neither irrational nor enthusiastic, was the purported demonstration that God *is* reality, and the material world an illusion.

He did not convince his contemporaries. Benjamin Hoadly pronounced for the orthodox rationalists that *Alciphron* was 'the most plain attempt to bring obscurity and darkness into all science, as well as to make nonsense essential to religion, that this last age has produced'. The book was, in the opinion of Swift and Gay, 'too speculative' to make much of a popular impact. If Berkeley had thundered like Carlyle, he might have made such an impact; but then he would not have been a man of his age. If he hoped on solid rational grounds to overthrow scientific materialism, he was about two centuries too early.

Berkeley had suggested that unclearness in any matter of religion may not be a valid objection against it. Perhaps this is only the Deity's way of stimulating us. Why should it be easy? While partially anticipating Butler, Berkeley, it is interesting to note, opposed the 'analogical' school of William King and Peter Browne, who influenced Butler. They were concerned to prove that we cannot know God at all except by analogy; Berkeley thought we can know Him directly. Both were in rebellion against the conventional rationalistic proofs of God, from nature. Butler, cautious, conservative and pragmatic, would lay no such axe to the root of the naturalist's universe as would Berkeley. He sought to save religion by the very method of science. Like Warburton,

[1] *Alciphron*, vii. 13.

but in a much more fundamental way, he would confute the deists by their own arguments. He would, for example, begin his discussion on immortality by using a Newtonian argument (inertia) to suggest the probability of the soul's survival. Unlike Berkeley, he accepted and argued from the world of physical experience, of scientific facts. He sought to apply the method of science to religion and show that this indicated, not the certainty of Christianity, but its probability—a probability as great as that of natural religion's alleged proofs, which were, when properly examined, by no means as clear as deists thought. Butler is not abandoning natural religion, but he is showing that it cannot be resorted to as a safer bulwark than revealed religion.

Those who know Butler best deny that the famous *tu quoque* argument was all he had. Certainly the deeper piety in him, communicated by his style, was a sense of the wonder and mystery in the world, a mood of true humility, a recognition of the limitations of man. He keeps with reason because, as he says, it is all we have, and it is something; but he knows it is not very much. So far as his formal argument runs, however, it is mostly the *tu quoque*. There are as many difficulties in natural as in revealed religion. Christianity is above our comprehension—and so is Nature.[1] Abstract reason is a poor guide to truth; let us consult experience, observe the world as it is, and then we perceive that it is not so clear. Nature is full of strange confusions and anomalies. Butler found so little evidence of plan or design in it, of purpose or even justice, that James Martineau was later to call his book a 'terrible persuasive to atheism'; James Mill, as his famous son recorded, thought it slew the Christians along with the deists; and William Pitt remarked that it 'raised in his mind more doubts than it answered'. Butler, of course, did not seek this reaction; if men took it that way, it was because they were too inured to rational proofs to do without them. Butler did not think Nature argued for God directly and obviously; he thought it showed how very mysterious to men are his ways. But this is, on reflection, quite reasonable; we know little, we may learn more, we

[1] Butler, *Works*, i. 202.

have no right to expect to know all at once. Obscurity in
the world is surely no argument for atheism.

Butler stressed this obscurity, however, for a purpose,
and one that could be interpreted as a strategy of despera-
tion: he wished to save an admittedly obscure Revelation by
pointing to an equally obscure Nature. He offered the suggestion that natural was in as parlous a state as revealed
religion; he permitted the inference that the reverse was
also true. He thought we are justified in taking both on
partial faith. Are we not equally justified in rejecting both?
Butler seems to have assumed that no one could possibly
be an atheist; he showed quite convincingly, with a practical
solidity that Berkeley lacked, how difficult it was to be a deist
(i.e. one who took natural religion to be certain while revealed
religion was otherwise); and he concluded with the modest,
non-dogmatic suggestion that we have every right to be
Christians on something less than certain proof. Butler
thought such proof might eventually be forthcoming, when
we know much more than we do now. But, as regards Biblical
literalism, was it not true that the advance of knowledge was
apparently in the other direction? Butler sidestepped the
embarrassing question of historical evidence; he directed his
fire against the enemy's vulnerable position in arguing from
natural design. And a formidable fire it was.

He also threw in other pregnant ideas, such as the
psychological justification for religion: man yearns for it,
and therefore it must be true.[1] Butler was a great moralist
as well; and on the ethical side he advanced, quite as much
as Hume, the study of human nature, seeking to discover by
empirical analysis the *science* of ethics. His stress on Conscience as the divinely implanted regulator of the varying
ingredients of human nature brings him, as has often been
noted, fairly close to the 'moral sense' deism of the Shaftesbury school.

The famous *Analogy*, which has freely been called not
only the greatest apologetic work of the century but 'the
greatest product of British ethical thought', disarmed
criticism by its very modesty and certainly dealt another

---

[1] *Ibid.* ii. 209–11; William J. Norton, *Bishop Butler, Moralist and Divine*,
pp. 215–17.

staggering blow to the rickety house of 'scientific' deism. But, as we have noticed, positive deism was always a contemptible foe. Did Butler restore the confidence of Christians against the potent destructive attacks of critical deism? Quite evidently not. His book received little immediate notice and excited little response. Was this not because it was an uncomfortable book to orthodox as well as deists? It was not easy to explain to those living in the high noon of the Enlightenment that most things are really dark. Few Christians were prepared to doubt that the advance of science proved the truth of religion. Frail and dubious indeed must the supports to religion offered by Berkeley and Butler have seemed to those reared on the confident assertions that science and history showed the demonstrable truth of Christianity.

It is doubtful whether these writings had much immediate influence. A few years later (1743) Henry Dodwell, jr., wrote in more popular style the book called *Christianity Not Founded on Argument*. Possibly those were right who accused Dodwell of intending to cast ridicule on Christianity.[1] However that may be, the answers showed emphatic rejection of the notion that Christianity could not or should not be defended on rational grounds. Deist and Orthodox had, after all, a great deal in common: they could agree that Berkeley was incomprehensible and Butler paradoxical, that Hume was not to be taken seriously, and that Law and Wesley were mad. In brief, that it was monstrous to overthrow that common ground of 'reason' where Christian and anti-Christian liked to meet and fight their duels, under a set of rules both sides accepted.

In the American colonies, Samuel Johnson of Connecticut and New York, a study in the religious currents of the age, learned to mistrust the 'deplorable progress of infidelity and apostasy in this age of mighty pretense and reasoning', which he traced to 'the well-meaning but too conceited Mr. Locke'. Earlier, Johnson had nearly been converted to 'Dr. Clark's and Bishop Hoadly's way of thinking'.[2] This tentative approach to liberal rationalism, and the drawing back

---

[1] John Leland, *Remarks on . . . Christianity Not Founded on Argument*, pp. 3–6.
[2] Herbert and Carol Schneider, eds., *Samuel Johnson*, i. 21; ii. 15.

from it during the 1730's during the deistic furore, was evidently fairly typical of intelligent Anglicans. With his friend Berkeley he enjoyed philosophizing but learned to draw a firm line on matters of faith. Distrusting the mob and the enthusiasm of the Great Awakening evangelists, he found refuge in this Berkeleian Anglicanism balanced between cool reason and blind faith. A moderate Arminian like Berkeley, he rejected both deistic Pelagianism and enthusiastic Calvinism. Here was a tenable if precarious position for an intellectual aristocrat; but Johnson had to watch the great majority proceeding towards either infidelity or emotionalism. Berkeley and Butler might save Christianity for conservative intellectuals; it was unlikely that they could lead a popular revival. They thought that Wesley was a monstrous enthusiast. Nor did Berkeley and Butler point in exactly the same direction. Thus we see these tentative thrustings against the Age of Reason working at cross-purposes. They were portents of the future rather than forces in the present. Down to Paley at the end of the century, orthodoxy remained committed to a Christianity supported, however doubtfully, by the twin pillars of Newtonian science and Biblical literalism.

VIII

ARMINIANISM

The design of Christianity is to make men good and keep them so.
                                                                DENHAM

There are Christians who rob Christianity of its mysteries. . . . They
open the way to deism, that is to say, a disguised atheism.   BOSSUET

I

THE early Anglicans had been 'Calvinistic';[1] but in the
eighteenth century that fact seemed a little incredible
to members of this Church. One of them was most
surprised to learn from his researches that the Articles were
Calvinistic, that 'till about the time of Archbishop Laud the
Clergy were universally so', and that in those days the anti-
Calvinists were the despised Anabaptists.[2] Nothing, however, was less suitable to optimistic rationalism than the
Augustinian–Calvinistic scheme, with its gloomy annihila-
tion of natural man. Arminianism in its milder form per-
meated this era, and in one sense is not heresy but orthodoxy.
But towards mid-century an extremer form of this doctrine
(merging with Socinianism) became what John Wesley
called no better than 'deism in new dress'.

Wesley considered himself an Arminian; so the more
extreme version of this doctrine, which he declared to be
just as dangerous as the opposite extreme of Calvinism,
might better be called by the name of the ancient heresy of
Pelagianism. Freedom of the will, denial of original sin, and
the possibility of salvation by moral excellence alone—these
things the British-born theologian of the fourth to fifth
centuries had taught, the classic example of a Christianity
stressing God too little and Man too much. Arminius, the
early-seventeenth-century Dutch Remonstrant, may better
be compared to those Semi-Pelagians of the earlier time who

---

[1] Calvin did not invent the idea of predestination and damnation, but only
strongly reasserted traditional Christian dogma. See G. G. Coulton, *The Medieval
Scene* (Cambridge, 1930), pp. 18–20.

[2] Nichols, *Illustrations*, iv. 326.

sought a compromise on the vexed questions of free will
versus predestination, moral freedom *versus* absolute human
depravity. His was a mediating doctrine.[1] Augustine and
Calvin went too far in the other direction, annihilating Man
completely in their earnestness to glorify God.

But admittedly the precarious middle ground Arminius
sought to occupy—of which Wesley had a keen apprecia-
tion—'gliding by almost imperceptible degrees, reached a
position with little to distinguish it from Socinianism [or
Pelagianism]'.[2] This position was approached after 1720
by such learned and respectable theologians as John Taylor,
Nathaniel Lardner, and George Benson.[3] It began to
threaten, from within, the reduction of Christianity to no
more than a moral code: 'far more dangerous than open
deism itself', Wesley wrote.

The preceding half-century had seen the serious weakening
of Calvinism. It had all but disappeared within the Church
of England.[4] The jesting answer to what the Arminians
held had long been that they held the best bishoprics and
deaneries in England; and the notable Calvinist John
Edwards was forced in 1670 to resign from St. John's
College at Cambridge because of his views. This same John
Edwards long continued active, but by 1700 was about the
only remaining example of a prominent Anglican Calvinist.
High and Low Churchmen alike were Arminian. In 1707
Charles Leslie, the Tory, wrote that predestination 'is more
fatal to the souls of men, than idolatry itself, or the worst
form of popery', and devoted five issues of the *Rehearsal*

---

[1] See article 'Arminianism' in *Encyclopaedia of Religion and Ethics,* ed. James
Hastings, i.

[2] Ibid. See also Tayler, *Retrospect of Religious Life,* p. 202: 'The Arminian and
Socinian systems were not identical, but grew out of a common tendency of mind.'
A Socinian could not avoid being an Arminian also, in that denial of Christ's
divinity entailed denial of the orthodox ideas of the Atonement, of original sin
and justification by faith; and if conduct is the basis of God's judgement on man,
then men must (as it was commonly thought) be free moral agents.

[3] It was Taylor's book on original sin that inspired the replies of Jonathan
Edwards and John Wesley. Wesley (*Works,* ix. 192–3) concedes Taylor's learning
and ability. George Benson was a distinguished scholar, respected by all save for his
Socinianism.

[4] G. R. Cragg, *From Puritanism to the Age of Reason; A Study of Changes in
Religious Thought within the Church of England, 1660–1700,* contains an excellent
chapter on 'The Eclipse of Calvinism' during the period 1670–1700.

to excoriating John Edwards of Cambridge. High Church Tories were influenced by their traditional hatred of Calvinistic Puritanism. On the other side, the Latitudinarian 'men of moderation' were Arminians out of a calm and rational spirit, hostile to the 'enthusiasm' of Calvinism. Tillotson's sermons were as far as possible from a hell-fire religion, and it was the country parsons who were sometimes less mild. In the early eighteenth century Daniel Whitby was the leading spokesman on the question for the moderates. He gave the clue to his thought when he declared that eternal damnation and hereditary sin are contradictory to 'common reason'.[1] Whitby noted that most Anglicans were Arminians; and no better proof of this can be found than in Anthony Collins's *Discourse of Freethinking*, where, seeking as usual to show that there is controversy within the Church, the deist is able to name, on the Calvinist side, no one worth naming except the above-mentioned John Edwards.[2] In the Anglican ranks, then, Arminian sentiment was all but universal; on this doctrine Charles Leslie and Samuel Clarke, right wing and left, could agree.

Dissent was Calvinistic by tradition; in 1629 a Puritan Commons had defied the King by passing resolutions against 'Popery and Arminianism'. The tradition had not died, but had certainly been much modified. The typical Dissenter, no longer a defier of kings, struggled now to explain away his Calvinism, leaning heavily on the great Richard Baxter's compromise formula. The General (Arminian) Baptists vigorously asserted that Calvinism was monstrous, its corollaries an evil God and a hypocritical Christ.[3] Other Dissenting groups obviously wavered in their loyalty to Calvinism.[4] True, George Benson, who began (1723) as a Calvinist, was forced to leave his Abingdon congregation in

---

[1] Daniel Whitby, *Six Discourses* (Worcester, Mass., 1801), preface.

[2] Collins mentions Jane, Brideaux [*sic*], Carlton [*sic*], Davenant, South, and Edwards as Calvinists. None of these except John Edwards can be identified as a then living Calvinist of any note. The deist clearly went far afield here to make his case for dissension within the Church.

[3] John Smith, *An Essay on Universal Redemption*.

[4] Coomer, op. cit., pp. 78–79, gives some figures on Arminianism as well as Arianism within Dissenting congregations. For example, of 44 Presbyterian churches in the London area in 1730, 19 were evidently Calvinist, 12 Baxterian, 13 Arminian.

1729 because of his Arminianism. Thomas Bradbury, an enthusiastic Calvinist Whig who preached the 'divine right of the Revolution', was a breath of the militant Puritan past not entirely unique, especially among the Independents. In the polemical literature of theology a stubborn Calvinist representation persists right down through the century, proudly and disdainfully repeating the iron logic of election and reprobation and showing that any compromise must lead to deism or atheism.[1] Nevertheless, most of the erstwhile Puritans were uneasy about their Calvinism, and anxious at the least to modify its harsher aspects.

The popular formula of the Baxterians accepted Election but shied away from Reprobation; some, they would have it, are assured of absolute salvation, but the rest are not necessarily damned, and may be saved. The distinction was an uneasy one. The rigorous Calvinistic doctrine that some are saved and some are damned had become the rather flabby suggestion that some are just more saved than others. From an Arminian point of view John Wesley assailed this compromise as meaningless, while a full-blooded Calvinist would also scorn it.[2] It owed its popularity to the mood of those numerous Dissenters who wished neither to cast aside their Calvinist traditions nor to accept them in all their original severity.

The question was not one on which Scripture shed much conclusive light.[3] But the temper of the age inclined the scales against Calvin's extreme doctrine, which seemed like enthusiasm and still smacked of rebellion; it was castigated as 'Antinomianism'. This name was applied to the rigorous Calvinists in a bitter dispute which broke out among the Dissenters in 1695–1698 (the Crisp–Williams controversy), the Calvinists replying by calling their milder brethren

---

[1] See, for example, Joseph Hussey, *The Glory of Christ Unveiled*, 1706; John Gill, *The Doctrine of Predestination Stated* . . ., 1752; Rowland Hill, *A Full Answer to the Rev. J. Wesley's Remarks* . . ., 1777.

[2] See Isaac Watts, 'The Ruin and Recovery of Mankind' (*Works*, vol. ii; cf. the critique of Wesley, 'Predestination Calmly Considered', *Works*, vol. x). Or from a strictly Calvinist point of view, John Gill, op. cit.

[3] Whitby's claim (see op. cit.) that Calvinism was contrary to Scripture was countered by John Edwards's *The Arminian Doctrine Condemned by the Holy Scripture* (1711)—the results were inconclusive. Cf. Watts, *Works*, vi. 152.

Arians. But even within Dissent the extreme Calvinists were scarcely popular.

The two great objections which a rationalistic age lodged against Calvinism, in addition to its threat of 'enthusiasm', was that it made God the author of evil, and that in denying free will it wrecked moral responsibility.

Moral responsibility was felt to require free will. 'Without the liberty of human action there can be no religion', Clarke declared. 'What ends and purposes of religion mere clocks and watches are capable of serving, needs no long and nice consideration.' Berkeley classed 'fatalists' along with atheists, enthusiasts, and sceptics as enemies of religion.[1] The deterministic position was scarcely respectable because it was associated with such infidels as Spinoza and Hobbes; Anthony Collins the deist contributed an astute attack on free will in 1715. Not until Jonathan Edwards took up his pen on the American frontier was it made perfectly clear that moral responsibility does not require 'freedom of the will'—indeed, that freedom of the will actually itself destroys moral responsibility. And it should be noted that even Edwards's invincible logic was furiously resisted. Wesley was shocked by it. Yet it did much to fortify the Calvinist position, in time. The remarks of Jonathan Edwards, jr., on the confusion of the Calvinists prior to his father's great work on freedom of the will seem to be accurate enough.[2] Nor was this confusion overcome until the later years of the century, when the impact of Edwardian theology was fully felt.

Moral responsibility was a powerful objection, then, to the 'fatalistic' system of Calvin, in an age very conscious of the free human intellect; but on analysis some of these objections vanished. Even more important was the making God the author of evil. Here was the ancient Christian problem of evil—an unsolvable problem, as Bayle the sceptic and the scoffing deists liked to point out.[3] Dr. Doddridge,

[1] Clarke, *Works*, iii. 851; Berkeley, *Works*, ii. 23. In Dialogue VII, sects. 16–20 of *Alciphron*, the ordinarily subtle Berkeley seems to be much confused by the free-will problem, and ends by refuting the determinists in roughly the same manner in which Dr. Johnson was to refute his Idealism.

[2] Jonathan Edwards, jr., *Works*, ed. Tryon Edwards (Boston, 1854), i. 481 ff.

[3] Anthony Collins, *A Vindication of the Divine Attributes* (1710), pp. 4–6. This

himself torn between the two systems of Arminian and Calvinist, received a letter from a doubter who applied to him for aid, being afflicted with Arminianism; he could not, he wrote, believe in a malevolent Deity such as would

by design, create a race of creatures who he knew would offend him; for which offences he designed everlastingly to punish them; excepting some few, whom, for no other reason than his own good will and pleasure, he resolved to save. . . .

'I readily acknowledge', the good minister replied, 'that you have fallen on a considerable difficulty in the Christian scheme.'[1] For the Calvinist might, of course, retort that if you doubt this you must impugn the divine omnipotence, thus denying the providence of God and his government of the world. This considerable difficulty John Locke himself had not been able to solve; in his letter to Molyneux he had confessed himself unable to reconcile divine omnipotence with human freedom, though he declared himself morally convinced that both existed. It was natural that this classic Christian dilemma should arise anew in a rationalistic period; it might indeed be said to have been the leading philosophic problem of the century.[2]

If the Calvinist is almost forced to deny God's benevolence, the Arminian must evidently deny his omnipotence, although each side could offer various hopeful evasions of its dilemma. Most Christians preferred to think there was no real dilemma, and took the best of both worlds. Susanna Wesley's letter to her son John in 1725 expressed an abhorrence of predestination, because it makes God the author of sin, yet she insisted that divine foreknowledge exists and is not inconsistent with human freedom: God's knowing that something will occur does not mean that he

work was written against aspects of William King's *De Origine Mali*, perhaps the most notable effort to solve the Christian problem of evil in this period. In it Collins takes his usual sly pleasure in complicating the problems of the orthodox. See also Charles Blount, *Oracles of Reason*, p. 194.

[1] Doddridge, *Correspondence and Diary*, ii. 429–30.

[2] Ernst Cassirer notes the immense amount of attention paid to the problem of evil in the eighteenth century, from Leibniz on, as if 'the fate of metaphysics and religion must hinge on this fundamental problem' (*Philosophy of the Enlightenment*, pp. 148 ff.). Aldridge, *Shaftesbury and the Deist Manifesto*, pp. 322 ff., discusses the optimistic theodicy of Shaftesbury.

causes it to occur. So also Wollaston: 'It involves no contradiction to assert that God certainly knows what any man
will choose.'[1] Nevertheless, uneasiness remained.

The reaction against Calvinism involved the danger of
pushing the opposite position too far. Do that, and you ended
in the making of Christianity into no more than a genteel
code of ethics: 'to make men good and keep them so'. Along
with predestination and the grim doctrine of salvation for the
elect only, 'original sin' would *logically* depart, and then all
sinfulness, leaving men not really in need of salvation at all.
The middle ground, as Wesley and Watts knew, was hard
to keep. So Richard Baxter, author of the compromise, had
complained apropos of this question that 'If you discover an
error to an injudicious man he reeleth into the contrary error,
and it is hard to stop him in the middle verity'.

'Original sin' was doubtless the real nub of the whole
controversy involving free will and *unde malum*. John Taylor
struck to the heart of matter and opened up the greatest
controversy when he wrote his important work on original
sin in 1738. It is very evident that those who insisted, against
Taylor, on the inherent sinfulness of man were very much
on the defensive. Some years later John Wesley, aware of
the danger in giving up 'original sin', noted how few replies
Taylor had received. Such as were made were weak. Watts's
Ruin and Recovery of Mankind is a study in hesitant Calvinism. Aware that the consequence of abandoning the
sinfulness of man must be deism, Watts tries his best, but,
we feel, without real conviction, to prove that mankind is
degenerate and the earth a poor place on which to live. He
balks at the idea of inherited sinfulness yet he thinks it is
necessary to believe this. Lockean psychology as it was
being developed by David Hartley made inherited sin most
implausible.

Yet if man was not naturally a sinful creature, Christianity
seemed to disappear in a vapour of moral platitudes. Wesley
pointed out to these ultra-Arminians that they destroyed
religion: if we are not sinful, why do we need a saviour? what

---

[1] *The Religion of Nature Delineated*, p. 186. Wollaston dealt elaborately, if
superficially, with the problems of free will and evil in this popular work. See also
Clarke, *The Being and Attributes of God* (*Works*, ii. 566 ff.).

is necessary except a code of moral conduct such as any
deist could produce? On the other hand, the great evangelist
rejected with horror the Calvinistic system. To believe that
God had created man sinful seemed to him so monstrous
that, he thought, one must be either a Manichee or an atheist
to believe it.[1] He protested that Jonathan Edwards had
made God the author of sin. 'O poor encouragement to de-
spairing sinners!' was his comment on predestination; the
doctrine of election seemed to him a fatalism that negated all
striving and made preaching a superfluous function.

For the best purposes of religion, the great evangelist
knew, man had to be sinful, yet made so by his own free
will, and redeemable, if he really wished it, by the same.
Yet what was so desirable psychologically was evidently
illogical; at least, it meant embracing free will and thus
giving up divine omnipotence. It is a well-known fact that
Wesley's Arminianism, an honest effort to save religion from
the twin dangers of Calvinism and Pelagianism, the one destroying hope and the other leaving nothing to be striven for,
divided the evangelical movement and began a controversy
between its two greatest architects. George Whitefield was
compelled to take his colleague to task (sweetly enough) for
misreading the doctrine of election and embracing the
heresy of universal redemption.[2] Strategically, Whitefield
felt that Arminianism made men complacent, whereas
election tended to 'rouse the soul out of its carnal security'.
Was not any Arminianism certain to lead away from the
all-important sense of sin? Or was Wesley right in holding
that Calvinism killed all hope and thus led to indifference?
Did Arminianism not surrender the vital concept of an
almighty God? But what of Calvinism's frightful inference
that the Deity was a mocking malignity? This disturbing
controversy remained unsettled and gave rise to such bitter
polemics as only rival theologies can produce.

2

The truth is that this age inclined to the Arminian side
because it did not have that profound sense of man's worth-

---

[1] Wesley, *Works*, x. 311.
[2] George Whitefield, *A Letter to the Rev. Mr. John Wesley* ... (1752).

lessness on earth which leads to the Augustinian–Calvinist position. John Locke, in *The Reasonableness of Christianity*, set the tone in declaring that happiness is possible in this life. The Platonists agreed: obey the inner law of your own nature, planted there by God, and happiness will be the result. There was no 'sense of sin' in these theologies. Even Bishop Butler's system seemed to find no place for original sin nor any very pressing need for atonement. Therefore did Jonathan Edwards of Massachusetts, from his radically Calvinistic vantage-point, accuse the entire century of Arminianism.[1]

For this it has been blamed by some moderns concerned to beat a retreat back along the road taken in the eighteenth century. But it could not very well have been otherwise. We may argue that if Christianity is not large enough to accommodate men in their optimistic as well as their pessimistic moods, it may expect to confront crises. For men will periodically weary of the gloomy view and strike out confidently to build their happiness here on earth. It is not very relevant to protest that this is an illusory pursuit. Happiness in heaven or on earth may both be illusions, but they will be sought, the one yielding in turn to the other as conditions of life change. In this eighteenth century there was no possible way of rejecting, as Jonathan Edwards almost alone rejected, the plea of Dr. Turnbull, cited by Edwards himself, to 'Let not the vices of mankind be multiplied or magnified. Let us make a fair estimate of human life....' The eighteenth century was a swing in the pendulum towards optimism and the pursuit of happiness.

In New England the Old Puritanism made the pulpits ring with protests against the soft and easy spirit of the age. In 1743 William Balch was brought severely to task for allegedly teaching 'that man is naturally virtuous, that morality is the height of Christianity'. In Old England the Puritan spirit had been considerably damaged, and we hear fewer protests of this sort. Eventually, however, 'Arminian-

---

[1] *Works*, i. 467: 'Arminianism has gradually more and more prevailed, till they are become almost universally Arminians. And not only so but Arminianism has greatly prevailed among the Dissenters, and has spread greatly in New England, as well as Old.'

ism', associated with Socinianism and Arianism, began to go so far that orthodox Christians drew back in alarm from the Denhams, Lardners, Taylors, and Fosters. The terms of the question were drastically changed by David Hartley and Joseph Priestley, after mid-century. Priestley, following the naturalistic, 'associationalist' psychology of Hartley, did not believe in free will at all. By 1770 Hartley's ideas, wrote John Wesley, were 'now adopted by almost all who doubt of the Christian scheme'.[1] Here was an optimistic determinism, proclaiming that man is the creature of his social environment—but that this social environment may be changed, to the end that the world and human nature may be freed from evil. Regardless of what logical inconsistencies there were in the exuberant notions of Priestley, his message, obviously, was significant. The pioneers of a naturalistic psychology—Hartley, Hume, Thomas Reid—were carefully studying human nature, and agreeing that man is intrinsically neither bad nor good, but a bundle of impulses both good and bad—potentialities to be developed. Responsibility, as Priestley himself said, was being transferred from God to the social reformer. Human nature was being viewed as perfectly plastic; and the vision of 'perfectibility' was opening up.

It is superfluous to ask what place the old concept of a soul depraved from birth, as a consequence of Adam's sin, could have under the new and exciting dispensation of social progress.

When William Wilberforce at the end of the century came to write his report on what was wrong with Christianity, at the beginning of his indictment he noted the refusal of most educated Christians to believe in the corruption and weakness of human nature. 'The bulk of Christians are used to speak of man as of a being naturally pure, and inclined to all virtue. . . .' They would have been shocked to have been called deists, yet, since they felt no sin, they did not think of Christ as Saviour, but simply as an excellent moral

[1] *Works*, x. 469. Hartley's *Observations on Man* was written in 1749; Priestley's *Philosophical Necessity* in 1777. Both are discussed in Basil Willey's *The Eighteenth Century Background*, chaps. viii and x.

teacher.[1] Complaining that the nominal Christians had lost all knowledge of real Christianity, Wilberforce with sure instinct picked out the decay of the sense of sin as the basic cause. Controversy had done its share to make men weary of theology; religion was being pushed off to one side of life by an increasing absorption in purely secular politics and business; but what really signalled the decline was a general and growing inability to believe in Christianity's central idea—man as a weak and wretched creature in a doleful world, in dire need of being rescued and assured of a better world to come.

Viewed in this light, such men as the learned and pious Benson and Taylor, and even Joseph Priestley, and in America Jonathan Mayhew, with their explaining away of sin and their free offer of salvation to all who will but strive, may well have been seeking to save something for Christianity against the optimistic, secular spirit of the age.[2] Nevertheless, Wesley and Wilberforce had a right to wonder what was left of Christianity when you went so far in appeasing the times. Priestley's God was a placable one, most anxious for man's happiness, a 'wise and kind parent' fitting us for happiness by mild corrections.[3] Such an anaemic religion, as Erasmus Darwin said, seemed like 'a featherbed for a dying Christian'.

Was this mild, Arminian Christianity no better than deism, or was it a defensible effort to adapt Christianity to modern circumstances? The reduction of religion to morality, and the optimistic view of human nature, were related to deism. On the other hand, Calvinism also could lead to extreme religious scepticism, singular as this may seem. A Calvinistic background was notable in the cases of both Bayle and Mandeville. Mandeville was prepared to reject Christianity as a working social force because it seemed to him that the great majority of men were without grace, unregenerate. Natural man being totally depraved, and most

---

[1] William Wilberforce, *A Practical View of the Prevailing Religious System* . . . (3rd edition, London, 1854, first published 1797), pp. 19–20 ff., 50 ff.

[2] Samples of the theology of Benson, Taylor, Lardner, and Belsham, with comments by Bishop Watson the editor, may be found in *Collection of Theological Tracts* (1785), *passim*. Cf. Priestley, *Memoirs*, i. 15–57.

[3] Ibid. i. iii.

men being in the natural state, Calvinism leads logically
to either a dictatorship of the regenerate (tried in Geneva
and in Massachusetts but wholly impractical) or else a
drastic divorce between religion and society, the 'principle
of segregation' between the 'order of nature' and the 'order
of grace'.[1] 'The church is God's enclosed garden', as Roger
Williams had written, 'but the world is the devil's wilderness
where good wheat and tares flourish and decay together.'[2]
Thus in positing too great a gap between man and God,
between nature and grace, Calvin's uncompromising
demands could break down religion as an active social
principle, leading to the conclusion that the society of men
is the 'devil's wilderness'. This might lapse into Mandeville's
deistic cynicism.

Jonathan Edwards the Calvinist found himself close to
Mandeville in denying virtue to natural man in his ordinary
social acts, which are entirely selfish. John Taylor the
Arminian pounced upon this weakness in Calvinism which
constantly insisted upon the utter corruption of men in the
natural state. This doctrine cuts off hope and encourages
corruption by insisting upon it. What wonder if Christians
are wicked (asks Taylor) when (Calvinist) Christians tell
them that they are inevitably so?[3] To which Edwards would
rejoin that unless we view the heart of man as corrupt and
all goodness as the gift of God, we must take the heart of
man as good and leave no place for God. No doubt rigorous
logic was on the Calvinist's side. But was it not true that
these rigorists did fatal damage to religion? A recent writer
has pertinently observed of the modern neo-Protestants'
overstress on Deity's transcendence, with the accompanying
belittlement of man's natural capacities, that one can carry
this sort of thing too far; the twentieth-century reaction
against liberalism is again in danger of upsetting the balance

[1] Calvin had declared that there are degrees of inferior grace, enough for social
purposes, but of no value to sanctification. A. S. P. Woodhouse's introduction to
Puritanism and Liberty (London, 1938), espec. pp. 58–60 and 85–86, has a superb
discussion of this.

[2] Quoted by Arthur Barker, *Milton and the Puritan Dilemma, 1641–1660*
(Toronto, 1942), pp. 91–93, another thoughtful analysis of this problem in
Calvinism.

[3] John Taylor, *The Scripture-Doctrine of Original Sin*, pp. 230–1, 257–9, 350.
Cf. Edwards's reply, *The Doctrine of Original Sin Defended*.

against man.[1] One can belittle man too much. Arminianism of Wesley's sort was in truth properly balanced on the razor's edge of this perennial Christian equation between God and Man.

It is equally certain, however, that the later eighteenth century toppled over on the opposite side, the optimistic man-centred side. Undoubtedly a mild and worldly religion reflected the economic facts of a prosperous and complacent age, dominated by the *bourgeoisie*. The reduction of religion to nothing more than prudent conduct was naturally accompanied by its elimination as an independent force in various spheres of activity. 'Political arithmetic' has begun by 1750 to grow into the science of economics. By about the same date politics has very nearly completed its separation from religion. It is time to turn to some consideration of religion's, and religious liberalism's, relationship to these other spheres of life.

[1] H. D. Lewis, *Morals and Revelation* (London, 1951), essay on 'Morality and Religion'.

IX

THE SECULARIZATION OF POLITICS

*Religion, ceasing to be the master interest of mankind, dwindles into
a department of life which it is extravagant to overstep.*

TAWNEY, *Religion and the Rise of Capitalism*

I

TAWNEY'S key statement provides the starting-point
for any consideration of religion and society in the
earlier eighteenth century. 'What was in question',
another student of intellectual history observes of this
period, 'was a colossal secularization of thought in every
possible realm of ideas at the same time, after the extra-
ordinarily strong religious character of much of the thinking of the seventeenth century.'[1] The trend was especially
notable in politics. It was also true that economic life cast
off what remained of a medieval heritage: Christian charity
and the doctrine of stewardship received a new interpretation
which had little to do with the giving of alms or the limita-
tion of profits (Tawney's 'new medicine for poverty').

Pious and orthodox Christians participated in this broad
movement. 'Liberalism' in this sense, viz. Whiggism in
politics and a trend towards *laissez-faire* in economics, is the
dominant philosophy in eighteenth-century England, and
by and large a conservative one. For however radical English
ideas seemed to European absolutists in this era, they were
associated at home with a conservative oligarchy. Liberty
and constitutional government were congenial to this ruling
group; democracy and social equality were abhorrent. The
'masses' were barely beginning to push themselves on to the
stage of history, and were in fact regarded by the new bourgeois potentates as peculiarly vicious. The humanitarian
movement, along with the beginnings of a demand for
political democracy, had to await the last quarter of the

[1] Herbert Butterfield, *The Origins of Modern Science, 1300–1800* (London, 1950),
p. 166.

century for real growth. Until then, the England that inspired Voltaire and Montesquieu with its liberalism remained, on a modern view, sunk in complacency, amid social evils which cried for attention but received little.

There remains the question, whether the religious freethinkers exerted any radical influence on political or social questions. We might expect that the Tolands, Tindals, and Chubbs, the deists and Socinians, would show an equal zeal for humanistic reform in these matters as in religion. But it is not so easy to equate the radical or liberal tradition in religion with such a tradition in politics or social questions. Let us, however, examine that question in its place. We need first to consider the whole picture, first the political, then the socio-economic.

2

'The ecclesiastical and civil state', wrote Clarendon, in his famous *History of the Rebellion*, 'was so wrought and interwoven together, and in truth so incorporated in each other, that like Hippocrates' twins they cannot but laugh and cry together.' In the 1680's John Phillips had observed that 'You cannot come to hear or read a sermon . . . but let the text be what it will, half the sermon is matter of state.' In 1700, G. M. Trevelyan remarks, at the basis of politics lay 'the undying feud of Anglican and Puritan, of Church and Dissent'.[1] As late as 1753 it was still most convenient to define political parties in religious terms, the Whigs being moderate Churchmen and Dissenters.[2] Nevertheless, between Clarendon and the Duke of Newcastle much has changed. Our period is one of transition. As Trevelyan observes, 'the world of Marlborough and St. John, of Defoe, Swift and Sacheverell' is hardly religious in the same sense 'as the world of Laud and Baxter, of Cromwell and George Fox'; yet to a degree, still, 'the rivalry of Church, Dissent, and that vague *tertium quid*—Free Thought—is the very pulse of the

---

[1] G. M. Trevelyan, *England under Queen Anne*, vol. iii, *The Peace and the Protestant Succession*, p. 263.

[2] *The Balance, or the Merits of Whig and Tory*, 1753; quoted in G. H. Guttridge, *English Whiggism and the American Revolution* (Berkeley and Los Angeles, 1942), p. 4.

machine of politics'. By 1720 the question of the succession
was placed beyond serious dispute; Jacobitism had died save
as a romantic pose, though as that it was to have a remarkable vitality; and the old High Church dogma of divine
right had become an anachronism. Yet the strong habitual
association between religion and politics only very gradually
waned.

'It seems very natural', Defoe had written, 'that as a sense
of religion dies, the love of virtue must also decay.' 'The ruin
of a state', thought Swift, 'is generally preceded by . . .
contempt of religion.' Whiston took it for granted that
atheism leads to men becoming 'cannibals and lawless
monsters.' Thus religion was necessarily related to politics
as long as it was felt that the very bonds that attach men to
each other are religious. The end of Christianity would
surely mean the end of society; if there is no respect for God,
how can there be any respect for the judge, or the father?
This feeling was ubiquitous, and indeed long remained so.
Gladstone held it as strongly in the nineteenth century as
Berkeley did in the eighteenth.[1] But religious liberalism made
a dent in it by suggesting that morality may be detached
from formal religious belief. Shaftesbury and Mandeville,
those 'two authors of infidel systems', Berkeley feared, setting out from opposite principles, are calculated to draw all
mankind, by flattering either their vanity, or their passions,
into one or another system'.[2] There was some substance in
Berkeley's fears. Religion itself, as we have seen, tended to
turn into little more than moral instruction.

Nevertheless, respectable men continued to defend the
necessity for an established religion. 'A constitution of civil
government without any religious establishment is a chimeri-
cal project, of which there is no example', wrote Bishop
Butler.[3] Religion is necessary to civilized society; a State
religion is necessary to a given State. This traditional reasoning was seldom challenged—not even, as we shall see, by
deists.

[1] George Berkeley, *A Discourse Addressed to the Magistrates and Men in Authority*,
forcefully presents the theme that if religion and the Church lose respect, the civil
magistrate cannot long retain any.

[2] Ibid., pp. 31–32.

[3] Joseph Butler, *Works*, ii. 308.

Political parties in the modern sense were very far from existing, either in practice or in theory. All deplored the presence of 'factions' and pleaded for unity—on their own terms, of course. Although such factions existed, everyone knows that the distinction between 'Whig' and 'Tory' was very confused between 1690 and 1714, and after that possibly even more confusing.[1] Clearly the really bitter feud among Englishmen involved High Church Jacobites, on the one hand, and on the other the Hanoverians, embracing the Dissenters and moderate Anglicans. The former found their greatest strength among the country squires and the inferior clergy, but Toryism also appealed to the *literati*, after 1720 especially, for they found the Whigs pedestrian and Walpole tight-fisted. The notable political development of the period is the emergence of a non-Jacobite Toryism—that is, an effort by the anti-Whigs to establish themselves on a new basis, discarding the impossible principles of divine right.[2] But this Hanoverian Toryism did not succeed until the time of George III.

The die-hard Tory—Non-Juror in the church, Jacobite in politics—accepted nothing of 1688/9. (It is important to realize that the events of the Glorious Revolution and the legislation that followed—Toleration Act and Bill of Rights —did not end the quarrel of Whig and Tory, or settle anything clearly. Nor did they abruptly achieve the divorce of religion from politics.) From the Tory point of view, Church and State and the landed interest had there fallen, all together and by the same hand. He did not doubt that Moderation, Dissent, Whiggery, Parliamentary supremacy, and the rule of Money all were part of the same infamous

---

[1] The story may be followed in such excellent books as William T. Morgan, *English Political Parties and Leaders in the Reign of Queen Anne*; Charles B. Realey, *The Early Opposition to Robert Walpole, 1720–7*; Keith G. Feiling, *A History of the Tory Party 1640–1714* and *The Second Tory Party 1714–1832*; Lewis B. Namier, *England in the Age of the American Revolution*.

[2] Not all the Jacobites of 1688 believed, strictly speaking, in *jus divinum*. Many of them subscribed to a variant of the compact theory, and rested their case for the Stuarts on precedent rather than divine right. Their position is clarified in an article by George L. Cherry, 'The Legal and Philosophical Position of the Jacobites', in the *Journal of Modern History* for Dec. 1950. However, all Jacobites believed that the lineal succession to the throne ought not to be altered, and Tory churchmen were much inclined to insist that there was a divine sanction to the monarchy.

plot. He wished to return to a simpler past where Altar, Throne, and Hearth were the supreme loyalties. It appeared to this Tory that in hereditary succession in both Church and State lay the only safety for society. Overthrow that principle and you enthrone anarchy, and a train of other evils, all stemming from the initial act of disobedience. 'The first Whig was the Devil', Johnson and Boswell solemnly agreed.[1]

So far as concerned the Church, extreme Jacobite Tories argued that if divine right fell, the Establishment lost all its sacred character and in fact might as well be abolished.[2] For religion cannot command respect when bishops are made by the Court, by politicians and not the anointed king; as that intrepid Tory Charles Leslie put it, its 'foundations they cannot think divine, while they see the Church deposable by the State . . .'.[3] This charge that the Whiggish Church was 'Erastian' was not without force. A Shaftesbury or a Thomas Gordon would openly admit that the Church was now a matter of political convenience; Whig bishops denied it, but could with difficulty evade the charge that the Church could not now pretend to exist independent of any political régime. The liberal Whiston conceded that 'political bishops' were an evil, and pointed to the results in a certain Dr. Cannon, who said he would have been a Catholic at Paris or a 'Muselman' at Constantinople, who cheerfully signed the Anglican articles without faith, 'taking religion to be an engine to promote peace in this world, rather than happiness in the next'.

Francis Atterbury's *Letter to a Convocation Man* (1697) started a long argument in which the Tories failed, naturally, to establish that the Church had always before been independent of secular control.[4] Yet their real point remained:

---

[1] This devil theory of the Whigs was not original with Dr. Johnson, but a familiar piece of Tory ideology; see Charles Leslie's *Rehearsal*, vol. i, nos. 54, 68, 83.

[2] Thus Dr. Hickes, the eminent Non-Juror, in Nichols, *Illustrations*, iii. 277. The sad reply of his correspondent was, 'should all be for abolishing Episcopacy who do not believe in it *jure divino*, I am persuaded it would not stand long'. Tory theory was divorced from Tory practice here as elsewhere, for Tory-minded churchmen did not ordinarily demand the abolition of the Established Church, though in theory they held it no true church or a critically degraded one.

[3] Leslie, 'Case of the Regale and the Pontificate', in *Theological Works*, iii. 295–7.

[4] See Hunt, op. cit. iii. 1 ff.; Sykes, *Church and State*, chap. iii; Carpenter,

there had never before been such a spectacle of a change in government leading to a change in the Church. 'The Erastian principle', Tories cried, had now perverted religion; it had 'turned the gentry deists, and the common people Dissenters', Leslie mourned. Who could respect a political church?

To the extreme Tory, Dissent still meant treason and anarchy. He was 'really unable to comprehend why anyone should desire to remain outside her [Church of England] communion save from pure malignity'.[1] Religious toleration and the 'natural rights' philosophy of the Whigs both became to him pure evil. The great sin of the Puritan in Tory eyes had been, as Clarendon wrote, 'preaching rebellion to the people as the doctrine of Christ'. Out of this had issued the Lockean philosophy in which rebellion was not any of Christ's affair (the neo-Calvinist theory of 'segregation', mentioned previously). Here was nothing but bloody anarchy. Defoe pointed out that it was ridiculous to identify the respectable Augustan Dissenter with a revolutionary, yet Tories continued to do it. Readers of the *Rehearsal* would gather that every Nonconformist was a regicide. 'Republican and Whig are Jack Presbyter's lay-elders, rebellion is his lay-face, as schism his ecclesiastical.'[2] This same Sir John Presbyter, in a Tory satire of the day, had no answer when robbed by bandits who appealed to their 'natural rights':

> Those cobwebs you have all swept down
> By sweeping off your Sov'reign's crown—

the cobwebs being law and order.[3] Religion and government were indeed inseparable to the old Tories, for the simple reason that a schismatic was demonstrably a rebel. When Dr. Sacheverell rallied the mob against Dissenters and Whigs, it was impossible to separate the religious from the

---

Thomas Tenison, chap. xi, and David G. Douglas, *English Scholars* (London, 1939), pp. 260 ff.; for discussions of this important controversy. Wake and then Gibson took up the Whig side. They were certainly successful in refuting Atterbury's historical arguments. But the proroguing of Convocation was an evident sign that the Whig bishops did not enjoy the support of the lower clergy.

[1] W. F. Lord, 'The Development of Political Parties during the Reign of Queen Anne', *Transactions of the Royal Historical Society,* xiv (n.s.), 1900, p. 75.

[2] Leslie, *Theological Works,* vi. 354, 445, &c.

[3] H. N. Fairchild, *Religious Trends in English Poetry,* i. 50–51.

political motives, for the Sacheverellites admitted no such distinction. They looked upon the existing Church of England, as Defoe said, as 'schismatical . . . all her members perjured revolters, both from their religion and their sovereign'. Leslie identified the Whigs with atheists, or at the best deists.[1]

Enough, perhaps, of an attitude that lingered on with a 'sunset charm', as J. N. Figgis put it—assuming that such rancorous distortions can have charm—as a romantic pose, long after it had the least basis in reality. 1715 disposed of the last remnants of Jacobite reality.[2] Even before that, more rational Tories were modifying their position. It was becoming impossible to believe in absolute monarchy and the old doctrine of the duty of absolute obedience. Swift, though a Tory, rejected non-resistance as nonsense: 'What, not be able to depose a Nero or Caligula?'[3] Benjamin Hoadly's *Original and Institution of Civil Government* (1710) included an easy victory over the 'patriarchal' theory of Filmer, who attempted to justify absolutism by an appeal to history, and whom Locke had already routed. Hoadly's presentation of Whig political philosophy drew many indignant rejoinders, and yet nearly all of them rested their opposition on grounds that were utilitarian: any right of revolution means anarchy, and the worst of tyrants is better than anarchy.[4] Such

---

[1] Defoe's *Review*, vol. v, 30 Aug. 1705; *Rehearsal*, i. 40. Thomas Wright, *Caricature History of the Georges*, pp. 5–6, gives the following Tory song:
> Bold Whigs and fanatics now strive to pull down
> The true Church of England, both mitre and crown,
> To introduce anarchy into the nation
> As they did in Oliver's late usurpation.

[2] Realey, op. cit., pp. 149–52, 230, points out the complete collapse of Jacobitism as a political force by 1725. The statement that 'Jacobitism remained a serious and powerful political cause until 1746' (F. J. C. Hearnshaw, *Conservatism in England*, p. 128) is very dubious indeed. Sir Charles Petrie, *The Jacobite Movement: The Last Phase, 1716–1807* (London, 1950), concedes that Jacobite strength declined very greatly for the twenty years after 1720 (pp. 21, 30 ff.). He finds (pp. 49–50) that the negative factor of dislike for the Whig régime, or apathy towards it, was significant in the '45. In Ireland and Scotland, of course, active Jacobitism did exist.

[3] *Sentiments of a Church of England Man*, in *Works*, ii. 215–16. The examples of Nero and Caligula were the customary ones invoked by the Tories themselves, who had commonly declared that one ought to obey even the worst possible tyrant rather than take up arms against constituted authority.

[4] Numerous criticisms of this sort are presented by Hoadly, with his replies *Works*, vol. ii.

hysterical extremism had perhaps been plausible in 1660 but could not be taken seriously by sober men in 1720. It was most significant that Tories were ceasing to defend non-resistance as a religious duty and were arguing for it as a social expediency, where their case was much weaker.[1]

Before long Tories were deciding that one ought to obey the constituted authority, but not because it is that of the anointed king. Defoe and the Whigs boldly pressed home the counter-charge of the Whigs, that divine right means tyranny.[2] The shift to Hanoverian Toryism, to an acceptance of the Revolution and the Settlement, considerably lessened the difference between Whig and Tory, and was bitterly criticized by the dwindling band of Jacobite diehards, but was inevitable. The Tories were, indeed, in a quandary, and Tindal the deist rubbed salt in their wounds when he chided the Jacobite clergy with now themselves preaching revolt against the throne—*New High Church Turned Old Presbyterian!* (1709). Tories soon accepted the permanence of the new order. Thomas Sherlock, whose father had been one of the first to recant his non-juring position (in 1691), soon led the clerical Tories towards a more moderate position.[3] Swift, Bolingbroke, and Berkeley accepted for Toryism the basic Whig axiom that government is 'natural' and not (immediately) divine.[4] Bolingbroke, chief architect of the new Toryism, praised the Act of Settlement, the 1688 Revolution, and the existing Constitution without stint; his ingenious position was that Walpole and the Whigs were upsetting the proper balance of the 1688 constitution and were creating a new sort of Parliamentary tyranny. There remained, of course, important differences of emphasis. The Tory continued to feel, as Berkeley felt, that unlimited freedom must end in anarchy or tyranny, being 'sufficient to dissolve any human fabric of polity or civil

[1] See Berkeley, *Discourse of Passive Obedience*. The most penetrating analysis of the breakdown of divine-right theory remains J. N. Figgis, *The Divine Right of Kings*. Figgis makes it clear that on any grounds but religious injunction, divine right was doomed.

[2] Defoe, *Review*, 8 Sept. 1705.

[3] Edward F. Carpenter, *Thomas Sherlock*, pp. 6–13; Thomas Sherlock, *Works*, iii. 336–9.

[4] Bolingbroke, *Collection of Political Tracts*, pp. 242 ff., 267.

government'. The Tories had not abandoned their instinct to seek discipline and unity, in government and religion both. They did slowly abandon their effort to impose it at the point of the sword, as God's evident mandate. They accepted toleration as a going concern while resisting as best they could its consequences.[1] Schism remained in their eyes an evil, but scarcely a mortal sin. Whigs and Tories were beginning to become 'liberals on the Left and Right'. David Hume's effort to define the parties about mid-century was notable in indicating how little now separated them.[2]

The Tories, then, might be 'Erastians' too. 'I leave it among the divines to dilate upon the danger of schism as a spiritual evil', Swift wrote, 'but I would consider it only as a temporal one.'[3] Swift had assailed Tindal's *Rights of the Christian Church* as Erastian, but his own outlook was in fact equally so. He differed from the Whig bishops in that he thought political convenience better served by not tolerating religious dissent. The truth is that for both Whig and Tory, *jus divinum* became irrevocably obsolete. Soame Jenyns put it baldly enough a few years later:

> I would by no means Church and King destroy
> And yet the doctrine taught me when a boy
> By Crab the Curate, now seems wondrous odd,
> That either came immediately from God.[4]

3

The moderate or Whig clergy accepted both deaths— the death of political divine right joyfully, that of religious divine right with a certain embarrassment, if they were

---

[1] There was a strong inclination to demand prosecution of deists and enforcement of the disqualifying acts against Dissenters. See the *Weekly Miscellany, passim.* Yet cf. Berkeley, *The Querist*, nos. 83 and 84, and *Memoirs of the Duke of Wharton*, pp. 360–76, for examples of Tory repudiation of religious persecution.

[2] 'Of the Parties of Great Britain', in *Essays, Moral, Political and Literary*, i. 139: a Tory is 'a lover of monarchy, though without abandoning liberty, and a partisan of the family of Stuart; as a Whig may be defined to be a lover of liberty, though without renouncing monarchy, and a friend to the settlement in the Protestant line'. Hume thought the Tories stressed order more than liberty, and the Whigs vice versa.

[3] *Works*, ii. 212.

[4] Quoted in Feiling, *Second Tory Party*, p. 9. The *Monthly Review*, Aug. 1749 (i. 315), notes of a divine-right political treatise, 'This author proceeds on the *old* principle of passive obedience.' (Italics ours.)

Anglicans. Benjamin Hoadly, Bishop of Bangor, was the most notorious of the Whig bishops. Hoadly, however, denied that he was Erastian. He declared himself horrified at the thought of 'debasing the most sacred thing in the world into a political tool, as an engine of state'.[1] Frank acceptance of the Church as simply a social and political convenience was confined to free-thinkers, and no bishop or other respectable Whig wished to be known as one of them. Yet Hoadly seemed logically to leave no real place for the Church. His *Original and Institution of Civil Government* (1710) presented the Whig view that government is of human origin, not divine, and that there is a right of revolution against unjust rulers (to which end he argued against a 'strict construction' of such passages as Romans xiii. 1). The end of government is the happiness of society; freedom of religion is essential to this happiness. Hoadly was consistent when, a few years later, in the famous Bangorian controversy, he defined the Church as invisible and wholly spiritual—in effect, as his critics noted, dissolving the Church of England as a society. But in practice neither the secular nor the ecclesiastical Whigs wanted to do away with the Church.

In Whiggism was a strong tradition of hostility to clerical interference in politics. From Milton to Harley it had believed that the clergy 'ought not to be suffered to meddle with politics', for they were no friends to 'the rights and liberties of the people'.[2] The Whig publicists Tutchin, Trenchard, and Gordon preached this in its most extreme form. 'Shun the side which has got the majority of these spiritual guides with them', Trenchard advised. 'However useful their profession may be to our souls, we find the generality of them no great friends to our bodies. . . .'[3] Yet it appeared that a Whiggish church guided by Hoadlys and Wakes, in which 'fanatics' were kept from power, was an asset. Conversely, Tories began to complain that Whig bishops minded their flocks too little and politics too much.[4] The Walpole organ, Osborne's *London Journal*, praised

[1] Hoadly, *Works*, ii. 425.
[2] See G. M. Trevelyan, *The Peace and the Protestant Succession*, p. 58; John Dennis, in *Somers Tracts*, vol. xiii.
[3] *Independent Whig*, ii. 276; cf. *Observator*, ii, no. 34, and iii, no. 83.
[4] Bolingbroke, *A Collection of Political Tracts*, pp. 205–6.

Hoadly as the 'great apostle and converter of the clergy to the principles of the Revolution and the sentiments of liberty...'.[1] Thomas Gordon contrasted 'proud, persecuting, covetous, rebellious, perjured priests' like Sacheverell and Atterbury with those bishops who were 'loyal, moderate men; men of conscience and moderation'. A church of the latter sort, Gordon baldly affirmed, is a useful institution, though perhaps not a divine one.[2] The creed of this 'independent Whig' was plain enough, but not very palatable. It appeared to make the Church the spiritual arm of the Walpole government. There is evidence enough, indeed, that this is about what it actually became. (Walpole was angered when Bishop Gibson presumed to cross him on a purely episcopal question.) But it was embarrassing to admit it.

'We are not to look into the Scriptures for the English Constitution', John Tutchin dryly remarked in 1703. He nevertheless felt obliged to argue that non-resistance is unscriptural; the Whigs usually proposed their own version of the famous injunction to obey the powers that be.[3] Even the Whigs, then, did not leave religion out of politics where they could cite it to their advantage. But the essence of Whiggism was the resort to nature for a demonstration of government's origins. A purely natural government, however, left no very clear place for an established church, short of the abhorred Erastian position, which to this era seemed like the worst cynicism. It is embarrassing to read some of the Whig efforts to justify the Establishment. Bishop Warburton's was the most notable of these efforts during this period.[4] Aware of the Erastian danger, or at least aware of the opprobrium attached to it, Warburton insisted he would have the Church be 'neither a slave nor a tyrant'. Yet his justification for it turns out to be entirely 'civic utility'. And he

---

[1] Quoted by Laprade, *Public Opinion in Eighteenth Century England*, pp. 373–4.
[2] *Independent Whig*, ii. 374, 415, &c.
[3] *Observator*, ii, no. 47. See also Bishop Fleetwood, *Works*, iii. 123–42. Fleetwood argues that Romans xiii means submission to the Hanoverians, which indicates the strong Whig tendency to think of their revolution as the last. John Locke had also rebutted divine right on scriptural grounds as well as natural, by way of being sure.
[4] *The Alliance between Church and State* (1736). Commentaries may be found in Evans, *Warburton*, chap. iii, and Sykes, *Church and State*, pp. 316–26.

concedes that it does not matter what the Established Church is, so long as it teaches some sort of God and his Providence over human affairs. The largest religious body ought to be made the official State church, just because it is convenient for the State to deal with such a body.

Warburton sought to deduce all this, of course, from natural law; the same Nature in which Locke had so clearly found the source of civil government ought to show the reason for an established church. But it is painfully evident that Warburton began with his institution and then tried hard to wring a rationale out of poor Nature. It is a laboured apology, for all Warburton's characteristic ingenuity, and it scarcely succeeded in making the Church more than a tool of politics. As against such tortured apologetics, the Dissenting case for full religious liberty was far more convincing.[1] The High Churchmen were right in feeling that the Church of England was lost if it threw away its claim to a special divine sanction. On utilitarian grounds, nothing was easier than to show the silliness of any established church. Paley will say, what in the last analysis the Anglican liberals could only say, that the Church is merely a 'scheme of instruction'.[2] Why then should the Anglican scheme of instruction be officially preferred over any other Christian scheme of instruction?

The reason given by Walpole, and then Burke, was, of course, just that it is not expedient to move what is at rest: when it is not necessary to change it is necessary not to change. An effectual if illogical 'balance' had been attained, which statesmen were not going to disturb. Against this sort of political logic the more militant Dissenters would beat in vain. There could be no question about the politics of all Dissenters. 'There is not one Jacobite to be found among them, or ever was, that I have heard of', Defoe asserted safely enough. 'They must be for King George, and that for ever.'[3] High Church intolerance had forced them to look to

---

[1] See, for example, Isaac Watts, 'A New Essay on Civil Power in Things Sacred', *Works*, vol. vi—which disposes of the question in a few lucid pages.

[2] William Paley, *Principles of Moral and Political Philosophy* (1785), vi. 10.

[3] Defoe's *Writings*, ed. Lee, ii. 86; *Review*, 25 Sept. 1705. There had once been Quaker Tories, in the time of Charles II, but High Church intolerance had ended this.

the Whigs for protection. Contented and prosperous, the Dissenters were far from being the rebels and subversives of old Tory propaganda, and, as has been noted, they were not especially anxious to demand more concessions either. Between 1689 and 1714 their position was still precarious, and from time to time the Tories and the mob howled against them (there were in fact such mobs as late as 1733). The Tories succeeded during their brief season of power between 1711 and 1714 in passing the Occasional Conformity Act and the Schism Act. The death of Queen Anne and the coming of the Hanoverians saved the Dissenters, and the obnoxious measures were repealed a few years later (1718–19).

But the Dissenters' political value declined during the Whig supremacy, and Walpole would not move farther, towards repeal of the Test and Corporation Acts. Anglican Whigs had once fought such bills as the Occasional Conformity measure because they needed Dissenting support against Jacobites and Tories.[1] That was no longer necessary. The danger was now that of giving further offence to the quiescent but potentially hostile group of Tory Anglicans, who would have been incensed at additional concessions to schism. When in the 1730's some Dissenters tried to renew the offensive for full religious and civil equality, they failed because of languid support from their own eminently contented fellows and the hostility of the Whig ministers.[2]

However weakly the Establishment might be justified in theory, it existed, and Walpole certainly did not intend to make enemies by attacking it; everyone knows that that genial politician desired to awaken no sleeping animosities. The Dissenters, he knew, were his in any event, and he propitiated them by gifts of money and by lax enforcement of the disqualifying laws.[3] The balance was on dead centre,

---

[1] Carpenter, *Thomas Tenison*, pp. 118–19.

[2] The effort to repeal the Test Act was very nearly successful in 1735; Hervey noted that at this time anti-clericalism was strong and 'the churchmen had never so strong reason to believe the decay of their interest in this kingdom'. But an alarmed Church rallied to defeat this and other bills in 1736 (Mortmain and Tithe bills). See John Hervey, *Memoirs of the Reign of King George II* (London, 1931), ii. 121–32; Sykes, *Bishop Gibson*, pp. 164 ff.

[3] Occasional conformity, the practice at which Tories had aimed, permitted one to pass technically as an Anglican by rare appearances at the parish church. The Schism

and the languid protests of a Dissenting group which was on the whole prosperous and contented, against some mild burdens, were not calculated to disturb it.

4

It was notoriously difficult to tell a Whig from a Tory in this period. Tacitly accepting the Revolution, the Tories had scarcely yet found any new principles. Within the Church, the moderate Tory Sherlock, a favourite of Queen Caroline, did not greatly differ from the once despised Whig bishops; and in 1736 the Church united in defence of its privileges. The Tory traditionalists showed a tendency to look back beyond the Stuarts to Hooker's more flexible philosophy.[1] In political theory Whig and Tory could come close to agreement on a moderate version of the compact; thus it is not easy to say whether the political philosophy expressed in Synge's *A Gentleman's Religion* is Whig or Tory. The civil magistrate, this typical 'gentleman' held, derives his power from the consent of the people, but when once established 'it is to be looked upon as ratified and confirmed by God's own appointment', and requires obedience— obedience up to what point is left unsaid.[2] Here was a formula on which Whig and Tory might agree. It left the Hanoverians firmly in power but satisfied Tory desires for authority. The desire of the Whigs to justify no more revolutions after 1688 was as marked as the gradual admission by the Tories that they could not after all undo 1688. In their theory of the Church, both were confused. Conservative churchmen mourned the decay of the Church, and were much inclined to blame the Whigs, but had no practical solution. Liberal Churchmen rested so strongly on religious freedom, private judgement, and natural right

Act would have struck at the Dissenting academies. The Test and Corporation Acts, which remained on the books, prohibited Dissenters from holding public office unless they would take the sacrament after the manner of the Anglican Church. Lax enforcement, as expressed in permitting occasional conformity and in passing annual indemnity acts for the protection of office-holders who did not fill the requirement, did not of course eliminate the fact that a really conscientious Dissenter could not legally hold office.

[1] Nichols, *Illustrations*, iv. 327.
[2] Synge, *A Gentleman's Religion*, pp. 208–9.

that they left the Establishment no very dignified excuse for existence. Without exactly intending it, both groups might be said to have been putting the Church in that position which J. Middleton Murry has called 'the absolute nadir of the Christian religion'—when, early in the nine-teenth century, the Erastian Church knew no better function than that of preaching political conservatism as an arm of the State.

Thus, although the dissociation of Church and State was by no means complete, politics could laugh and cry without religion by 1750; it was the latter that was becoming sub-ordinate. Perhaps we might risk the generalization that in 1670 one was a Tory because one was a High Church Anglican, while in 1770 one was an Anglican because one was a Tory. Toland and the free-thinkers had always poked fun at the idea that because one man kneels in church and another does not they should form themselves into separate political parties. They had done so because the Tory mind had stubbornly denied that stable government could be had except on a basis of religious obedience to the monarch. Reinforced by civil war and fear of anarchy, this Stuart theory was fed on the association of Dissent with rebellion in the age of the Puritan Revolution and took a good while to die. Shaken by the desertion of James II, Tories impo-tently witnessed the triumph of anti-hereditary principles and a revolution in the Church hierarchy which filled the sees with men scarcely to be distinguished from Dissenters. They had, indeed, much to complain of during the rule of the cynical Walpole. But they could not turn back the clock. Tarred with the brushes of popery and tyranny, they were seriously discredited, the more so as stable and prosperous government prevailed despite their laments. Gradually they accepted the finality of the Revolution, and abandoned Jacobitism.

The Whigs for their part always accepted the divorce of religion from politics; but not of Church from State. Illogic-ally enough, they kept the Established Church, though they could really only justify it as a pleasant custom. Dissenters and even deists accepted this without protest. Perhaps they were mindful of a warning issued by John Wesley some years later. 'Do you imagine there are no High Churchmen left?' he asked the politically radical Nonconformists of 1775. 'Did they all die with Dr. Sacheverell? Alas, how little do you know of mankind!'[1] That is to say, the return of 'fanaticism' continued to be a possibility all through the century; Tory High-Church emotions smouldered but did not die; it was always dangerous to disturb the 'balance' by any additional pressure in the direction of liberalism.

Certainly the events of 1790 verified Wesley's judgement. It goes without saying that few liberals wanted any sweeping social or political changes. They were content to rest with what they had, without further baiting the Tory bull.

[1] Wesley, *Works*, xi. 138.

X

RELIGION AND THE RULING CLASS

I believe, sir, you will agree with me, that never had any nation a fuller
enjoyment of liberty than we have had since the Revolution.
JOHN LELAND, 1754

In some other countries the upper part of the world is free, but in
Great Britain the whole body of the people is free.
JOSEPH BUTLER

COMPLACENCY, of the sort expressed above by Leland
and Butler, was the keynote of an age which found
itself generally prosperous, with few really acute social
problems such as might threaten the security of society, and
a mild but stable government. But we need to add that, to
Bishop Butler, liberty consisted in submission to the
authority of government and in the preservation of a class
hierarchy, with the poor kept in their appointed place. The
sanction of religion was given to the class structure and
submission to one's assigned station. Butler, quite conventional in his views here, declared that the relationship between
rich and poor had not been essentially changed by the new
urban environment—it still should be as it had been on the
manor.[1]

In economics, as well as politics, the period was one of
relative quiet, a moment of equilibrium underneath which,
indeed, momentous preparations were going on for great
changes which would come near the end of the century.
Some historians, insisting quite properly that the industrial
revolution was not made overnight, have pushed back the
origins of that process to the beginning of the century. This
does not disturb the fact that industrialism's striking social
consequences were not felt until later, that large capitalistic
units were as yet exceptional, not typical, that class divisions
were not yet generally sharp as between owner and worker,
and that the horrors of the early factory system were not yet

[1] Joseph Butler, *Works*, ii, 258, 295, 314, 329; see also Norton, op. cit., p. 150.

very noticeable. In brief, while industrial capitalism had arrived, its problems had not become acute.[1]

It is possible to trace the turn towards *laissez-faire* back to the Restoration, and to say that 'the economic drift of the century was towards a sharper demarcation of classes and towards depriving the poor of such economic protection as the Tudor and early Stuart governments had managed to keep for them'.[2] This was certainly true; within the nation 'the principle and practice of free trade and exchange made great headway' in the eighteenth century, though by no means complete.[3] On the other hand, it is possible to say that (relatively) there was 'little or no social discontent'.[4] It is not true that there was absolutely no discontent. There was the mob, which Fielding named the Fourth Estate—Sacheverell's mob, the Spitalfield weavers, the anti-Jewish riots of 1753, mobs against Dissenters and against Catholics—the sort of thing that culminates finally in that extraordinary outburst of 1780, the Gordon riots: rioting that is aimless and leaderless and futile, yet certainly significant. It was a sign of growing inequality and growing insecurity for many of the poor. Although everyone agrees that this was a time of exceptional prosperity for England at large, with a rising standard of living over all, it is equally evident that this prosperity was fluctuating and 'very unstable', with the poorer classes subject to great hardships, and in general to less security than before.[5]

---

[1] Such studies as J. U. Nef, *The Rise of the British Coal Industry* (1932), have revealed the earlier roots of the industrial revolution; see also Nef's article, 'The Progress of Technology', in *Economic History Review*, Oct. 1934. Alfred P. Wadsworth and Julia de L. Mann, *The Cotton Trade and Industrial Lancashire 1600–1780*, show that by 1750 Lancashire had achieved in most sectors of its industry 'a fairly high level of capitalistic organization' (p. 211). Cf. Paul Mantoux, *The Industrial Revolution in the Eighteenth Century*, pp. 68, 376, *passim*.

[2] E. Lipson, *Economic History of England* (1931), iii. 264–65, 312–13; Feiling, *History of the Tory Party*, p. 20.

[3] John M. Clark, in Clark *et al.*, *Adam Smith, 1776–1926*, p. 61.

[4] G. M. Trevelyan, in A. S. Turberville, ed., *Johnson's England*, i. 7. See also the same author's *English Social History* (London, 1947), pp. 294–5.

[5] Mantoux, op. cit., pp. 72–73; Max Beloff, *Public Order and Popular Disturbances 1660–1714*; W. C. Sydney, *England and the English in the Eighteenth Century*, ii. 192–5; R. F. Wearmouth, *Methodism and the Common People of the Eighteenth Century*, sect. i, chaps. i–iii. Chap. iii of Eli Ginzberg, *The House of Adam Smith*, on 'The Laboring Poor', is an eloquent summary as seen through the unorthodox eyes of the great Scottish economist.

But in so far as the lower classes protested it was not in the name of any coherent philosophy of social change. Revolutionary sentiment was lacking, and what little thought there was among these classes was towards a restoration of 'the old governmental control over economic activity and social life' rather than towards any new order.[1] In 1751 a writer thought he detected a spirit of 'mutiny and independence' among 'the gross body of the people'.[2] Quite evidently there was such a vague discontent abroad, but it was as yet formless and without direction. There was a proletariat before the factory age, capable of commenting on their exploitation by those who

> . . . gain all [their] wealth and estate
> By many poor men that work early and late.

But only the dimmest origins of a trade-union movement existed. What is beyond dispute is the fact that the poor, as always, existed—the poor who, as Cowper wrote,

> . . . inured to drudgery and distress
> Act without aim, think little and feel less.

The innumerable local riots show that they sometimes felt, but also that they did generally think little and act without aim.

It was not the Fourth Estate's century, but the Third's. The dominant classes in England exhibited an understandable complacency. John Toland, deist and Whig, thought that English liberty 'wants very little of perfection', and was rendered indignant by even those good-natured slights on the home of freedom contained in Defoe's *True-born Englishman*.[3] 'What can you desire more than you have already?' John Wesley asked the malcontents in 1774.[4] The only reproach that literary Tories could think of was—too much wealth and indulgence, leading to a corrosion of moral fibre, to 'vain, luxurious, and selfish effeminacy'.[5] This Tory

---

[1] Beloff, op. cit., pp. 153–5. Wearmouth, op. cit., p. 51, makes the statement that 'the suffering masses of the eighteenth century never tried to alter the Constitution and never openly desired a change in the form of administration'.

[2] John White, *Free and Impartial Considerations* . . ., pp. 7–8.

[3] Toland, *The Art of Governing*, p. 161; *State-Anatomy of Great Britain*, pp. 44–45.

[4] Wesley, *Works*, xi. 139.

[5] Such charges were common; see the pages of the Tory *True Briton* (in *Memoirs*

protest against a commercial age was fairly faint, if not so
faint as the complaints from the voiceless poor. The Tory
who lamented Whig materialism did not often extend his
criticism to a championing of the poor. He might, indeed,
charge the Whigs with callous heartlessness; we see in this
period the beginning of the Tory indictment of bourgeois
economics on humanitarian grounds which culminates in
Carlyle and Ruskin a century later: Swift's bitter satire of
'political arithmetic' in his *Modest Proposal* is of course a
case in point. But Henry Fielding, for example, worried
mainly about the effect of bourgeois 'luxury' on the lower
classes, making them restless and unruly; he agreed that
the poor have themselves to blame for their plight, and his
remedy was to lower wages while punishing the 'incorrigible
idle', which was what any bourgeois would have said.[1] The
real source of Tory pessimism would appear to have been
much less any real sympathy for the poor than their own
plight—the plight of rural gentlemen, not to mention pro-
fessional authors. 'For many years, a country squire has been
an object of ridicule', one of them noted in 1750, in a tract
advising country squires how to live respectably in the face
of rising prices.[2]

Whiggism meant commercialism, a thing resented by the
'Old England' Tories as much for social as for economic
reasons. Through trade, the commoners had acceded to
political power.[3] The English merchant, who now boasted
that 'our trade is the most considerable of the whole world',
could also note with satisfaction that, in Defoe's words,
'trade in England makes gentlemen'. 'Money was becoming
more and more the measure of prestige and power.' The new
aristocracy of trade was purchasing land on a large scale and
thus directly invading the aristocracy.[4] The rural squires,

---

of the Life of the Duke of Wharton); John Brown's famous *Estimate of the Manners
and Principles of the Times*, or Henry Fielding's *An Enquiry into the Late Increase of
Robbers*, &c.   [1] Fielding, op. cit., pp. 17–19, 35–36, 88–90.

[2] John Trusler, *The Way to be Rich and Respectable*. The author's advice included
a recommendation to stay at home on the estate, pursuing the simple and robust life,
instead of going to foppish London each year. As L. B. Namier points out, the
squires actually did cease even to attend Parliament in these years.

[3] Fielding, op. cit., preface.

[4] Mantoux, op. cit., p. 163; Lucy S. Sutherland, *A London Merchant, 1695–
1774*, pp. 5–6.

simple of mind and taste, looked upon this urban moneyed class as something of a scandal, dishonest and wasteful. What the City thought of the rural squires is reflected in Addison's Tory foxhunter, and in the Whig myth as later classically perpetuated by Macaulay.

On the other hand a rising capitalist class in industry was very apt to think of itself as frugal and virtuous as against a profligate nobility; these *nouveaux riches* were likely to be Dissenters, especially in the rising manufacturing towns of west, midland, and north. In any event it was clear to all that the Whigs were the party of commerce and finance. The Whig power, Tories declared, was based on 'setting up a monied interest in opposition to the landed'.[1] The bitterness of the Tories towards this plutocracy was often intense. Pope, it seems, would have been glad to abolish money altogether! The Whigs for their part feared the economic implications of a Tory victory. The Jacobite was pictured with 'a sponge in his left hand' to repudiate all the acts benefiting trade and to abolish the Bank of England. The price of stocks fell with the successes of Dr. Sacheverell. Toland referred to 'priests' (Tory High Churchmen) as enemies of trade.[2]

The growth of luxury, of an ignoble materialistic spirit, was commonly related by critics of Whiggism to the decay of religion.[3] In this age the Tory philosophy attacked commercial capitalism from the viewpoint of an older order dominated by the country gentleman. In that rural squire-archy religion had played a part, if not an extraordinary one. The parson, of course, was a fixture in that stable, stratified rural society. He was scarcely as benighted as Macaulay imagined, even if he 'did not think of himself in any special sense as a messenger of the Lord, but as a country gentle-man . . . who had a social status to maintain, and who happened to have certain clerical duties to perform'. The English country gentleman 'looked upon religion as neces-sary to a decent and respectable living and as essential to a well-ordered state. . . . A pattern of life that ignored religion

---

[1] Swift to Pope, in Pope's *Works*, iii. 123.
[2] *Spectator*, no. 3; *Observator*, ix. no. 53; Toland, *State-Anatomy*, p. 44.
[3] See for example John Brown, *Estimate*, pp. 98 ff.

was unthinkable to them'.[1] But a gentleman was not a religious fanatic, and the squires had very little taste for theology, preferring books of 'practical divinity' such as Jeremy Taylor's *Holy Living*, or *The Whole Duty of Man*. A gentleman was a Christian in conduct, which meant that he went to church and treated his tenants with a certain amount of Christian kindness. Such charity by no means included any notion of equality. Class lines were tightly drawn, and the parson no more than the squire dreamed of crossing them. Not only was the class system supported by appeals to Scripture, but it is to be suspected that 'sin was the prerogative of the lower orders'.[2] We shall not find any questioning of the class system even among the most humane and sensitive of the eighteenth-century gentry; the gentle poet Cowper, prince of humanitarians, will insist that 'differences of rank and subordination are, I believe, of God's appointment, and consequently essential to the well-being of society'.[3] This was accepted by all, and it may reasonably be said that one of religion's functions—if not the only one —was to help maintain this proper subordination of rank. The Anglican catechism enjoined each person to do his duty in that state of life unto which it should please God to call him. But the parson's duties included philanthropy and kindness to the poor, and this element of stewardship was equally a part of the Christian tradition.

Religion had long sat rather lightly on the squires, because religious fanaticism was associated with the Roundheads. It was the latter whose change in religious intensity was apparently the most marked. The Dissenters had become, certainly, far quieter and more conservative. The Tory myth of Jack Presbyter as a radical was, of course, just that; and Dissent had always been primarily a middle-class faith. Presbyterianism was 'not a religion for gentlemen'.[4] Neither

---

[1] Elizabeth K. Nottingham, *The Making of an Evangelist*, p. 53; Louis B. Wright, *First Gentlemen of Virginia* (San Marino, California, 1940), pp. 66, 134–5. James Woodforde's *Diary of a Country Parson*, ed. J. Beresford, is famous as the best picture of a parson's life in the eighteenth century.

[2] Nottingham, op. cit., p. 50. We are reminded of the Duchess's famous rejoinder to Wesley, that 'it is monstrous to be told that you have a heart as sinful as the common wretches that crawl on the earth'—Tyerman, *Whitefield*, i. 160–1.

[3] L. C. Hartley, *William Cowper, Humanitarian*, p. 39.

[4] Clark, *History of English Nonconformity*, ii. 6.

was it a religion for the riff-raff. Its class bias had always been evident and strong. 'Freeholders and tradesmen are the strength of religion and civility in the land', Richard Baxter had written, 'and gentlemen and beggars, and servile tenants, are the strength of iniquity.' On the other side of that coin, we find Tory-Anglican contempt for 'shop-prating weavers and cobblers'.[1]

The erstwhile weavers and cobblers had quite commonly become men of substance in the eighteenth century. The greater capitalists were very apt to be Dissenters. As of 1719, Philip Doddridge noted that Dissent's position had become 'highly respectable'.[2] Not only the Presbyterians and Independents but also Quakers and Baptists tended to become well-to-do and respectable. The Quakers, it was observed, were changing their plain clothes for buttons and ruffles.[3] Some prosperous Dissenters conformed in this period, but whether they did or not made little difference, for they were no longer Roundheads, and all but the most prejudiced Anglicans recognized that Puritanism had lost its sting.

Poverty the Dissenters regarded with contempt. On the familiar Puritan terms worldly success was the proof of spiritual success, but no one can fail to sense that in the eighteenth century the equation has become far more crassly materialistic. It was the somewhat astonishing rule among the Dissenters that a brother who became bankrupt 'must expect to be cut off from our body . . .'.[4] True, the great Nonconformist prophets—Baxter, Bunyan, Penn—had clearly expressed the traditional warnings against excessive greed and against unscrupulous economic practices. Christian economic ethics are sufficiently ambiguous, and from Calvin

---

[1] Quoted in the valuable work by Richard B. Schlatter, *Social Ideas of Religious Leaders, 1660–1688*, p. 167.

[2] Doddridge, *Correspondence and Diary*, i. 29. See Tawney, op. cit., pp. 252–3, and R. V. Holt, *Unitarian Contributions to Social Progress in England*, chap. 2.

[3] César de Saussure, *A Foreign View of England in the Reigns of George I and George II*, translated and edited by B. Van Muyden (New York, 1942), p. 327. Such observations were numerous; see Schlatter, op. cit., pp. 232–5. Arthur Raistrick, *Quakers in Science and Industry*, stresses the role played by Quakers in industry, trade, and finance; the concluding chapter is a thoughtful examination of both the reasons for this Quaker eminence in capitalism and the consequences to religion.

[4] Davis, *Isaac Watts*, p. 38.

one might derive a kind of socialism (as the Christian Socialists later did) as well as capitalism.[1] But the stern admonitions against excessive wealth, the warnings against exploiting the poor, the prohibitions of usury and other such practices, while they are still occasionally heard in the eighteenth century, are not much honoured. We feel inclined to believe Collins the deist when he writes that he never heard of but one clergyman in all England who thought usury to be a sin.[2] Defoe's 'complete English tradesman' was in theory, and no doubt sometimes in practice, 'a fair downright honest man', who 'never grinds the faces of the poor'.[3] He was taught the doctrine of Christian stewardship. But we shall have to give some place to the complaint of the American Quaker, John Woolman, that too often a capitalist on the make ignored it, that 'in the mouth of many it is but a cant, unmeaning expression'.

Doubtless the stewardship doctrine influenced many employers and tradesmen to greater humanity.[4] It is equally clear that the middle class had discovered a 'new medicine for poverty' far different from indiscriminate charity. 'Damn the poor'—'God cannot love the wretch he starves'—such was Alexander Pope's interpretation of the outlook of the moneyed class.[5] Pope was a prejudiced witness where Whigs and merchants were concerned, but he seems to have been right. The Puritan's individualism did lead him to regard the poor as men of no virtue and grace. Middle-class opinion was unanimous, 'from Locke and Defoe to Chalmers', that the poor had only to blame their 'personal follies and Christian ingratitude'.[6] 'Everyone but an idiot knows that the lower classes must be kept poor or they will never be industrious.' Arthur Young's famous remark was all too typical.[7]

[1] See Ernst Troeltsch, *The Social Teachings of the Christian Churches*, ii. 641–9.

[2] *Discourse of Freethinking*, p. 74.

[3] Daniel Defoe, *The Complete English Tradesman*, ii. 143.

[4] Isabel Grubb, *Quakerism and Industry before 1800* (London, 1930), argues that in this respect the Friends were better than average.

[5] Pope, *Works*, iii. 138–9. Cf. Basil Williams, *The Whig Supremacy*, pp. 123–33.

[6] Wadsworth and Mann, op. cit., p. 385. See John Clayton, *Friendly Advice to the Poor*, 1755.

[7] *Arthur Young on Industry and Economics*, ed. Elizabeth P. Hunt, presents

For the ruling classes, religion had ceased to be austere. The religion of most people of means in this period was a mild and comfortable one, well expressed in the *Gentleman's Religion* observation that 'I find no reason to think that [God] has decreed us all, or any of us, to be absolutely miserable whilst we remain in this world'.[1] The sanctity of property was strongly stressed in religious utterances. Sermons on the 'temporal advantages of religion' were common. The left hand of Christianity, a prudent man's faith, held riches and honour. The social outlook of such a Whig as Bishop Hoadly reflected the comfortable conviction that religion's tasks were to defend property and liberty and prosperity, as established by the Glorious Revolution, from Tory threats.[2]

This Whig system was not, needless to say, a democratic one. The Puritan had believed in democracy no more than the Anglican, but that God had placed men in 'their several stations and callings'. 'A noble, a gentleman, a yeoman, the distinction between them is rightly of great interest to the nation', Cromwell had said. Political power, according to the dominant Roundhead faction, rightly belonged only to propertied men. Diggers and Levellers had been crushed by the powerful reaction against extremes of 'enthusiasm'. When, a century after 1640, the Methodists appeared, a group whose intent was quite innocent of any social or political radicalism (Wesley being almost the prince of conservatives in such matters), they still were not merely suspected but bitterly reviled and persecuted by all as dangerous revolutionaries, because they sought to reach the masses and because their religious outlook seemed to involve 'enthusiasm'. Nothing better illustrates both the fear of the people and the still existing association of religion with political and social attitudes.[3]

examples of Young's astonishing but typically class-conditioned view of the poor—e.g. pp. 45, 55, 95, 112.

[1] Synge, op. cit., pp. 184, 185 ff.

[2] Hoadly, *Works,* ii. 111–17; Nichols, *Anecdotes,* i. 140, 379.

[3] The unbelievable animus against the Methodists may be followed in Wearmouth, op. cit. That Methodists were regarded as 'dangerous to the person and Government of His Majesty King George' (ibid., p. 153) rested on grounds explained by Dr. Johnson when he observed that 'the doctrine of inward light, to which some Methodists pretend, is entirely incompatible with political and religious security'.

The rationalists of our period, whether orthodox or deistic, were by no means political radicals. Worshipping liberty and property, they were quite satisfied with the Whig régime as it existed after 1714. What of those who lacked property? Little sympathy was wasted on them. For these 'idle and vicious', there were harsh penal laws and the workhouses. The 'drones' of political arithmetic were entitled to no sympathy. A sober and honest man could presumably rise in society. Such at least is the outlook we find reflected in the sermons of the day. 'Submission and humility', along traditional Christian lines, are enjoined upon servants; 'the state of servitude is absolutely necessary, by the order and appointment of the wise Creator and Disposer of all things'. But by industry and honesty a servant may rise. The master has a duty to be fair and just to his servants.[1]

This code, as the industrial revolution was to show, had its equivocations for those unfortunate enough not to have already risen to wealth. The early eighteenth century did not yet witness the tensions of the factory age; yet there were enough social evils. A few only were prepared to go beyond the narrower version of the stewardship idea to begin the humanitarian movement.

We have only to glance at the *bourgeoisie* in other lands to recognize aspects of both religion and social philosophy characteristic of this class in all places. The French bourgeois also thought the workers were paid too much, and were lazy and vicious.[2] In religion, the outright deist shocked him—a dangerous philosophy; yet there was, as M. Roustan has noted, a bit of the *philosophe* in him—tolerance suits him, he is too hard-headed for mysticism, he prefers a religion that does not get in the way of business and is not too expensive. It does not surprise us that the English merchant Braund owned a copy of a deist book.[3] It would have surprised us very much had he not remained outwardly orthodox—or if he had owned a copy of Law or Whitefield. The merchant

---

[1] William Fleetwood, *Works*, i, Discourses xiv, xv, xvi; ii. 261 ff.
[2] Marius Roustan, *Pioneers of the French Revolution*, translated by F. Whyte (Boston, 1926), chap. vii, also p. 229.
[3] Sutherland, op. cit.

was, after 1710, constantly congratulating himself on England's prosperity, which he attributed mainly to 'the security and liberty which the nation gained at the Revolution'.[1] This happy situation he did not wish to disturb by a movement either forward or backward. A religion which preached submission and sobriety to the poor, yet sanctioned his own aggressive acquisitiveness and made few demands on his purse, was what the dominant bourgeois wished. Evidently both a Whiggish Church of England and a debilitated Dissent were willing enough to provide something of the sort. As for the few who enjoyed being outright deists, they generally contented themselves with exposing the hypocrisy of this arrangement, without suggesting a change.

[1] Alexander Mackenzie, *Characteristics of the Present State of Great Britain*, pp. 100, 101, 199, &c.

XI

RELIGION AND SOCIAL REFORM

> We can never estimate the religion of any age or society without
> observing its attitude towards the poor.
>
> G. G. COULTON, *The Medieval Village*

I

ARTHUR YOUNG spoke for his age. Despite an occasional
shedding of the poet Thomson's 'social tear', too often
open to Mandeville's suspicions about its sincerity,
there was no real humanitarian movement until the last
quarter of the century. There was the beginning of one,
the fruit of a religious philanthropy, at the beginning of the
century. The men whom Thomson celebrated in verse—
Thomas Bray, James Oglethorpe, and the Wesleys, to name
the foremost—set going the charity schools, founded the
societies for reforming manners and propagating the gospel,
established hospitals and ultimately inquired 'into the horrors
of the gloomy jail'. They founded the colony of Georgia.
Add to them such nonconforming philanthropists and
reformers as the celebrated Quaker John Bellers and the
unitarian Thomas Firmin.[1] But this impulse had very nearly
died by 1730. Although some claim a tradition of religious
charity stretching across the century from Robert Nelson
to Hannah More, it would seem that this tradition thinned
down to the faintest trace between the first decade or two
and the last. As Thomson wrote,

> Much still untouched remains, in this dark age;

and amid many evils there were remarkably few men to
employ 'the patriot's weeding hand'.

Until after 1750 at the earliest, there was no disposition
to 'pry into the state of society'. 'It was beyond the range of

---

[1] Consult L. C. Hartley, *William Cowper, Humanitarian*; Mary G. Jones, *The
Charity School Movement*; Betsy Rodgers, *Cloak of Charity: Studies in Eighteenth
Century Philanthropy*; V. W. Crane, *The Southern Frontier* (Durham, North Carolina,
1928), chap. xiii; A. Ruth Fry, ed., *John Bellers, 1654–1725*.

their mentality to conceive that the poor were poor because Society was an ill-regulated machine.'[1] Bellers and Firmin did, indeed, advocate constructive social projects for the employment of the poor in experimental 'colleges of industry', and thus won a niche for themselves as dim precursors of Owenite socialism. Mid-century is a dividing point beyond which the mind would move towards new concepts of economic science and social determinism. But this, the time of David Hartley and David Hume, is the earliest we can date the origins of a really systematic approach to economic science and to social amelioration. In general, to the eighteenth century humanitarianism means charity, not social engineering.

There was little enough of that, assumed in theory to be the duty of all Christians. The charity-school movement was the finest fruit of early-century humanitarianism: 'the glory of the age we live in', Addison called it in 1712. But after 1723 it deteriorated sadly, until these schools, in most of England, became scandalous, the prototypes of Dickens's Dotheboys Hall. Mandeville did not exaggerate much when he called them just a fashion of the hour.[2] The zeal of the little group that established them was not enough to sustain them against public indifference and political hostility. To the Whigs they were a Tory project, suspected of teaching Jacobitism. But for the reasons why Whigs neglected them (quite often turning them, after 1723, into workhouses) we must turn to the prevailing social philosophy: 'The conviction that the education of the poor was economically unsound and socially destructive was well entrenched.'[3] Would it not unfit them for their role as manual labourers? There was an equivocation in the middle-class philosophy: the theory that the workers may rise by their own efforts

---

[1] M. G. Jones, op. cit., p. 8.

[2] Mandeville's *Essay on Charity and Charity Schools* (1725) is included in *The Fable of the Bees*—see F. B. Kaye's standard edition.

[3] M. G. Jones, op. cit., p. 13. We owe to A. D. Lindsay (*The Modern Democratic State*, New York and London, 1947, i. 135) the observation that as late as 1822 an English clergyman opposed educating the lower classes as 'dangerous to the public peace', while Merle Curti in his *The Social Ideas of American Educators* (New York, 1935) recounts a similar opposition, based on fear of spoiling the workers for their lowly tasks.

clashed with the conviction that each class ought to keep its place, and the latter was stronger. The real desire of the middle class was for a working class that would be industrious and sober but well disciplined and tractable. Constant complaints about the 'idleness and stubbornness of the poor' appear from 1680 on: they will not work steadily, 'and when they do work they will often mar what they do'.[1] The charity schools were used only to inculcate religious lessons which were economically useful: not to steal from your master, to make dutiful servants, to waste no time at work. This was the only kind of education wealthy people would invest in; and after 1723 even this was neglected. The 'blackguard boys', armies of homeless, lawless, degenerate children, roamed the country. The remedy for them was thought to be the workhouse.

The idea of catechistical instruction in the charity schools had not been favoured by the noblest minds of the earlier period—Bellers, Firmin, and John Locke. They had favoured work projects, where relief might be combined with practical education.[2] It is doubtful if these worthy men would have approved the workhouses as they existed after 1723, becoming as these did in time 'a symbol of dread and despair', classically delineated in Crabbe's *The Village*. Their great merit was that they reduced the rates and drove the poor to work. Philanthropy, on the dominant middle-class view, had nothing to do with the giving of alms. ('Giving Alms No Charity' was the title of a Defoe tract.) Philanthropy consisted in lowering wages. For this would increase commerce and industry, which in turn would provide work for the poor. Defoe, the typical burgher, holds that the only cause of unemployment is the laziness of the poor and the profitableness of begging. He is against workhouses where the poor would be put to work making things, because of the competition with private industry. The right remedy for idleness, he suggests, would be forced-labour battalions for all vagabonds.[3] Possibly respectable Christian employers

[1] Dorothy Marshall, *The English Poor in the Eighteenth Century*, p. 8.

[2] Charles Povey, *The Present State of Great Britain*, presents the case for such 'hospitals of industry'.

[3] Defoe, *Everybody's Business is Nobody's Business*, 1725. This tract as well as *Giving Alms No Charity* is in his *Works*, edited by John S. Keltie.

did not openly subscribe to Bernard Mandeville's cynical
view that the poor must be kept poor, otherwise there would
be no one to do the dirty work. But they did feel that the
poor must be kept poor so that they would be industrious,
and would work for low wages (punitive workhouses keeping
them from the recourse of idleness), so that trade and
industry might prosper. They believed that in augmenting
his own fortune with the aid of these low wages a rich
employer is 'increasing the riches and power of his country
and giving bread to thousands of his industrious country-
men'.[1] It would seem that Mandeville's 'private vices equal
public benefits' had won the field; and it soon received, at
least partly, the sanction of Adam Smith.

Christian stewardship had manifestly assumed paradoxical
forms, if it still existed. The greatest Christians continued
to set an example of charity. Butler and Law gave freely of
what they had; Cowper lived up to his maxim, 'If you
abound, impart.' John Wesley endowed stewardship with
meaning, for the Methodists, if their message was in some
respects the typically middle-class one of 'work and earn',
insisted that the rich must give freely, and enjoined secrecy
to avoid the Mandeville accusation that charity was really
selfish. Certainly the Christian spirit produced some attention to social evils. 'In sermon after sermon preachers painted
the terrible punishments which awaited the uncharitable
in the after-world.'[2] However, this view of social evil was
sharply limited. It was limited, first, by its own philosophical
belief that evils are of divine decree, inherent in an order of
things beyond human control or questioning:

> Let poverty or want be what it will,
> It does proceed from God; therefore's no ill.

Therefore there was no thought of social changes, but only
of what mitigation private benevolence might provide.
More serious than this, the new wealthy had come to hold
with Defoe that real charity was not the giving of alms;
it was evidently the indulging of their own greed, with the

---

[1] John Moore, *A View of Society and Manners in Italy* (1790 edition), i. 327-8.
[2] Rodgers, op. cit., p. 7.

comfortable thought that the more they made the better off
the poor were.

In order to influence them towards reform it became
necessary to appeal to their self-interest. 'If compassion
cannot move you', William Sharp pleaded in 1755, 'let consideration of interest prevail with you.' Bishop Berkeley, in
The Querist, makes his appeal to the intelligent interest of
the upper classes, in a series notable for trying to think out
a national economic programme for depressed Ireland. But
the dominant classes did not see their self-interest as lying
in such things as education, penal reform, or projects for
the unemployed. Betsy Rodgers points out that such middle-
class philanthropists as there were usually had 'little sympathy for the objects of their charity'. If they built hospitals
it was because they feared under-population (high wages);
if they made the prisons cleaner they also made them less
cheerful. Captain Thomas Coram and Jonas Hanway,
founders of hospitals for prostitutes and foundlings, had to
overcome severe prejudice and endure the criticism that
paupers would not try to improve themselves if they had
'such a commodious access to ease and relief'. Yet some such
projects did succeed; and after 1760 the philanthropic movement regained momentum.

The notable late-century movement of social consciousness was created by religious philanthropists, among them
Wilberforce, Granville Sharp, Clarkson, Howard, and
Miss More. This was mainly a conservative Church of
England group, though with a persistent Quaker influence.
In contrast with this religious philanthropy we should note
the cult of benevolence. The pleasures of charity were 'the
most lasting, valuable and exquisite'[1] of all. This effort to
apply Shaftesbury's ethic of virtue as its own reward de-
served, it is to be feared, the sneers of Mandeville, for it
does not appear to have produced any zealots of philanthropy
or reform, and was more apt to be a fashionable pose.
Zeal, indeed, was the enemy of enemies to the neo-classic
gentlemanly code Shaftesbury was so closely related to. A
'virtuoso' of reform would have committed the unpardonable

---

[1] See *Gentleman's Magazine*, August 1732, 'Benevolence'; Robert Eden, *The
Harmony of Benevolence*.

sin of enthusiasm. Bishop Gibson was afraid of being thought enthusiastic because he ventured to attack immorality at the Court!

2

The religious liberals, for their part, were scarcely reformers. That numerous evils existed, ripe for the reformer, need not be argued at length. The condition of the poor was 'nasty and scandalous', Henry Fielding conceded.[1] The eighteenth-century historian of the poor laws gives a picture of callousness and cruelty by the workhouse overseers, chiefly concerned to reduce the rates.[2] There was the harsh penal code, with its death sentence for even petty robbery. The pressing of sailors was defended by so 'liberal' a Whig as John Tutchin.[3] As is well known, the Asiento treaty of 1723 gave England's merchants a lucrative stake in the slave trade; except for some Quakers and a poet, no one protested against the slave trade until after 1770. In brief, English society was afflicted with all those evils that were later to challenge the energies of the evangelical humanitarians and the utilitarian reformers. It is obvious enough that 'much still untouched remained'. How far did those who were radicals in theology partake of radicalism in social, economic, and political reform? The answer would seem to be, scarcely at all.

At least it is hard to find evidence of that 'tremendous interest of most of the deists in the public good' quite commonly alleged.[4] The English deists were neither reformers nor democrats. There is little social significance to be drawn immediately from their writings and activities. 'Drawn from virtually every scale of society . . ., virtually unknown to each other',[5] they formed no such cohesive society as did the French *philosophes*, nor did they ever have such definite social and political goals. Their numbers included aristocratic dilettanti like Shaftesbury and Bolingbroke; university

[1] Fielding, op. cit., pp. 48 ff. An outstanding brief description of the age's social evils may be found in W. C. Sydney, *England and the English in the Eighteenth Century*, ii. 192–5.

[2] Richard Burn, *History of the Poor Laws*, 1764.

[3] *Observator*, iii, no. 85 (7 Feb. 1705).

[4] A. C. McGiffert, *Protestant Thought before Kant*, p. 229.

[5] Mossner, *Butler*, p. 45.

men such as Tindal, Woolston, and Middleton; scribblers
on the make, the Tolands and Morgans; self-taught amateur theologians like Annet and Chubb, the latter being
a journeyman glovemaker by trade. What seems true of
all is a lack of interest in practical projects of reform.
Thomas Firmin, the unitarian philanthropist, is the
exception.

Perhaps this does the deists an injustice. In a period that
produced few new political or social ideas, Bolingbroke,
Shaftesbury, Mandeville, and Toland all have a certain social
significance, though it is not in a single direction. But
between religious radicalism and socio-political radicalism
there is no necessary connexion. Americans are familiar
with the fact that Washington, Hamilton, and John Adams,
as well as Paine and Jefferson, were (roughly) religious
deists. The leading 'free-thinker' of the nineteenth century
in the United States, Robert Ingersoll, was conservative
enough in his political views. The social and political inferences from deism were most ambiguous. To give only the
most obvious example, the two most persistent ethical ideas
in deistic thought were the contradictory ones that man is
selfish and needs to be tricked by his rulers (Mandeville,
leading to Alexander Hamilton) and that man is benevolent
(Shaftesbury, leading to Thomas Jefferson).[1] Again, the
Newtonian, deistic assumption of 'the harmonious order of
nature' might mean almost anything: a drive to do away with
injustices, or the worst sort of *laissez-faire* complacency.
The contradictory impulses here are nowhere better shown
than in Adam Smith; whether to assume benevolence or
self-love, whether to play the reformer or the apologist for
economic egoism—this unresolved dilemma is responsible
for the ambiguities in the great economist, which make him
still a controversial figure.

Doubtless deism had a certain implicit democratic content.
First of all, the deists always fought the battle for free speech
and for toleration, though they might well draw the line at

---

[1] It is true that Jefferson was the more typical deist. Such works as Adrienne
Koch, *The Philosophy of Thomas Jefferson* and D. J. Boorstin, *The Lost World of
Thomas Jefferson* indicate the influence on Jefferson of English deistic thought
(e.g. Shaftesbury's), much of which came through Joseph Priestley.

free speech for Jacobites and toleration for Roman Catholics. Charles Blount, the early deist, led the battle against the Licensing Act, 1679–93; Anthony Collins's plea for freedom of thought was famous, and all heterodox religious thinkers naturally desired freedom for their own views. Toland expressed an advanced and sincere idea of liberty of opinion, though he excluded Roman Catholicism from his range of toleration.

Then too, the philosophy of deism assumed what Professor Lovejoy has called 'intellectual equalitarianism'. Chubb would say that 'Christians stand to each other in the relation of brethren only, and not in relations of master and servant'. 'The gospel which Christ preached to the poor . . . was plain and intelligible, and level to the lowest understanding.'[1] 'Christianity Suited to Plain Men' had been the title of a section in Locke's *Reasonableness of Christianity*, where he declared that 'these are articles that the labouring and illiterate man may comprehend'. No priests are needed; all men have sufficient understanding to know the truth— here was deism's very creed. True or not, it had obvious democratic aspects.

But, with characteristic inconsistency, deism was also marked by a certain intellectual snobbishness. The same Chubb wrote that he expected his writings to appeal only to 'the more intelligent part of our species, who are not interested in popular opinion'.[2] Bolingbroke spoke of the 'rabble' as 'a monstrous beast' which 'has passions to be moved, but no reason to be appealed to'.[3] With Hume and Middleton, as has been noted, faith in the common understanding of men is abandoned completely—the masses need 'superstition', and 'philosophic' religion is only for the few.

Voltaire and Diderot had this contempt for the *canaille*, which did not prevent them from being tremendously significant as reformers and inciters to social change. One must not forget that the socially more militant French and

---

[1] Chubb, *True Gospel*, pp. 11, 49, 62–63. Also Toland, *Christianity Not Mysterious*, pp. xix, 141.

[2] Chubb, *Posthumous Works*, i. 63–65.

[3] Letter to Swift, 10 July 1721; see the latter's *Correspondence*, ed. F. E. Ball.

American deists went to school to the English.[1] The reason why the English deists were far less dynamic may be found partly in the difference between France and England. The French *philosophes* were bourgeois, but they struggled against religious intolerance, legal inequality, a privileged and snobbish aristocracy, and obsolete economic practices. In England such feudal objects of middle-class hostility existed to a far lesser degree. The 'harmonious order of nature' meant to Voltaire and his fellows a struggle against an obviously 'unnatural' régime; to Tindal, Toland, and theirs it meant more nearly just the régime that existed, the Whig England which, indeed, Voltaire himself thought ideal.

John Toland concerned himself with political matters more than any other English deist save Bolingbroke. Toland had an excellent education, and a very high opinion of his own talents.[2] Locke and Leibniz, who were his friends, thought him opinionated, conceited, and probably superficial. His integrity is beyond question: Harley was his patron, but he withdrew from that statesman when he turned Tory. Toland liked to think of himself as independent of parties, and could well claim to be no sycophant, despite his poverty and need for attachments. Yet he was committed wholly to the Whigs, and never went beyond Whig orthodoxy. His *sine qua non* principles were religious toleration, the Protestant succession, and civil liberty. Editor of the works of Harrington and Sydney, author of a life of Milton, he denied that he was an extreme republican, or that he agreed with what he called the 'democratical schemes of government' of Milton and Harrington. Believing in the classical 'mixed' system, he regarded the nobility as a natural pillar of society; and, as he said, all true 'republicans' admired, 'almost to adoration', the Hanoverian settlement. He was perfectly satisfied with Hanoverian, Whig England, praising it as 'the most free and best constituted in all the

---

[1] Torrey, *Voltaire and the English Deists*, carefully demonstrates Voltaire's debt to the English.

[2] Anna Seeber, *John Toland als politischer Schriftsteller*, is an excellent source; see also F. H. Heinemann, 'John Toland and the Age of Reason', in *Archiv für Philosophie*, Sept. 1950. Our analysis of Toland is based on a number of his political pamphlets; see bibliography for titles.

world'. He did not attack the Established Church, but agreed with Warburton that 'some public and orderly way of worshipping God, under the allowance, endowment and inspection of the civil magistrate' is necessary to a State. Toland the deist assumed that it belongs to the nature of man to have a religion; therefore it belongs to the nature of a State to have some common religion.[1] He would, however, grant full toleration, within Protestantism—like all deists he was violently anti-Catholic. He does indeed approach a theory of pure religious freedom. Like Pope, he argues that a variety of religious opinions is as natural as a variety of tastes, and is not an evil. The advanced element in his views on tolerance is his argument that there is no final and fixed religious truth, but a constant progress, analogous to the situation in science. His exclusion of Catholics is based on their alleged political subversiveness.

Toland's opinions on free speech, civil liberty, and religious toleration indicate deism's contribution to these causes. However, the deists were far from alone in favouring such things. This was a normal Whig outlook. Toland, enthusiastic but somewhat complacent Whig, self-styled 'fighter for the truth and assertor of liberty' (his self-composed epitaph), hardly original in any opinion but persistent and even courageous in the Whig faith, may perhaps stand as a typical specimen. He indicted the 'spirit of bigotry and persecution', insisted that a government need not have but one religion (though it should have a public church), and castigated the Tories as despots and Papists in disguise. But he never got beyond these ordinary Whig principles. In some of his pamphlets written around 1700 he did show an awareness of the inadequacies of the 1688 Revolution, noting the need for parliamentary reform.[2] But after the Hanoverians came he had no complaints. Disliked for his religious views, he would scarcely have warranted any special comment on account of his political ones, and seems to have had no socio-economic ones beyond a Whiggish enthusiasm for commerce. He was a rather typical Whig.

---

[1] See also Bolingbroke's approval of a state church, *Works*, iii. 485 ff.

[2] *The Danger of Mercenary Parliaments*, 1700, and *The Art of Governing by Parties*, 1701.

It was generally assumed, at least by Tories, that 'free-thinkers' were Whigs, and Tory propaganda liked to associate Whigs and atheists, in which there was of course no truth.[1] The great majority of Whigs repudiated deism, and welcomed the support of the Tindals and Tolands about as much as a modern New Dealer or Socialist welcomes the support of Communists. Walpole Whiggism and deism came closest together, perhaps, in the crude but gusty writings of Thomas Gordon, the popular 'Independent Whig'. Intemperate attacks on the clergy and on the Tories were blended with a cool Erastianism and a crude deism.[2] But Gordon soon proved to be an embarrassment to the Whigs.

However, not all deists were Whigs. Bolingbroke and Hume, the neo-Tories, discovered that their emancipation from religious orthodoxy did not necessarily mean devotion to Robert Walpole or the Duke of Newcastle. One could easily take the conservative side—the side, as Hume put it, that leaned more to authority than to liberty—without taking the devout position. One could, and can—to put it simply enough—believe in Christianity and be a liberal, or a radical, and one can reject religion without rejecting a variety of views on political and social questions which are ordinarily thought of as highly conservative. There had been a strong tendency for Tories to believe in strictly orthodox Christianity because they had identified this with a secure (divine right) monarchy. But that tendency waned as politics drew apart from religion. (Very pious people in the Dissenting tradition had always been Whigs.) It may be noted, and has been, that the sceptic is very apt to be a Tory. Basil Willey has commented on the 'cosmic toryism' of those who held with Pope that 'whatever is, is right'. Hume's scepticism leads to the mood of relying on custom because of a mistrust of reason. Hume, Middleton, and Bolingbroke doubted

---

[1] Swift, commenting on the appearance of Shaftesbury's *Characteristics*, called it 'free Whiggish thinking' (*Correspondence*, i. 111). See also his attack on Collins.

[2] 'He that can read, and has a common portion of reason', Gordon thought, 'may find such plain and easy directions in the New Testament, as will instruct him how to find the ready way to Heaven; by which he will avoid the tedious ambiguities of a mercenary guide.' *Independent Whig*, ii. 374. Yet there ought to be a church, and bishops—'I will not presume to determine, whether . . . by a divine or human institution.' Ibid., p. 415.

human wisdom, in the mass, too much to believe very readily in the progress of human society.

If the attack on such evils as the slave trade and noisome jails came mainly from Anglicans and Quakers, the impulse to political reform and democracy came, after about 1770, mainly from the left wing of Dissent—from the group that included Priestley, Cartwright, Jebb, and Price.[1] Unitarians, apostles of a Pelagianized Christianity, they were not deists strictly speaking, but held, as Priestley was to warn Paine, that it is as dangerous to believe too little as it is to believe too much; nevertheless they were too heterodox to be admitted as Christians by the orthodox. By their time, deism in England was, as such, dead, but some of its elements surely lived on in the drastic Nonconformity of the Priestley group. Deism had never struck any deep roots, had always been disreputable, and had, without establishing any valid philosophy, lived chiefly on sensationalism, which soon lost its appeal. In a society as prosperous and secure as that of England in this period, it was not easy to maintain even a scandalous notoriety very long by making faces at the gods. The gods were too plainly smiling on England (propertied England, at least) to merit such ingratitude.

Deism had not supplemented this religious iconoclasm with any clear, constructive, social or political ideology. It was a middle-class ideology which did not even appeal to the middle class, wherein lies the secret of its failure. Respectable opinion of the deists was always that expressed by a magazine at the height of the movement in 1733: 'a set of men who, from no better motive than vanity, or malicious wickedness, are labouring to subvert society'.[2] The diagnosis was excellent, except that the deists were not really labouring to subvert society, for they had no political or social programme to offer. It is quite true that their radicalism was capricious and based chiefly on personal vanity.

English deism struck fire in France and America, where it was assimilated to social radicalism under different

---

[1] See R. V. Holt, op. cit., chap. iii; Anthony Lincoln, *Some Political and Social Ideas of English Dissent, 1763–1800*. John Jebb was a liberal, unitarian Anglican; nor did Major Cartwright have a nonconformist background.

[2] *Weekly Miscellany*, 1 Dec. 1733.

conditions. Such radicalism, it appears, had no opportunity in England—where the middle classes, unlike the French, were content, and where the lower classes, unlike the American, had not yet approached the threshold of power.

The unitarians who from 1768 on exerted a democratic force in England were, as we said, perhaps deistic in the widest sense. Christianity had become worldly; the pursuit of happiness in this world had become its theme. A long review of one of James Foster's books in 1749 noted that if men were 'cautious and prudent, diligent and industrious', they would be 'crowned with prosperity'.[1] Such a faith was most acceptable to the complacent *bourgeoisie*. But this mild, worldly religion, which served so well for a prosperous burgher, also suited those who wished secular reforms in society. The 'dying Christian', in Priestley's case, made way for the energetic reformer. Many new things might emerge once religion had been reduced to a 'compartment', to mere vague morality. The real point of departure towards the modern idea of secular progress would appear to be the exclusion of Christian ideas from society. Christianity as increasingly 'Arminianized' was a moral code increasingly indistinguishable from secular behaviour. Christianity was absorbed by, dissolved into, secularism when it ceased to represent anything more than 'prudence'. No longer influencing culture as an independent force, it was in this sense 'compartmentalized'. A secularized and compartmentalized Christianity might be adopted by secular profit-seekers or secular reformers; it no longer had a will of its own.

In America we observe such a figure as Jonathan Mayhew, who was to some orthodox clergymen 'no better a Christian than a Turk', but who certainly considered himself a Christian. His energies were however directed entirely towards secular goals: political freedom, full civil liberties.[2] If Priestley and Mayhew and Cartwright were not deists, they devoted themselves to goals no deist could disapprove: the happiness and freedom of men on earth. But they were beginning to add some positive social ideas to deism's negativism.

---

[1] *Monthly Review*, i. 368.
[2] See *A Discourse concerning Unlimited Submission*, 1750, and other writings by Mayhew.

The critical moment in the emergence of a positive spirit of reform undoubtedly came later than the deists' heyday, and consisted in the awareness of evil as being social and remediable. It begins about 1750. The religious people who carried it forward most notably were those left-wing Dissenters who began to call themselves unitarians. By the end of the century the identification of unitarian with democrat had become a natural one. The young Coleridge heard it said of himself that 'In religion he is a Unitarian, if not a Deist; in politics a Democrat, to the utmost extent of the word'.[1] But who were the young Coleridge's idols? Hartley, Priestley, and William Godwin. He had, we surmise, scarcely heard of Toland and Tindal, Collins and Chubb. No doubt their mistake had been in not tying their religious radicalism to a political credo equally advanced and energetic. The early deists should have realized that, if Christianity was fading, the centre of importance would shift from religion to secular faiths.

The failure of deism also profited the Methodists. They alone reached the working classes. For their pains they were denounced in the most immoderate language, as anarchists, enthusiasts, fanatics, revolutionaries. In this denunciation 'liberals' of all sorts joined. Charles Chauncy and Samuel Johnson in America, William Warburton and Conyers Middleton in England, showed sufficiently that all middle-class liberals, whether deist or Arminian, shared a distrust of the mob when stirred by a Whitefield, that 'Jack Cade in a cassock'. In America, it is true, the Great Awakening had some rather striking social, economic, and political aspects.[2]

---

[1] Quoted in E. K. Chambers, *Samuel Taylor Coleridge* (Oxford, 1938), p. 29. On the growth of democratic ideas among the 'rational Dissenters' (who were unitarian in theology but did not admit to deism) see Anthony Lincoln, op. cit.— a thoughtful and scholarly work. The American Revolution was a turning-point in the emergence of an outspoken political radicalism within Dissent (though by no means embracing the majority of Dissenters).

[2] John C. Miller's article on 'Religion, Finance, and Democracy in New England' in vol. vi of the *New England Quarterly*, and Oscar Zeichner's *Connecticut's Years of Controversy, 1750–76*, bring out class lines as between the aristocratic Old Lights and the lower-class New Lights, the religious quarrel often blending into the economic and political. See also the excellent social analysis in Wesley M. Gewehr, *The Great Awakening in Virginia, 1740–90*.

Wesley, however, was very far from being a social or political radical, and certainly never went farther than the idea of making the poor sober and industrious so that they might raise themselves by self-help. In the long run, he doubtless aided capitalism, by disciplining the poor and spreading the gospel of thrift and steady habits. But the democratic ingredients contained in his genuine love and concern for all of God's children, regardless of class, rendered him suspect as a bloody-handed revolutionary. Wesleyanism made it obvious that English free thought had never reached, and never even tried to reach, the lower classes. It was as far beyond the wishes of Bolingbroke or Shaftesbury to do so as it was beyond the talents of Chubb or Annet.[1]

Militant deism, doubtless, did have a certain social role to play—in the French Revolution, with its Jacobin Supreme Being, and at about the same time in America, with the activity of Tom Paine and Elihu Palmer.[2] In a somewhat extraordinary example of a nation influenced by its own ideas as reflected back through foreign sources—an example which is a tribute to the impotence of the earlier English deists—Voltaire and Paine began to reach the English working classes, in some degree, about 1796. These prophets of French and American liberalism had absorbed deistic ideas from the English deists, but not until they had related them to a social and political ideology did the English masses hear about them. This popular deism was not very important. Paine was effective through *The Rights of Man*, not *The Age of Reason*; if this extreme deist was to become the very 'centre and life' of the 'radical' political movement of the 1790's, it was not because he attacked religion, but because he spoke out against political corruption and inequality.[3] This English radicalism paid relatively little attention to religion. Who

---

[1] Bolingbroke, *Works*, iii. 55; Aldridge, *Shaftesbury*, p. 367; both these citations refer to passages in which these free-thinkers dwell on the desirability of keeping free-thought out of the hearing of the 'vulgar', lest it excite them to discontent.

[2] G. A. Koch has told, sympathetically enough, the story of the effort to make deism into a popular republican cult in the United States, and the failure of that movement, in *Republican Religion*. John Morley's brilliant essay on 'Robespierre', in *Biographical Studies* (London, 1923), contains a more severe indictment of the French deistic cult.

[3] Walter P. Hall, *British Radicalism, 1791–1797*, pp. 85–95.

could still believe that 'priests' were the chief enemies of man?

What was significant was the reduction of religion to an adjunct of politics, by men of both camps, the conservative and the liberal. Clearly Edmund Burke was a Christian because he was a conservative in politics—because, that is, he saw in the Church a useful tool of political conservatism and because the French radicals were inclined to deism.[1] In like manner Paine, it would appear, was an anti-Christian chiefly because he associated that faith with the aristocracy he hated. Of this degradation of religion we have already spoken. It was, perhaps, the inevitable consequence of a period when religion and politics, while in fact separating, were still linked in men's minds as the Hippocrates' twins of Clarendon; when new economic and social forces were creating new conflicts and struggles which had nothing to do with theologies, but still bore their imprint.

[1] H. G. Schenk, *The Aftermath of the Napoleonic Wars* (London, 1947), chap. i, pp. 5 ff. especially, discusses Burke's religion and the whole ideological basis of the period's return to religion, for political reasons, as a buttress against the forces of change unleashed by the French Revolution. These conservatives felt, as it has been said of Gentz, more strongly about the value of religion than about religion itself.

XII

CONCLUSION

The thing we call heretic has one very good side. It means a person who has at least wished to see with his own eyes. The question is only whether the eyes were good. LESSING

The Unitarian Church forgets that men are poets. EMERSON

IT is not easy to summarize the results and the significance of the eighteenth-century religious debate. On the simplest view, the Christian religion had been vindicated, reason had triumphed, and deism had been beaten off with its own weapons. It was assumed that Butler and others had answered every deist argument. In 1744 John Jackson, Samuel Clarke's old lieutenant, thought that Christianity had profited from the attacks of deists and emerged stronger than ever.[1] It was assumed that Hume's scandalous essay on the impossibility of miracles stood refuted.[2] In 1820, in Boston, Francis Wrangham edited *The Pleiad*, a reprinting of the outstanding eighteenth-century anti-deist tracts, in the firm belief that these immortal writings had dealt the *coup de grâce* to infidelity for all time.

It was not for another century that Christianity was forced to yield its stronghold on what Gladstone called the 'impregnable rock' of attested evidence. In 1865 a leading Anglican divine still argued that religion rested squarely on Scriptural revelation, attested divine by miracle and prophecy.[3] Deism had started a great critical movement, but it lacked the tools to finish the job. 'Though silenced, it was not answered', a distinguished contemporary theologian has said of deism, 'and though dead, it yet speaketh.'[4] But the opinion prevailed that it had been answered, and the discrediting of Scripture as immediately inspired had to await a later scholarly movement. Before the time of the higher

---

[1] *An Address to Deists*, pp. 159–60.
[2] Noted by A. C. McGiffert, *Protestant Thought before Kant*, pp. 219–21.
[3] See A. L. Lilley, *Reason and Revelation*, p. 7.
[4] F. R. Tennant, *Miracle and Its Philosophic Presuppositions* (Cambridge, 1925), pp. 96–97.

criticism, popular free-thought in the deistic tradition never quite died out, but was a fairly negligible thing in the nineteenth century. Possibly it was true, as John Stuart Mill claimed in his *Autobiography*, that a large number of the 'brightest ornaments' secretly were sceptics or deists, fearing to be so publicly because of the social and political consequences that might ensue if the masses lost their faith.

Deism had certainly failed to prove its case, though it had shaken Christianity badly. The greatest virtue of the deists was undoubtedly that suggested by Lessing: they dared to think for themselves, to see with their own eyes. And though their eyes might have been poor, their insistence upon using them passed into the great and successful Western tradition of free inquiry as no negligible contribution.

Perhaps Emerson put his finger on their greatest fault. Certainly the psychological deficiencies of deism as a religion are obvious. But Lessing himself recognized the failure of the 'free-thinkers' even as thinkers. They had their own sort of bigotry—as Montesquieu recognized when he said that Voltaire had his own church. Berkeley's picture of the 'minute philosopher' hit near the mark of deistic pretentiousness. The deist committed all the sins of intellectual arrogance and narrowness; he seldom rose above the sneer; he revelled in what the sage Franklin called beating your mother to prove your manhood. He was willing to consign all the Hebraic-Christian past—more than two millennia of religious development—to the trash-heap; the world, it would seem, had been waiting for a Toland or a Chubb to bring it light! These faults sterilized deist thought. In part, it is true, they were the faults of an age wholly lacking a historical sense, but the deists were not able to rise above this blemish. When Turgot and Lessing found that Christianity had after all at least marked a stage in moral progress, strict deism was finished. The perspective of historical development was destined to supersede the infantile perspective of a priestly conspiracy. 'It is ill reasoning against religion', wrote Montesquieu, 'to compile a long list of the evils it has inflicted, without doing the same for the blessings it has bestowed.'[1] In general, this was the method of deism.

---

[1] See *Esprit des lois*, Bk. xxiv, chap. 2.

It aimed at tearing down Christianity by an unfair attack, and in place of it offered a pathetically inadequate and confused religion, a dogma—this is the worst we can say of the deists —more sterile and far less emotionally satisfying than traditional Christianity.

Although some assumed that Christianity had held fast with reason, the deist period also had much to do with the reaction against reason. 'Reason', a representative clergyman thought in 1781, 'has impertinently meddled with the Gospel, and that with such overbearing sedulity as to darken it more and more. . . .'[1] Dr. Johnson agreed that there had been too much impudent speculation on sacred matters. A certain crisis in civilization had been reached when 'an inquisitive and free-thinking age', as one orthodox writer called it, had come in sight of reasoning itself out of its religion, with David Hume going so far as to state flatly that one must now cease to inquire or cease to believe. Few accepted Hume's unpleasant alternative; but while they liked to pretend that belief had been sustained by inquiry, they exhibited also a certain desire to avoid further trials by reason. This was simply retrograde and reactionary. But it was related to a more constructive realization that reason is not all of religion. The despised Methodists did at length open the eyes of men to quite another way of religion. Oliver Goldsmith was one who thought that much could be learned from the Methodists; he was writing in 1759–60 that 'reason is but a weak antagonist when headlong passion dictates; in all such cases we should arm one passion against another . . .'.[2] Indeed, here speaks also the prudent man of the Enlightenment; but reason itself had led towards an awareness of the emotions.

The whole story of the drift towards romanticism is much too complex to discuss here. The deistic controversy had played its part in that process, indirectly. 'I had to deny knowledge to make room for faith', said Kant; and perhaps the strongest single ingredient in romanticism's revolt against the age of reason was this urgent desire to save the religious experience from the rationalist theologians and

---

[1] Joseph Milner, *Gibbon's Account of Christianity Considered*, &c., p. 154.
[2] See *The Bee*, no. 7 (17 Nov. 1759); *Works*, ed. Gibbs (1884), i. 271.

sceptics. But something of deism remained, if we think of that side of deism which sought for a broad, non-sectarian spirit in religion—the quest for that 'natural religion' which depended on no special theology. Romantic religion was an answer to deism, yet a retention of some portions of it, with a new emphasis. The emphasis shifted from head to heart, from universal reason to private intuition, from the rational proofs to the individual experience, but it was a similar quest the romantics carried on for a single, non-dogmatic faith. The pious mystic William Law had spoken of 'an instinct of goodness in the soul' common to all men. In 1776 Soame Jenyns argued that Christianity is not proved by the prophecies and miracles but by 'internal marks of divinity'. 'If one listened only to what God says to man's heart, there would never have been but one religion on earth.' The creed of the Savoyard Vicar, describable as romantic deism, was deeply significant for the great figures of the next epoch. Wordsworth and then the Transcendentalists held it. Pantheistic and mystical, the 'immanent' theology of a Schleiermacher would have shocked an eighteenth-century deist as much as an orthodox Christian.[1] But it had developed out of deism.

It is said that deism was overthrown by romantic subjectivism, wherein each man would have his own private religion, as sharply opposed to deism's insistence on a single rational standard.[2] But this view seems to overlook romanticism's tendency to believe that there was universal, objective truth, written in each heart to be sure but not wholly private; the individual being indeed the very basis of the universe, yet an intrinsic part of a greater organic structure. In any event the quest was similar to deism's in the rejection of formal theological creeds in favour of some simpler, immediate, and universal religion. Emil Brunner has pointed out that generally speaking the nineteenth century agreed with the eighteenth in holding all religion to be essentially one, a monistic view to which theology becomes irrelevant.[3]

[1] See Richard B. Brandt, *The Philosophy of Schleiermacher* (New York and London, 1948), pp. 307, &c.

[2] Lovejoy, *The Great Chain of Being*, pp. 288 ff., especially pp. 310–11.

[3] See his essay in Cavert and Van Dusen (eds.), *The Church Through Half a Century*.

The quest for the basic Christian 'spirit' beyond creeds continued. 'Ask me not, then, whether I am a Catholic or a Protestant, Calvinist or Arminian', John Adams wrote. 'As far as they are Christian, I wish to be a fellow-disciple with them all.'

This mood had grown up in the second half of the eighteenth century, when the evaporation of reason and the Bible as clear standards made for a tendency to feel that there is no such thing as heresy, that each man seeks God in his own way, that quibbling over theological details is bootless. In 1749 the exclusion of a unitarian by an Independent church occasioned an indignant exclamation by an English journal of by no means radical sentiments: 'To how great a height does the spirit, we dare not say Christian spirit, of these trifling zealots carry them! Even in this enlightened age!'[1] A few years later a foreign visitor, the Duc de la Rochefoucauld, thought that 'almost all the English have a different faith' and were quite undisturbed by this singular lack of doctrinal unity. This tolerance of mere theological differences represented a sort of triumph for deism. It undoubtedly rested on a good deal of indifference to all except a minimum of moral rectitude; it also represented a reaction against tedious, inconclusive wrangling among the clerics.

The reader may refer to our chapter on 'Arminianism' for remarks on the weakening of Christianity through the century; also to the sections on secularizing influences. As to the latter, politics, of course, continued to crowd out religion. We recall that in 1673 'divinity' was the commonest table-talk; it remained so in the rural areas, at least, for a long time after that. But in 1762, a century later, a visitor to England noted that when strangers struck up a conversation a political discussion was sure to follow.[2] If, as Leslie Stephen remarked, the first half of the century had been a period of political stagnation, the last half was quite otherwise. George III, Pitt, and Edmund Burke, not to speak of two revolutions abroad, made politics practically exciting

---

[1] *Monthly Review*, i. 456. See also Robert Clayton, *An Essay on Spirit*, dedication.
[2] Count Frederick Kielmansegge, *Diary of a Journey to England in the Years 1761–1762*, translated by Countess Kielmansegg (London, 1902), p. 255.

and theoretically interesting. Then the grand idea of progress, social reform, and 'perfectibility' struck the young intellectuals; and in the thought of so representative a radical
as Joseph Priestley religious reform is quite secondary to
this exciting vision of social utopia. The 'true Christianity'
purged of 'corruptions' which Priestley wrote of went with
perfectibility, practical science, political reform; its purpose
was to cast a kind of virtuous effusion over the dream of social
progress. The earlier deists had had few glimpses of this
vision. Still, they had been by and large optimistic, secular-
minded, concerned to elevate politics above religion.

The faults of a Pelagianized Christianity are obvious.
Having proclaimed its own victory over the deism it pro-
fessed to abhor, Christianity then so diluted itself that
Wesley exaggerated very little in describing it as deism in
disguise. A rational, liberal Christianity sacrificed the
'mysteries', the sense of sin, and contempt for material
things. It thereby lost most of its excuse for existence. The
crisis in Christianity at the end of the century has been
commonly enough recognized. Coleridge and Carlyle felt it
their mission to call England back to some sort of real
religion. The religious future lay with the evangelicals and
the Anglo-Catholics, to both of whom the eighteenth-century
clergy became a byword of reproach for a shocking lapse into
paganism and indifference.

All this lies far beyond our purview. But it is perhaps
relevant to conclude by mentioning some possible applica-
tions to the present. Today, amid a powerful reaction among
Christian theologians against religious 'liberalism', the status
of some ideas first strongly presented by the liberals of the
eighteenth century is worth noting.

The Bible as immediate and literal revelation has, of
course, fallen. The 'neo-orthodox' of our day share with the
liberals an awareness that the Bible is a human document.
(However, liberals of the later nineteenth century learned to
read it as poetry, as great inspirational literature, in a way
quite foreign to the deists.) The concept of revelation has
become a historic one: 'something that *happens*, the living
history of God in His dealings with the human race'.[1] The

[1] Emil Brunner, *Reason and Revelation*, p. 381.

Bible is a witness to this revelation; it is not *the* revelation.
The deists both won and lost here. The Bible is not defended
any more, by educated Christians, in the sense in which it
was fervently defended by the eighteenth-century orthodox;
it even seems most strange to us that intelligent men so
close in some ways to the modern epoch could have defended
it in that way. But neither, of course, is the Bible regarded
as the deists regarded it, as a fraud in so far as it pretended to
be anything unique—as (at best) simply one statement of a
general 'religion of nature'. Christians may hold that the
historical experience of the Hebrews is without parallel in its
religious significance, and in that view they would be supported by historical science and the opinion of most informed
men.

Modern Protestant theology is no longer, then, Bible-
centred; Chillingworth's famous dictum has become obsolete. An idea of the shift can be gained by noting that modern
defenders of the doctrine of the Trinity do not care at all
that the doctrine is not scriptural. How that would have
bewildered Dr. Clarke! The Trinity is defended on the
grounds simply that the Christian religious experience needs
this doctrine to be apprehended fully. Modern Protestant
Christianity has appealed to experience. So radical a revision
the eighteenth-century divines could not have faced; it has
been forced on moderns. To dispense with Scripture as
direct revelation, the former thought, was to yield all.
Courageously, Lessing in that century declared that 'the
Christian religion is not true because the evangelists and
apostles taught it, but they taught it because it is true'.
Today, Dean Inge can declare what seems obvious, that 'the
craving for signs and wonders is a weakness of religion'.
But it is still not clear that the older clergy were not right;
we may wonder whether a religion that cannot be literally
believed in can ever again command such unquestioning mass
allegiance as was once the case.

If historical investigation has destroyed the orthodox view
of the Bible, it has also, at points, discredited the deists.
The deistic interpretation of Christ is a case in point. The
ethical Jesus of religious liberalism, so vital to deism and
moralistic Christianity, does not seem to be historical, as

Albert Schweitzer, Johannes Weiss, and others have shown.
'Liberal ethical Christianity can be gleaned even from the
Sermon on the Mount only by selection.'[1] The 'eschato-
logical' or 'apocalyptic' Jesus emerges instead—hardly the
teacher of secular morality. So the test of truth was often
fatal to deism as well as to orthodoxy.

Doubtless each era sees what it desires to see in Christ.
Eighteenth-century deism was a part of the broader movement of liberalism within Christian culture which succeeded
in eliminating the prophetic, other-worldly element in Christianity and adapting religion to the purposes of optimistic
secularism. Today, and especially since 1914, 'recoil from
liberalism is the most important feature' of theology.[2] Quite
simply, the explanation lies in the collapse of secular progress as a tenable faith. But we can hardly avoid feeling that
in rejecting liberalism and turning to a radical critique of
secular optimism Christianity is moving closer to its original
and essential character. For Christ and his followers did not
come, in the beginning, to bring peace, but a sword; they
had no vision of earthly and worldly progress, but rather
a keen sense of the disintegration of such things for want of
deep spiritual insights. Neither the deists nor the Pelagians
properly understood the spirit of Christianity. A 'religion of
humanity' may be very well; it is a quite different thing, as
Comte recognized, from Christianity.

Perhaps the chief legacy of religious liberalism is faith in
reason. That is still in dispute. Reason is mistrusted extremely by the Barths and Brunners who have in our time
sought to cast out the old sins of an excessive, man-centred
liberalism vitiating the essential nature of Christianity. The
great religious revival which took place early in the nineteenth century revolted against the 'barren rationalism'
and 'narrow intellectualism' of the Enlightenment period
only to find itself eventually weakened by its own sort of
narrowness, in the guise of Biblical literalism, intellectual
narrowness, and inability to accommodate itself to new discoveries of the human intellect in science (and, we might
add, an aesthetic narrowness repellent to all humanistic

1 E. R. Goodenough, in *Review of Religion*, xii. 314.
2 Van Dusen, *The Church Through Half a Century*, p. 84.

studies).[1] The neo-orthodox revival of the twentieth century revolted against the meek submission of liberal Christianity to science and secularism, only, it may be, to fall once again in danger of glorifying the irrational. The new irrationalism is resisted by many Christians who find themselves wondering, quite as those Restoration and Augustan divines did, how a religion unsupported by reason can possibly stand.

'Reason' is a vague enough term. The theistic belief that God is rationally demonstrable, via such arguments as the teleological, succumbed to the blows of Hume and Kant, and may or may not be recoverable.[2] That religion is primarily intellectualistic—i.e. only a form of philosophy—few would any longer care to claim. But in the long run, surely, the rational theologians of the eighteenth century were right in this, their basic claim: that Christianity must not fear the test of untrammelled inquiry, or abandon reason as the touchstone of what is true and right. If it does, it is lost, at least until the dark ages return. The eighteenth-century Christians were wrong in thinking that the case for their religion was unassailable on the grounds of historical evidence, i.e. that the Bible was certainly a direct revelation. They lost, and the blow was a hard one. Christianity is still trying to recover. But it must still grapple with its fate with the weapons of reason, as opposed to authority, superstition, or 'enthusiasm'.

So perhaps we may properly conclude with a comment of Dr. Barrow's, quoted by the deist Bolingbroke: 'If we seriously weigh the case, we shall find that to require faith without reason is to demand an impossibility, and that God therefore neither doth nor can enjoin us faith without reason.'

[1] See McGiffert, *Protestant Thought before Kant*, quoted in J. H. Randall, *The Making of the Modern Mind*, pp. 408–9.

[2] See for example Edgar P. Dickie, *Revelation and Response*, p. 106; Charles Hartshorne, 'Two Levels of Faith and Reason', in *Journal of Bible and Religion*, xvi (Jan. 1948), p. 14. The whole of this issue is devoted to a symposium on the subject of religion and reason.

BIBLIOGRAPHY

I. PRIMARY SOURCES

A. *Personal Narratives, Correspondence, etc.*

BAXTER, RICHARD. *Reliquiae Baxterianae.* London, 1696. Published 1925 as *The Autobiography of Richard Baxter*, ed. by J. M. Lloyd Thomas. London: J. M. Dent & Sons, 1925.

BURNET, GILBERT. *History of My Own Time.* Edited by Osmund Airy. 2 vols. Oxford: Clarendon Press, 1897–1900.

CALAMY, EDMUND. *An Historical Account of My Own Life.* Edited by J. T. Rutt. 2 vols. London: Colburn & Bentley, 1829–30.

DODDRIDGE, PHILIP. *Correspondence and Diary.* Edited by J. D. Humphreys. 5 vols. London: Colburn & Bentley, 1829–31.

FRANKLIN, BENJAMIN. *Autobiography.* In *Representative Selections*, edited by F. L. Mott and C. E. Jorgenson. New York: American Book Co., 1936 (American Writers Series).

GIBBON, EDWARD. *Autobiography.* Everyman's Library, 1932.

HERVEY, JOHN (Lord). *Memoirs of the Reign of King George II.* Edited by R. Sedgwick. 3 vols. London: Eyre & Spottiswoode, 1931.

JOHNSON, SAMUEL. *Samuel Johnson, President of King's College; His Career and Writings.* Edited by H. W. and Carol Schneider. New York: Columbia University Press, 1929. (Vol. i contains his 'Memoirs' and personal correspondence.)

NICHOLS, JOHN (ed.). *Literary Anecdotes of the Eighteenth Century.* 9 vols. London: Nichols & Bentley, 1812–16.

—— *Illustrations of the Literary History of the Eighteenth Century.* 8 vols. London: Nichols & Bentley, 1817–58.

ORTON, JOB. *Letters to Dissenting Ministers and to Students for the Ministry.* Edited by S. Palmer. 2 vols. London, 1806.

—— *Letters to a Young Clergyman.* Boston, 1794.

PRIESTLEY, JOSEPH. *Memoirs.* 2 vols. Northumberland, Pa., 1806.

SWIFT, JONATHAN. *Correspondence.* Edited by F. E. Ball. 6 vols. London: G. Bell & Sons, 1910–14.

WESLEY, JOHN. *The Journal of the Reverend John Wesley.* Edited by N. Curnock. 8 vols. London: R. Culley, 1909–16.

WHISTON, WILLIAM. *Memoirs.* 3 vols. London, 1749–50.

WOODFORDE, JAMES. *Diary of a Country Parson.* Edited by J. Beresford. 5 vols. London: H. Milford, Oxford University Press, 1926–31.

WOOLMAN, JOHN. *The Journal, with Other Writings of John Woolman.* Everyman's Library, 1922.

B. *Writings: Tracts, Pamphlets, Sermons, etc.*

ABBADIE, JAMES. *A Sovereign Antidote against Arian Poison.* London, 1719.

ANNET, PETER. *Judging for Ourselves.* London, 1739.

—— *The Resurrection of Jesus, Considered . . . by a Moral Philosopher.* London, 1744.

—— *Critical Examination of the Life of St. Paul.* ('Translated from the French of Boulanger.') London, 1823.

ARSCOTT, ALEXANDER. *Some Considerations Relating to the Present State of the Christian Religion.* London, 1731. Reprinted in Philadelphia by Benjamin Franklin, 1732.

ATTERBURY, FRANCIS. *Miscellaneous Works.* Edited by J. Nichols. 5 vols. London, 1789–98.

—— *Sermons.* Edited by T. Moore. Vols. iii–iv. London, 1734.

BARON, RICHARD (ed.). *The Pillars of Priestcraft and Orthodoxy Shaken.* 4 vols. in 2. 2nd ed. London, 1768.

BAXTER, RICHARD. Chapters from *A Christian Directory.* Edited by Jeannette Tawney. London: G. Bell & Sons, 1925.

BELLERS, JOHN. *John Bellers, 1654–1725: Quaker, Economist, and Social Reformer.* Edited by A. Ruth Fry. (Bellers' writings, with a memoir.) London: Cassell & Co., 1935.

BENTLEY, RICHARD. *Remarks upon a Late Discourse of Freethinking.* 8th ed. Cambridge, 1743.

BERKELEY, GEORGE. *Works.* Edited by A. C. Fraser. 4 vols. Oxford: Clarendon Press, 1901.

—— *The Querist.* Dublin, 1752.

—— *A Discourse of Passive Obedience.* London, 1721.

—— *An Essay towards Preventing the Ruin of Great Britain.* London, 1721.

—— *A Discourse Addressed to Magistrates and Men in Authority.* Dublin, 1738.

BLOUNT, CHARLES. *The Oracles of Reason.* London, 1693.

—— *Miscellaneous Works.* London, 1695.

BOLINGBROKE, HENRY ST. JOHN (Viscount). *Works.* 4 vols. Philadelphia, 1841.

—— *A Collection of Political Tracts.* London, 1748.

Boyle Lectures. *A Defence of Natural and Revealed Religion.* Edited by J. Nichol and S. Letsome. 3 vols. London, 1739.

BRADBURY, THOMAS. *Fifty Four Sermons.* 3 vols. London, 1762.

BROWN, JOHN. *An Estimate of the Manners and Principles of the Times.* Dublin, 1757.

—— *Essays on the Characteristics.* London, 1751.

BURN, RICHARD. *History of the Poor Laws.* London, 1764.

BURNET, THOMAS. *The Theory of the Earth.* 2 vols. London, 1684–90.

BURY, ARTHUR. *The Naked Gospel.* London, 1690.

BUTLER, JOSEPH. *Works.* Edited by W. E. Gladstone. 2 vols. Oxford: Clarendon Press, 1897.

CALAMY, EDMUND. *Fourteen Sermons.* London, 1710.

—— *Thirteen Sermons Concerning the Doctrine of the Trinity.* London, 1721.

CHANDLER, SAMUEL. *Defence of Christianity from the Prophecies of the Old Testament.* London, 1725.

—— *A Vindication of the Christian Religion.* London, 1725.

CHEYNELL, FRANCIS. *Rise, Growth and Danger of Socinianism.* London, 1643.

CHILLINGWORTH, WILLIAM. *The Religion of Protestants a Safe Way to Salvation.* London, 1638.

CHUBB, THOMAS. *The True Gospel of Jesus Christ Asserted.* . . . London, 1738.

—— *Posthumous Works.* 2 vols. London, 1748.

CLARKE, SAMUEL. *Works.* 4 vols. London, 1738.

CLAYTON, JOHN. *Friendly Advice to the Poor.* London, 1755.

CLAYTON, ROBERT. *An Essay on Spirit.* London, 1751.

CLIFFORD, MARTIN. *A Treatise of Human Reason.* Printed in *The Phenix,* vol. 2, 1708.

Cobbett's State Trials. Edited by Thomas B. Howell. Vol. xv. London, 1809–26.

COLLINS, ANTHONY. *A Vindication of the Divine Attributes.* London, 1710.

—— *A Discourse of Freethinking.* London, 1713.

—— *A Dissertation on Liberty and Necessity.* London, 1729. (Published 1715 as *A Philosophic Inquiry Concerning Human Liberty.*)

—— *A Discourse of the Grounds and Reasons of the Christian Religion.* London, 1737.

—— *The Scheme of Literal Prophecy Considered* . . . London, 1727.

—— *A Discourse Concerning Ridicule and Irony in Writing.* London, 1729.

DAVENANT, CHARLES. *Essays on Peace at Home and War Abroad.* London, 1704.

DEFOE, DANIEL. *Works*. Edited by J. S. Keltie. Edinburgh: W. P. Nimmo, 1872.
—— *Life and Recently Discovered Writings*. Edited by William Lee. 3 vols. London: J. C. Hotten, 1869.
—— *The Shortest Way to Peace and Union*. London, 1703.
—— *The Complete English Tradesman*. London, 1738.
DODDRIDGE, PHILIP. *Works*. 10 vols. Leeds, 1802–5.
—— *Three Sermons, Stating Briefly the Evidences of Christianity*. Chambersburg, Pa., 1796.
DODWELL, HENRY, jr. *Christianity Not Founded on Argument*. London, 1743.
EDEN, ROBERT. *The Harmony of Benevolence*. London, 1760.
EDWARDS, JOHN. *The Arminian Doctrine Condemned by the Holy Scripture*. London, 1711.
EDWARDS, JONATHAN. *Works*. Vol. i. Worcester, Mass., 1858.
EMLYN, THOMAS. *A Full Inquiry into . . . I John V, 7*. London, 1715.
Faults on Both Sides. London, 1710.
FIELDING, HENRY. *An Enquiry into the Causes of the Late Increase of Robbers . . . .* London, 1751.
FLEETWOOD, WILLIAM. *Works*. 3 vols. Oxford: Oxford University Press, 1854.
FOWLER, EDWARD. *Principles and Practices of Certain Moderate Divines of the Church of England. . . .* London, 1670.
GILL, JOHN. *The Doctrine of Predestination Stated . . . in Opposition to Mr. Wesley's Predestination Calmly Considered*. London, 1752.
GOLDSMITH, OLIVER. *Works*. Edited by J. W. M. Gibbs. 5 vols. London: G. Bell & Sons, 1884–6.
GORDON, THOMAS. *The Trial of William Whiston*. London, 1739.
—— *The Independent Whig*. 4 vols. London, 1747.
—— *A Collection of Tracts by John Trenchard and Thomas Gordon*. 2 vols. London, 1751.
GOUGH, STRICKLAND. *Enquiry into the Causes of the Decay of the Dissenting Interest*. London, 1730.
HERBERT OF CHERBURY (Edward, Lord). *Lord Herbert of Cherbury's 'De Religione Laici'*. Edited by Harold R. Hutcheson. New Haven: Yale University Press, 1944.
—— *De Veritate*. Translated and edited by M. H. Carré. Bristol, 1937.
HOADLY, BENJAMIN. *Works*. 3 vols. London, 1773.
HUME, DAVID. *Essays and Treatises on Several Subjects*. 2 vols. Edinburgh, 1817.
—— *Essays, Moral, Political and Literary*. Edited by T. H. Green and T. H. Grose. 2 vols. London: Longmans, Green & Co., 1889.
HUSSEY, JOSEPH. *The Glory of Christ Unveiled*. London, 1706.
HYDE, EDWARD (Earl of Clarendon). *The History of the Rebellion and Civil Wars in England*. Edited by W. D. Macray. 6 vols. London, 1888.
JACKSON, JOHN. *A Reply to Dr. Waterland's Defence of His Queries*. London, 1722.
—— *A Defence of Human Liberty*. London, 1730.
—— *An Address to the Deists*. London, 1744.
JENKIN, ROBERT. *A Brief Confutation of the Pretences against Natural and Revealed Religion*. London, 1702.
—— *The Reasonableness and Certainty of the Christian Religion*. 2 vols. 6th ed. London, 1734.
JENYNS, SOAME. *A View of the Internal Evidences of the Christian Religion*. London, 1776.
Joint Committee of Both Houses of Convocation of the Province of Canterbury. *Representation of the Present State of Religion . . . .* London, 1711.
KING, JOSIAH. *Mr. Blount's Oracles of Reason Examined and Answered*. London, 1698.

LAW, WILLIAM. *Liberal and Mystical Writings.* Edited by W. S. Palmer. London: Longmans, Green & Co., 1908.

—— *Remarks on The Fable of the Bees.* Edited by F. D. Maurice. Cambridge: Cambridge University Press, 1844.

—— *A Short but Sufficient Confutation of the Rev. Dr. Warburton's Divine Legation of Moses.* London, 1757.

LELAND, JOHN. *A View of the Deistical Writers.* 2 vols. London, 1807.

—— *The Divine Authority of the Old and New Testament Asserted.* . . . 2 vols. London, 1739.

—— *Remarks on* . . . *'Christianity Not Founded on Argument'.* London, 1744.

LESLIE, CHARLES. *Theological Works.* 7 vols. Oxford: Oxford University Press, 1832.

LOCKE, JOHN. *An Essay Concerning Human Understanding.* Edited by A. C. Fraser. 2 vols. Oxford: Clarendon Press, 1894.

—— *Works.* 10 vols. London: Thomas Tegg, 1823.

LOWMAN, MOSES. *A Dissertation on the Civil Government of the Hebrews.* London, 1740.

MACKENZIE, ALEXANDER. *Characteristics of the Present State of Great Britain.* London, 1758.

MANDEVILLE, BERNARD. *The Fable of the Bees, or Private Vices Public Benefits.* Edited by Frederick B. Kaye. 2 vols. Oxford: Clarendon Press, 1924.

—— *A Letter to Dion.* London, 1732.

MATHER, COTTON. *The Christian Philosopher.* London, 1721.

MAYHEW, JONATHAN. *A Discourse Concerning Unlimited Submission* . . . . Boston, 1750.

MIDDLETON, CONYERS. *Miscellaneous Works.* 4 vols. London: R. Manby, 1752.

MILBOURNE, LUKE. *Mysteries in Religion Vindicated* . . . . London, 1692.

MILNER, JOSEPH. *Gibbon's Account of Christianity Considered, together with Some Strictures on Hume's Dialogue concerning Natural Religion.* London, 1781.

MORE, PAUL ELMER, and CROSS, F. L. (eds.). *Anglicanism; The Thought and Practice of the Church of England Illustrated from the Religious Literature of the Seventeenth Century.* Milwaukee: Morehouse Publishing Co., 1935.

MORGAN, THOMAS. *The Moral Philosopher.* 3 vols. London, 1738–40.

—— *A Collection of Tracts* . . . *Occasioned by the Trinitarian Controversy.* London, 1726.

—— *A Brief Examination of the Rev. Dr. Warburton's Divine Legation of Moses.* London, 1742.

NYE, STEPHEN. *A Brief History of the Unitarians, also called Socinians.* London, 1687.

—— (?) *Brief Notes on the Creed of St. Athanasius.* London, 1689.

—— (?) *Observations on Dr. Sherlock's Answer to the Brief History of the Unitarians.* London, 1691.

PAINE, THOMAS. *Representative Selections.* Edited by Harry W. Clarke. New York: American Book Co., 1944 (American Writers Series).

PALEY, WILLIAM. *Principles of Moral and Political Philosophy.* Vol. vi. London, 1785.

PENN, WILLIAM. *England's Present Interest Discovered.* London, 1675.

POVEY, CHARLES. *The Present State of Great Britain.* London, 1714.

POPE, ALEXANDER. *Works.* Edited by W. Elwin and W. J. Courthope. 10 vols. London: J. Murray, 1871–9.

PYKE, JOSEPH. *An Impartial View of the Principal Difficulties that affect the Trinitarian or clog the Arian Scheme.* London, 1721.

SAVILE, GEORGE (first Marquess of Halifax). *Complete Works.* Edited by Walter Raleigh. Oxford: Clarendon Press, 1912.

SHAFTESBURY, THIRD EARL OF (Anthony Ashley Cooper). *Characteristics of Men, Manners, Opinions.* Edited by J. M. Robertson. 2 vols. London: Grant Richards, 1900.

SHERLOCK, THOMAS. *Works*. Edited by T. S. Hughes. 5 vols. London, 1830.
SHERLOCK, WILLIAM. *A Vindication of the Holy and Ever-Blessed Trinity*. London, 1691.
—— *A Short Summary of the Principal Controversies between the Church of England and the Church of Rome*. London, 1687.
SIMON, FATHER RICHARD. *Critical History of the Old Testament*. London, 1682.
—— *Critical Inquiries into the Various Editions of the Bible*. London, 1684.
—— *A Critical History of the Text of the New Testament*. London, 1689.
SMALBROKE, RICHARD. *A Vindication of the Miracles of Our Blessed Saviour*. 2 vols. London, 1729–31.
SMITH, JOHN. *An Essay upon Universal Redemption*. London, 1701.
Somers Tracts. Vol. xiii. London, 1815.
SOUTH, ROBERT. *Sermons*. 2 vols. London: H. G. Bohn, 1870.
—— *Tritheism Charged upon Dr. Sherlock's New Notion of the Trinity*. London, 1695.
SQUIRE, FRANCIS. *An Answer to . . . The Independent Whig*. London, 1723.
STEELE, RICHARD (1629–92). *The Religious Tradesman*. Charlestown, Mass., 1804.
STEELE, SIR RICHARD (1672–1729). *Tracts and Pamphlets*. Edited by R. Blanchard. Baltimore: Johns Hopkins University Press, 1944.
SWIFT, JONATHAN. *Works*. 2 vols. London: H. G. Bohn, 1853.
SYKES, ARTHUR ASHLEY. *The External Peace of the Church*. London, 1716.
—— *Essay upon the Truth of the Christian Religion*. London, 1725.
SYNGE, EDWARD. *A Gentleman's Religion*. Oxford, 1800. First published 1710.
—— *The Authority of the Church in Matters of Religion*. London, 1718.
TAYLOR, ABRAHAM. *Lime Street Lectures*. American edition, as *The Insufficience of Natural Religion*. Boston, 1755.
TAYLOR, JOHN. *The Scripture-Doctrine of Original Sin*. . . . London, 1738.
TEMPLE, WILLIAM. *Observations upon the United Provinces of the Netherlands*. 5th ed. Amsterdam, 1696.
TINDAL, MATTHEW. *A Defence of the Rights of the Christian Church*. London, 1709.
—— *New High Church Turned Old Presbyterian*. London, 1709.
—— *The Nation Vindicated from the Aspersions Cast on It*. . . . London, 1711.
—— *Christianity as Old as the Creation; or, the Gospel a Republication of the Religion of Nature*. 2nd ed. London, 1732.
TOLAND, JOHN. *Christianity Not Mysterious*. London, 1702.
—— *Amyntor; or a Defence of Milton's Life*. London, 1699.
—— *Memorial of the State of England*. London, 1705.
—— *A Collection of Several Pieces*. 2 vols. London, 1726.
—— *Anglia Libera*. London, 1701.
—— *The Art of Governing by Parties*. London, 1701.
—— *The Danger of Mercenary Parliaments*. London, 1700.
—— *The Destiny of Rome*. London, 1718.
—— *The State-Anatomy of Great Britain*. London, 1717.
—— *Pantheisticon*. London, 1720.
—— (ed.). *The Oceana of James Harrington and His Other Works*. Dublin, 1737.
TRUSLER, JOHN. *The Way To Be Rich and Respectable*. London, 1750.
WARBURTON, WILLIAM. *The Alliance between Church and State*. London, 1736.
—— *The Divine Legation of Moses*. London, 1738.
WATERLAND, DANIEL. *A Vindication of Christ's Divinity, Being A Defence of Some Queries Relating to Dr. Clarke's Scheme of the Holy Trinity*. Cambridge and London, 1719.
—— *Scripture Vindicated, in Answer to . . . 'Christianity As Old As the Creation'*. London, 1731.
—— *A Critical History of the Athanasian Creed*. Cambridge, 1728.

WATSON, RICHARD (ed.). *A Collection of Theological Tracts.* 6 vols. Cambridge, 1785.
WATTS, ISAAC. *Works.* 6 vols. London, 1810–11.
WEBBER, FRANCIS. *The Jewish Dispensation Considered and Vindicated.* . . . London, 1738.
WESLEY, JOHN. *Works.* 14 vols. London: Mason, 1829–31.
WHISTON, WILLIAM. *Primitive Christianity Revived.* 4 vols. London, 1711.
—— *Athanasius Convicted of Forgery.* London, 1712.
—— *An Essay towards Restoring the Truth of the Old Testament.* London, 1722.
—— *A New Theory of the Earth.* London, 1696.
WHITBY, DANIEL. *Six Discourses.* Worcester, Mass., 1801.
—— *Last Thoughts.* London, 1728.
WHITE, JOHN. *Free and Impartial Considerations upon the Free and Candid Disquisitions relating to the Church of England.* London, 1751.
WHITEFIELD, GEORGE. *A Letter to the Rev. Mr. John Wesley* . . . . (1752).
WILBERFORCE, WILLIAM. *A Practical View of the Prevailing Religious System* . . . . 3rd ed. London: H. G. Bohn, 1854. First published 1797.
WOLLASTON, WILLIAM. *The Religion of Nature Delineated.* 7th ed. Glasgow, 1746.
WOODWARD, JOHN. *An Essay toward a Natural History of the Earth.* London, 1695.
WOOLSTON, THOMAS. *Free Gifts to the Clergy.* London, 1724.
—— *Discourses on the Miracles of Our Saviour.* London, 1729.
—— *Defence of His Discourses.* London, 1729.
—— *The Old Apology for . . . the Christian Religion . . . Revived.* Cambridge, 1705.
WORCESTER, SAMUEL. *A Letter to the Rev. William E. Channing.* Boston, 1815.
WRANGHAM, FRANCIS (ed.). *The Pleiad.* Boston, 1820.
YOUNG, ARTHUR. *Arthur Young on Industry and Economics.* Edited by Elizabeth P. Hunt. Bryn Mawr, Pa., 1926.

c. *Contemporary Periodicals*

Defoe's Review (Columbia University Press, published by Facsimile Text Society, 1938–9). 22 vols., 1704–13. (See also *Life*, ed. Lee, above, for other periodical writings by Defoe.)
Freethinker (London, 1739). 3 vols., 1718–19.
Gentleman's Magazine. 1731–50.
Grub Street Journal: James T. Hillhouse, *The Grub Street Journal.* Durham, N.C.: Duke University Press, 1928.
Independent Whig (London, 1747). 4 vols., 1720.
Monthly Review. 1749–50.
Observator. Vols. 2–3, 9–10, 1703–4, 1710–11.
Rehearsal. 1704–9.
Spectator. Edited by G. G. Smith. Everyman's Library, London and New York, 4 vols., 1909.
True Briton: Memoirs of the Life of the Duke of Wharton. 1731.
Weekly Miscellany. 1732–3.

II. SECONDARY WORKS
A. *Biographies, Studies of Individuals*

(General sources: *Dictionary of National Biography*; obituaries in *Gentleman's Magazine*; sketches in John Nichols, *Illustrations of Eighteenth Century Literary History*.)

BEATTIE, LESTER M. *John Arbuthnot, Mathematician and Satirist.* Cambridge, Mass.: Harvard University Press, 1935.
BERNHARD, HAROLD E. *Charles Chauncy, Colonial Liberal, 1705–87.* Chicago: University of Chicago Press, 1948.

BINGHAM, E. R. 'Political Apprenticeship of Benjamin Hoadly', *Church History*, xvi (September 1947).

BREDVOLD, LOUIS I. *The Intellectual Milieu of John Dryden*. Ann Arbor: University of Michigan Press, 1934.

BULLOCH, JOHN M. *Thomas Gordon, the Independent Whig*. Aberdeen: Aberdeen University Press, 1918.

CARPENTER, EDWARD F. *Thomas Tenison, Archbishop of Canterbury,. 1636–1715*. London: S.P.C.K., 1948.

—— *Thomas Sherlock*. London: S.P.C.K., 1936.

CLARK, JOHN MAURICE, et al. *Adam Smith, 1776–1926*. Chicago: University of Chicago Press, 1928.

CORNISH, JOSEPH. *Life of Thomas Firmin*. London, 1780.

DAVIS, ARTHUR P. *Isaac Watts*. New York, 1943.

EVANS, ARTHUR W. *Warburton and the Warburtonians*. London: Oxford University Press, 1932.

FISHER, MITCHELL S. *Robert Boyle, Devout Naturalist*. Philadelphia: Oshiver Studio Press, 1945.

FOXCROFT, HELEN C. *Life and Letters of the First Marquess of Halifax*. London: Longmans, Green & Co., 1898.

—— *A Character of the Trimmer*. Cambridge: Cambridge University Press, 1946.

FRASER, ALEXANDER C. *Life and Letters of George Berkeley*. Oxford: Clarendon Press, 1871.

GINZBERG, ELI. *The House of Adam Smith*. New York: Columbia University Press, 1934.

HARTLEY, L. C. *William Cowper, Humanitarian*. Chapel Hill: University of North Carolina Press, 1938.

HOBHOUSE, STEPHEN H. *William Law and Eighteenth Century Quakerism*. London: G. Allen & Unwin, 1927.

HOPKINSON, ARTHUR W. *About William Law*. London: S.P.C.K., 1948.

JOHNSTON, GEORGE A. *The Development of Berkeley's Philosophy*. London: Macmillan & Co., 1923.

LOOTEN, C. *La Pensée religieuse de Swift*. Paris, 1935.

MAXWELL, J. C. 'The Ethics and Politics of Mandeville', *Philosophy*, xxvi, no. 98 (July 1951).

MERRILL, WALTER M. *From Statesman to Philosopher: a Study in Bolingbroke's Deism*. New York: Philosophical Library, 1949.

MILLER, PERRY. *Jonathan Edwards*. American Men of Letters Series, 1949.

MORGAN, IRVONWY. *The Nonconformity of Richard Baxter*. London: Epworth Press, 1946.

MOSSNER, ERNEST C. *Bishop Butler and the Age of Reason*. New York: Macmillan Co., 1936.

NORTON, WILLIAM J. *Bishop Butler, Moralist and Divine*. New Brunswick: Princeton University Press, 1940.

NOTTINGHAM, ELIZABETH K. *The Making of an Evangelist: a Study of John Wesley's Early Years*. New York, 1938.

OSMOND, PERCY H. *Isaac Barrow, His Life and Times*. London: S.P.C.K., 1947.

SEEBER, ANNA. *John Toland als politischer Schriftsteller*. Württemberg, 1933.

SMITH, NORMAN KEMP. *John Locke, 1632–1704*. Manchester: Manchester University Press, 1933.

SUTHERLAND, LUCY S. *A London Merchant, 1695–1774*. London: Oxford University Press, 1933.

SYKES, NORMAN. *Edmund Gibson, Bishop of London, 1669–1748*. London, O.U.P., 1926.

TYERMAN, LUKE. *The Life and Times of John Wesley.* 2nd ed. 3 vols. London: Hodder and Stoughton, 1872–5.

—— *Life of George Whitefield.* 2 vols. London: Hodder & Stoughton, 1876.

WILBERFORCE, ROBERT I. and SAMUEL. *The Life of William Wilberforce.* 3 vols. Philadelphia, 1841.

WILD, JOHN. *George Berkeley; a Study of His Life and Philosophy.* Cambridge, Mass.: Harvard University Press, 1936.

B. *Other Secondary Works*

(General: *Encyclopaedia of Religion and Ethics,* ed. James Hastings; *A Dictionary of English Church History,* ed. S. L. Ollard.)

ABBEY, C. J., and OVERTON, J. H. *The English Church in the Eighteenth Century.* 2 vols. London, 1878.

ALDRIDGE, ALFRED O. *Shaftesbury and the Deist Manifesto.* Philadelphia: American Philosophical Society, 1951.

BECKER, CARL L. *The Heavenly City of the Eighteenth Century Philosophers.* New Haven: Yale University Press, 1932.

BELOFF, MAX. *Public Order and Popular Disturbances, 1660–1714.* London: Oxford University Press, 1938.

BETHELL, S. L. *The Cultural Revolution of the Seventeenth Century.* London: Dennis Dobson Ltd., 1951.

BLISS, ISABEL ST. JOHN. 'Young's *Night Thoughts* in Relation to Contemporary Christian Apologetics', *Publications of the Modern Language Association,* xlix (1934).

BRAITHWAITE, W. C. *The Second Period of Quakerism.* London: Macmillan & Co., 1919.

BURTT, EDWIN A. *The Metaphysical Foundations of Modern Physical Science.* New York: Harcourt, Brace & Co., 1925.

BURY, J. B. *The Idea of Progress.* London: Macmillan & Co., 1920.

BUSH, DOUGLAS. *English Literature in the Earlier Seventeenth Century, 1600–1660.* Oxford: Clarendon Press, 1945.

CASSIRER, ERNST. *The Philosophy of the Enlightenment.* Princeton: Princeton University Press. Translated by F. C. A. Koelln and J. P. Pettagrove.

CAVERT, S. M., and VAN DUSEN, H. P. (eds.). *The Church Through Half a Century.* New York and London: C. Scribner's Sons, 1936.

CHEYNE, T. K. *Founders of Old Testament Criticism.* London: Methuen & Co., 1893.

CLARK, HENRY W. *History of English Nonconformity.* Vol. ii. London: Chapman & Hall, 1913.

COLLIGAN, J. HAY. *The Arian Movement in England.* Manchester: Manchester University Press, 1913.

—— *Eighteenth Century Nonconformity.* London: Longmans, Green & Co., 1915.

COOMER, DUNCAN. *English Dissent under the Early Hanoverians.* London: Epworth Press, 1946.

CRAGG, G. R. *From Puritanism to the Age of Reason; a Study of Changes in Religious Thought within the Church of England, 1660–1700.* Cambridge: Cambridge University Press, 1950.

CRANE, R. S. 'Anglican Apologetics and the Idea of Progress', *Modern Philology,* xxxi (1934).

CRANE, VERNER W. *The Southern Frontier.* Durham, N.C.: Duke University Press, 1928.

DOWDEN, EDWARD. *Puritan and Anglican; Studies in Literature.* London: Kegan Paul & Co., 1900.

DRENNON, HERBERT. 'Newtonianism: Its Method, Theology, and Metaphysics', *Englische Studien,* vol. lxviii (1933–4).

FAIRCHILD, H. N. *Religious Trends in English Poetry*. New York: Columbia University Press, 1939.

FARRAR, A. S. *A Critical History of Freethought*. London: J. Murray, 1862.

FEILING, KEITH. *A History of the Tory Party, 1640–1714*. Oxford: Clarendon Press, 1924.

—— *The Second Tory Party, 1714–1832*. London and New York: Macmillan & Co., 1938.

FIGGIS, J. N. *The Divine Right of Kings*. 2nd ed. Cambridge, 1934.

GARDNER, WILLIAM B. 'George Hickes and the Origin of the Bangorian Controversy', *Studies in Philology*, xxix, no. 1 (1942).

GEORGE, M. DOROTHY. *England in Transition; Life and Work in the Eighteenth Century*. London: G. Routledge & Sons, 1931.

GEWEHR, WESLEY M. *The Great Awakening in Virginia, 1740–1790*. Durham, N.C.: Duke University Press, 1930.

HALL, WALTER PHELPS. *British Radicalism, 1791–1797*. New York: Columbia University Press, 1912.

HANSON, LAURENCE. *Government and the Press, 1695–1763*. London: Oxford University Press, 1936.

HAROUTUNIAN, JOSEPH. *Piety Versus Moralism; the Passing of the New England Theology*. New York: H. Holt & Co., 1932.

HARRISON, A. W. *Arminianism*. London: Duckworth, 1937.

HAZARD, PAUL. *La Pensée européenne au XVIIIème siècle*. 3 vols. Paris, 1946.

HEFELBLOWER, S. G. *The Relation of John Locke to English Deism*. Chicago: University of Chicago Press, 1918.

HOLT, RAYMOND V. *The Unitarian Contribution to Social Progress in England*. London: G. Allen & Unwin, 1938.

HUNT, JOHN. *Religious Thought in England from the Reformation to the End of the Last Century*. 3 vols. London: Strahan & Co., 1870–3.

IVIMEY, J. *A History of the English Baptists*. 3 vols. London, 1823.

JONES, LOUIS C. *The Clubs of the Georgian Rakes*. New York: Columbia University Press, 1942.

JONES, MARY G. *The Charity School Movement; a Study of Puritanism in Action*. Cambridge: Cambridge University Press, 1938.

JORDAN, WILBUR K. *The Development of Religious Toleration in England*. Cambridge, Mass.: Harvard University Press, 1940.

KOCH, GUSTAV ADOLF. *Republican Religion; the American Revolution and the Cult of Reason*. New York: H. Holt & Co., 1933.

KRAPP, ROBERT M. *Liberal Anglicanism, 1636–47*. Ridgefield, Conn.: Acorn Press, 1944.

LAPRADE, WILLIAM T. *Public Opinion and Politics in Eighteenth Century England to the Fall of Walpole*. New York: Macmillan Co., 1936.

LECHLER, G. V. *Geschichte des englischen Deismus*. Stuttgart, 1841.

LECKY, W. E. H. *A History of England in the Eighteenth Century*. 7 vols. New York: D. Appleton & Co., 1892–3.

—— *History of . . . Rationalism in Europe*. 2 vols. London: Longmans, Green & Co., 1904.

LEE, UMPHREY. *The Historical Background of Early Methodist Enthusiasm*. New York: Columbia University Press, 1931.

LILLEY, A. L. *Reason and Revelation*. London: S.P.C.K., 1932.

LINCOLN, ANTHONY. *Some Political and Social Ideas of English Dissent, 1763–1800*. Cambridge: Cambridge University Press, 1938.

LOVEJOY, ARTHUR O. *The Great Chain of Being*. Cambridge, Mass.: Harvard University Press, 1936.

LOVEJOY, ARTHUR TO. 'he Parallel of Deism and Classicism', *Modern Philology*, xxix (February 1932), 281–99.

MCCULLEY, GRANT. 'The Seventeenth Century Doctrine of the Plurality of Worlds', *Annals of Science*, i (15 October 1936).

MCGIFFERT, ARTHUR C. *Protestant Thought before Kant*. New York: C. Scribner's Sons, 1936.

MCKILLOP, ALAN D. *The Background of Thomson's Seasons*. Minneapolis: University of Minnesota Press, 1942; London: Oxford University Press, 1942.

MCLACHLAN, HERBERT J. *The Story of a Nonconformist Library*. Manchester: Manchester University Press, 1923.

—— *The Religious Opinions of Milton, Locke and Newton*. Manchester: Manchester University Press, 1941.

—— *Essays and Addresses*. Manchester: Manchester University Press, 1950.

—— *Socinianism in Seventeenth Century England*. Oxford: Clarendon Press, 1951.

MANTOUX, PAUL. *The Industrial Revolution in the Eighteenth Century*. Translated by Marjorie Vernon. New York: Harcourt, Brace & Co., 1948.

MARSHALL, DOROTHY. *The English Poor in the Eighteenth Century*. London: G. Routledge & Sons, 1926.

MILLER, SAMUEL. *A Brief Retrospect of the Eighteenth Century*. 2 vols. New York, 1803.

MORAIS, HERBERT M. *Deism in Eighteenth Century America*. New York, 1934.

MORGAN, WILLIAM T. *English Political Parties and Leaders in the Reign of Queen Anne*. New Haven: Yale University Press, 1920.

MORLEY, JOHN. *Biographical Studies*. London: Macmillan & Co., 1923.

NAMIER, LEWIS B. *England in the Age of the American Revolution*. London: Macmillan & Co., 1930.

ORR, JOHN. *English Deism; Its Roots and Fruits*. Grand Rapids, Mich., 1934.

PATTISON, MARK. *Essays*. Edited by H. Nettleship. Vol. ii. Oxford: Clarendon Press, 1889.

PEASTON, A. ELLIOTT. *The Prayer Book Reform Movement in the Eighteenth Century*. Oxford: Basil Blackwell, 1940.

POWICKE, FREDERICK J. *The Cambridge Platonists*. London: J. M. Dent, 1926.

RAISTRICK, ARTHUR. *Quakers in Science and Industry*. London: Philosophical Library, 1950.

RANDALL, JOHN HERMAN. *The Making of the Modern Mind*. Boston: Houghton Mifflin, 1940.

RAPHAEL, D. DAICHES. *The Moral Sense*. London: Oxford University Press, 1947.

REALEY, CHARLES B. *The Early Opposition to Robert Walpole, 1720–1727*. Philadelphia, 1931.

ROBERTSON, J. M. *A Short History of Free Thought*. New York: Macmillan Co., 1899.

—— *The Dynamics of Religion*. London: Watts & Co., 1926.

RODGERS, BETSY. *Cloak of Charity; Studies in Eighteenth Century Philanthropy*. London: Methuen & Co., 1949.

SAYOUS, ÉDOUARD. *Les Déistes anglais et le christianisme, 1696–1738*. Paris, 1882.

SCHLATTER, RICHARD B. *Social Ideas of Religious Leaders, 1660–1688*. London: Oxford University Press, 1940.

SCUDI, ABBIE T. *The Sacheverell Affair*. New York: Columbia University Press, 1939.

STEPHEN, LESLIE. *A History of English Thought in the Eighteenth Century*. 2 vols. New York: G. P. Putnam's Sons, 1876, 1881, 1902.

STEVENS, DAVID H. *Party Politics and English Journalism, 1702–1742*. Chicago, 1916.

STOYE, JOHN W. *English Travellers Abroad, 1604–1667*. London: British Book Centre, 1952.

SUTHERLAND, JAMES. *Background for Queen Anne*. London: Methuen & Co., 1939.

SYDNEY, WILLIAM C. *England and the English in the Eighteenth Century*. 2 vols. London: Ward & Downey, 1881.

SYKES, NORMAN. *Church and State in England in the Eighteenth Century*. Cambridge: Cambridge University Press, 1934.

TAWNEY, R. H. *Religion and the Rise of Capitalism*. New York: Harcourt, Brace & Co., 1926.

TAYLER, JOHN J. *Retrospect of the Religious Life of England*. London: J. Chapman, 1845.

THOLUCK, AUGUST. *Vermischte Schriften*. Vol. ii. Hamburg, 1839.

THOMAS, H. H. 'The Rise of Geology and its Influence on Contemporary Thought', *Annals of Science*, v (15 July 1947).

TINKER, CHAUNCEY B. *Nature's Simple Plan; a Phase of Radical Thought in the Mid-Eighteenth Century*. Princeton: Princeton University Press, 1922.

TOLLES, FREDERICK B. *Meeting House and Counting House; the Quaker Merchants of Colonial Philadelphia, 1682–1763*. Chapel Hill: University of North Carolina Press, 1948.

TORREY, NORMAN L. *Voltaire and the English Deists*. New Haven: Yale University Press, 1930; London: Oxford University Press, 1930.

TREVELYAN, GEORGE M. *England under Queen Anne*. Vol. i, *Blenheim*; vol. iii, *The Peace and the Protestant Succession*. London: Longmans, Green & Co., 1930–4.

TROELTSCH, ERNST. *The Social Teachings of the Christian Churches*. 2 vols. Translated by Olive Wyon. New York: Macmillan Co., 1931.

TULLOCH, JOHN. *Rational Theology and Christian Philosophy in England in the Seventeenth Century*. 2 vols. Edinburgh and London: Wm. Blackwood & Sons, 1872.

TURBERVILLE, A. S. (ed.). *Johnson's England*. 2 vols. Oxford: Clarendon Press, 1933.

TUVESON, ERNEST. 'The Origins of the Moral Sense', *Huntington Library Quarterly*, xi (May 1948).

WADSWORTH, ALFRED P., and MANN, JULIA DE LACY. *The Cotton Trade and Industrial Lancashire, 1600–1780*. Manchester: Manchester University Press, 1931.

WALLACE, ROBERT. *Anti-Trinitarian Biography*. 3 vols. London: E. T. Whitefield, 1850.

WEARMOUTH, ROBERT F. *Methodism and the Common People of the Eighteenth Century*. London: Epworth Press, 1945.

WHITE, ANDREW D. *History of the Warfare of Science with Theology in Christendom*. 2 vols. New York: D. Appleton & Co., 1897.

WHITELEY, J. H. *Wesley's England*. London: Epworth Press, 1938.

WHITING, CHARLES E. *Studies in English Puritanism from the Restoration to the Revolution*. New York: Macmillan Co., 1931.

WILBUR, EARL M. *A History of Unitarianism*. Cambridge, Mass.: Harvard University Press, 1945.

WILLEY, BASIL. *The Seventeenth Century Background*. London: Chatto & Windus, 1934.
—— *The Eighteenth Century Background*. London: Chatto & Windus, 1940, 1941, 1950.

WILLIAMS, BASIL. *The Whig Supremacy, 1714–1760*. Oxford: Clarendon Press, 1939.

WILLIAMSON, GEORGE. 'The Restoration Revolt against Enthusiasm', *Studies in Philology*, xxx (1933).

WRIGHT, CONRAD. 'Edwards and the Arminians on the Freedom of the Will', *Harvard Theological Review*, xxxv (October 1942).

ZEICHNER, OSCAR. *Connecticut's Years of Controversy, 1750–1776*. Chapel Hill: University of North Carolina Press, 1949.

INDEX

PRINTED IN GREAT BRITAIN
AT THE UNIVERSITY PRESS, OXFORD
BY CHARLES BATEY, PRINTER TO THE UNIVERSITY